Bel Ami (A Ladi

The Works of Guy de Maupassant

(Volume 6)

Guy de Maupassant

Alpha Editions

This edition published in 2024

ISBN : 9789367249277

Design and Setting By
Alpha Editions
www.alphaedis.com
Email - info@alphaedis.com

As per information held with us this book is in Public Domain.
This book is a reproduction of an important historical work. Alpha Editions uses the best technology to reproduce historical work in the same manner it was first published to preserve its original nature. Any marks or number seen are left intentionally to preserve its true form.

Contents

I ....- 1 -

II ....- 14 -

III ....- 25 -

IV ....- 40 -

V ....- 52 -

VI ....- 79 -

VII ....- 100 -

VIII ....- 114 -

IX ....- 131 -

X ....- 150 -

XI ....- 161 -

XII ....- 178 -

XIII ....- 188 -

XIV ....- 204 -

XV ....- 212 -

XVI	- 227 -
XVII	- 238 -
XVIII	- 249 -

I

When the cashier had given him the change out of his five francpiece, George Duroy left the restaurant.

As he had a good carriage, both naturally and from his military training, he drew himself up, twirled his moustache, and threw upon the lingering customers a rapid and sweeping glance—one of those glances which take in everything within their range like a casting net.

The women looked up at him in turn—three little work-girls, a middle-aged music mistress, disheveled, untidy, and wearing a bonnet always dusty and a dress always awry; and two shopkeepers' wives dining with their husbands—all regular customers at this slap-bang establishment.

When he was on the pavement outside, he stood still for a moment, asking himself what he should do. It was the 28th of June, and he had just three francs forty centimes in his pocket to carry him to the end of the month. This meant the option of two dinners without lunch or two lunches without dinner. He reflected that as the earlier repasts cost twenty sous apiece, and the latter thirty, he would, if he were content with the lunches, be one franc twenty centimes to the good, which would further represent two snacks of bread and sausage and two bocks of beer on the boulevards. This latter item was his greatest extravagance and his chief pleasure of a night; and he began to descend the Rue Notre-Dame de Lorette.

He walked as in the days when he had worn a hussar uniform, his chest thrown out and his legs slightly apart, as if he had just left the saddle, pushing his way through the crowded street, and shouldering folk to avoid having to step aside. He wore his somewhat shabby hat on one side, and brought his heels smartly down on the pavement. He seemed ever ready to defy somebody or something, the passers-by, the houses, the whole city, retaining all the swagger of a dashing cavalry-man in civil life.

Although wearing a sixty-franc suit, he was not devoid of a certain somewhat loud elegance. Tall, well-built, fair, with a curly moustache twisted up at the ends, bright blue eyes with small pupils, and reddish-brown hair curling naturally and parted in the middle, he bore a strong resemblance to the dare-devil of popular romances.

It was one of those summer evenings on which air seems to be lacking in Paris. The city, hot as an oven, seemed to swelter in the stifling night. The sewers breathed out their poisonous breath through their granite mouths, and the underground kitchens gave forth to the street through their windows the stench of dishwater and stale sauces.

The doorkeepers in their shirtsleeves sat astride straw-bottomed chairs within the carriage entrances to the houses, smoking their pipes, and the pedestrians walked with flagging steps, head bare, and hat in hand.

When George Duroy reached the boulevards he paused again, undecided as to what he should do. He now thought of going on to the Champs Elysées and the Avenue du Bois de Boulogne to seek a little fresh air under the trees, but another wish also assailed him, a desire for a love affair.

What shape would it take? He did not know, but he had been awaiting it for three months, night and day. Occasionally, thanks to his good looks and gallant bearing, he gleaned a few crumbs of love here and there, but he was always hoping for something further and better.

With empty pockets and hot blood, he kindled at the contact of the prowlers who murmur at street corners: "Will you come home with me, dear?" but he dared not follow them, not being able to pay them, and, besides, he was awaiting something else, less venally vulgar kisses.

He liked, however, the localities in which women of the town swarm—their balls, their cafés, and their streets. He liked to rub shoulders with them, speak to them, chaff them, inhale their strong perfumes, feel himself near them. They were women at any rate, women made for love. He did not despise them with the innate contempt of a well-born man.

He turned towards the Madeleine, following the flux of the crowd which flowed along overcome by the heat. The chief cafés, filled with customers, were overflowing on to the pavement, and displayed their drinking public under the dazzling glare of their lit-up facias. In front of them, on little tables, square or round, were glasses holding fluids of every shade, red, yellow, green, brown, and inside the decanters glittered the large transparent cylinders of ice, serving to cool the bright, clear water. Duroy had slackened his pace, a longing to drink parched his throat.

A hot thirst, a summer evening's thirst assailed him, and he fancied the delightful sensation of cool drinks flowing across his palate. But if he only drank two bocks of beer in the evening, farewell to the slender supper of the morrow, and he was only too well acquainted with the hours of short commons at the end of the month.

He said to himself: "I must hold out till ten o'clock, and then I'll have my bock at the American café. Confound it, how thirsty I am though." And he scanned the men seated at the tables drinking, all the people who could quench their thirst as much as they pleased. He went on, passing in front of the cafés with a sprightly swaggering air, and guessing at a glance from their dress and bearing how much money each customer ought to have about him. Wrath against these men quietly sitting there rose up within him. If their pockets were rummaged, gold, silver, and coppers would be found in them. On an average each one must have at least two louis. There were certainly a hundred to a café, a hundred times two louis is four thousand francs. He murmured "the swine," as he walked gracefully past them. If he could have had hold of one of them at a nice dark corner he would have twisted his neck without scruple, as he used to do the country-folk's fowls on field-days.

And he recalled his two years in Africa and the way in which he used to pillage the Arabs when stationed at little out-posts in the south. A bright and cruel smile flitted across his lips at the recollection of an escapade which had cost the lives of three men of the Ouled-Alane tribe, and had furnished him and his comrades with a score of fowls, a couple of sheep, some gold, and food for laughter for six months.

The culprits had never been found, and, what is more, they had hardly been looked for, the Arab being looked upon as somewhat in the light of the natural prey of the soldier.

In Paris it was another thing. One could not plunder prettily, sword by side and revolver in hand, far from civil authority. He felt in his heart all the instincts of a sub-officer let loose in a conquered country. He certainly regretted his two years in the desert. What a pity he had not stopped there. But, then, he had hoped something better in returning home. And now— ah! yes, it was very nice now, was it not?

He clicked his tongue as if to verify the parched state of his palate.

The crowd swept past him slowly, and he kept thinking. "Set of hogs—all these idiots have money in their waistcoat pockets." He pushed against people and softly whistled a lively tune. Gentlemen whom he thus elbowed turned grumbling, and women murmured: "What a brute!"

He passed the Vaudeville Theater and stopped before the American café, asking himself whether he should not take his bock, so greatly did thirst torture him. Before making up his mind, he glanced at the illuminated clock. It was a quarter past nine. He knew himself that as soon as the glassful of beer was before him he would gulp it down. What would he do then up to eleven o'clock?

He passed on. "I will go as far as the Madeleine," he said, "and walk back slowly."

As he reached the corner of the Palace de l'Opera, he passed a stout young fellow, whose face he vaguely recollected having seen somewhere. He began to follow him, turning over his recollections and repeating to himself half-aloud: "Where the deuce did I know that joker?"

He searched without being able to recollect, and then all at once, by a strange phenomenon of memory, the same man appeared to him thinner, younger, and clad in a hussar uniform. He exclaimed aloud: "What, Forestier!" and stepping out he tapped the other on the shoulder. The promenader turned round and looked at him, and then said: "What is it, sir?"

Duroy broke into a laugh. "Don't you know me?" said he.

"No."

"George Duroy, of the 6th Hussars."

Forestier held out his hands, exclaiming: "What, old fellow! How are you?"

"Very well, and you?"

"Oh, not very brilliant! Just fancy, I have a chest in brown paper now. I cough six months out of twelve, through a cold I caught at Bougival the year of my return to Paris, four years ago."

And Forestier, taking his old comrade's arm, spoke to him of his illness, related the consultations, opinions, and advice of the doctors, and the difficulty of following this advice in his position. He was told to spend the winter in the South, but how could he? He was married, and a journalist in a good position.

"I am political editor of the *Vie Francaise*. I write the proceedings in the Senate for the *Salut*, and from time to time literary criticisms for the *Planète*. That is so. I have made my way."

Duroy looked at him with surprise. He was greatly changed, matured. He had now the manner, bearing, and dress of a man in a good position and sure of himself, and the stomach of a man who dines well. Formerly he had been thin, slight, supple, heedless, brawling, noisy, and always ready for a spree. In three years Paris had turned him into someone quite different, stout and serious, and with some white hairs about his temples, though he was not more than twenty-seven.

Forestier asked: "Where are you going?"

Duroy answered: "Nowhere; I am just taking a stroll before turning in."

"Well, will you come with me to the *Vie Francaise*, where I have some proofs to correct, and then we will take a bock together?"

"All right."

They began to walk on, arm-in-arm, with that easy familiarity existing between school-fellows and men in the same regiment.

"What are you doing in Paris?" asked Forestier.

Duroy shrugged his shoulders. "Simply starving. As soon as I finished my term of service I came here—to make a fortune, or rather for the sake of living in Paris; and for six months I have been a clerk in the offices of the Northern Railway at fifteen hundred francs a year, nothing more."

Forestier murmured: "Hang it, that's not much!"

"I should think not. But how can I get out of it? I am alone; I don't know anyone; I can get no one to recommend me. It is not goodwill that is lacking, but means."

His comrade scanned him from head to foot, like a practical man examining a subject, and then said, in a tone of conviction: "You see, my boy, everything depends upon assurance here. A clever fellow can more easily become a minister than an under-secretary. One must obtrude one's self on people; not ask things of them. But how the deuce is it that you could not get hold of anything better than a clerk's berth on the Northern Railway?"

Duroy replied: "I looked about everywhere, but could not find anything. But I have something in view just now; I have been offered a riding-master's place at Pellerin's. There I shall get three thousand francs at the lowest."

Forestier stopped short. "Don't do that; it is stupid, when you ought to be earning ten thousand francs. You would nip your future in the bud. In your office, at any rate, you are hidden; no one knows you; you can emerge from it if you are strong enough to make your way. But once a riding-master, and it is all over. It is as if you were head-waiter at a place where all Paris goes to dine. When once you have given riding lessons to people in society or to their children, they will never be able to look upon you as an equal."

He remained silent for a few moments, evidently reflecting, and then asked:

"Have you a bachelor's degree?"

"No; I failed to pass twice."

"That is no matter, as long as you studied for it. If anyone mentions Cicero or Tiberius, you know pretty well what they are talking about?"

"Yes; pretty well."

"Good; no one knows any more, with the exception of a score of idiots who have taken the trouble. It is not difficult to pass for being well informed; the great thing is not to be caught in some blunder. You can maneuver, avoid the difficulty, turn the obstacle, and floor others by means of a dictionary. Men are all as stupid as geese and ignorant as donkeys."

He spoke like a self-possessed blade who knows what life is, and smiled as he watched the crowd go by. But all at once he began to cough, and stopped again until the fit was over, adding, in a tone of discouragement: "Isn't it aggravating not to be able to get rid of this cough? And we are in the middle of summer. Oh! this winter I shall go and get cured at Mentone. Health before everything."

They halted on the Boulevard Poissonière before a large glass door, on the inner side of which an open newspaper was pasted. Three passers-by had stopped and were reading it.

Above the door, stretched in large letters of flame, outlined by gas jets, the inscription *La Vie Francaise*. The pedestrians passing into the light shed by these three dazzling words suddenly appeared as visible as in broad daylight, then disappeared again into darkness.

Forestier pushed the door open, saying, "Come in." Duroy entered, ascended an ornate yet dirty staircase, visible from the street, passed through an ante-room where two messengers bowed to his companion, and reached a kind of waiting-room, shabby and dusty, upholstered in dirty green Utrecht velvet, covered with spots and stains, and worn in places as if mice had been gnawing it.

"Sit down," said Forestier. "I will be back in five minutes."

And he disappeared through one of the three doors opening into the room.

A strange, special, indescribable odor, the odor of a newspaper office, floated in the air of the room. Duroy remained motionless, slightly intimidated, above all surprised. From time to time folk passed hurriedly before him, coming in at one door and going out at another before he had time to look at them.

They were now young lads, with an appearance of haste, holding in their hand a sheet of paper which fluttered from the hurry of their progress; now compositors, whose white blouses, spotted with ink, revealed a clean shirt collar and cloth trousers like those of men of fashion, and who carefully carried strips of printed paper, fresh proofs damp from the press. Sometimes a gentleman entered rather too elegantly attired, his waist too tightly pinched by his frock-coat, his leg too well set off by the cut of his trousers, his foot squeezed into a shoe too pointed at the toe, some fashionable reporter bringing in the echoes of the evening.

Others, too, arrived, serious, important-looking men, wearing tall hats with flat brims, as if this shape distinguished them from the rest of mankind.

Forestier reappeared holding the arm of a tall, thin fellow, between thirty and forty years of age, in evening dress, very dark, with his moustache ends stiffened in sharp points, and an insolent and self-satisfied bearing.

Forestier said to him: "Good night, dear master."

The other shook hands with him, saying: "Good night, my dear fellow," and went downstairs whistling, with his cane under his arm.

Duroy asked: "Who is that?"

"Jacques Rival, you know, the celebrated descriptive writer, the duellist. He has just been correcting his proofs. Garin, Montel, and he are the three best descriptive writers, for facts and points, we have in Paris. He gets thirty thousand francs a year here for two articles a week."

As they were leaving they met a short, stout man, with long hair and untidy appearance, who was puffing as he came up the stairs.

Forestier bowed low to him. "Norbert de Varenne," said he, "the poet; the author of '*Les Soleils Morts*'; another who gets long prices. Every tale he writes for us costs three hundred francs, and the longest do not run to two hundred lines. But let us turn into the Neapolitan *café*, I am beginning to choke with thirst."

As soon as they were seated at a table in the *café*, Forestier called for two bocks, and drank off his own at a single draught, while Duroy sipped his beer in slow mouthfuls, tasting it and relishing it like something rare and precious.

His companion was silent, and seemed to be reflecting. Suddenly he exclaimed: "Why don't you try journalism?"

The other looked at him in surprise, and then said: "But, you know, I have never written anything."

"Bah! everyone must begin. I could give you a job to hunt up information for me—to make calls and inquiries. You would have to start with two hundred and fifty francs a month and your cab hire. Shall I speak to the manager about it?"

"Certainly!"

"Very well, then, come and dine with me to-morrow. I shall only have five or six people—the governor, Monsieur Walter and his wife, Jacques Rival, and Norbert de Varenne, whom you have just seen, and a lady, a friend of my wife. Is it settled?"

Duroy hesitated, blushing and perplexed. At length he murmured: "You see, I have no clothes."

Forestier was astounded. "You have no dress clothes? Hang it all, they are indispensable, though. In Paris one would be better off without a bed than without a dress suit."

Then, suddenly feeling in his waistcoat pocket, he drew out some gold, took two louis, placed them in front of his old comrade, and said in a cordial and familiar tone: "You will pay me back when you can. Hire or arrange to pay by installments for the clothes you want, whichever you like, but come and dine with me to-morrow, half-past seven, number seventeen Rue Fontaine."

Duroy, confused, picked up the money, stammering: "You are too good; I am very much obliged to you; you may be sure I shall not forget."

The other interrupted him. "All right. Another bock, eh? Waiter, two bocks."

Then, when they had drunk them, the journalist said: "Will you stroll about a bit for an hour?"

"Certainly."

And they set out again in the direction of the Madeleine.

"What shall we, do?" said Forestier. "They say that in Paris a lounger can always find something to amuse him, but it is not true. I, when I want to lounge about of an evening, never know where to go. A drive round the Bois de Boulogne is only amusing with a woman, and one has not always one to hand; the *café* concerts may please my chemist and his wife, but not me. Then what is there to do? Nothing. There ought to be a summer garden like the Parc Monceau, open at night, where one would hear very good music while sipping cool drinks under the trees. It should not be a pleasure resort, but a lounging place, with a high price for entrance in order to attract the fine ladies. One ought to be able to stroll along well-graveled walks lit up by electric light, and to sit down when one wished to hear the music near or at a distance. We had about the sort of thing formerly at Musard's, but with a smack of the low-class dancing-room, and too much dance music, not enough space, not enough shade, not enough gloom. It would want a very fine garden and a very extensive one. It would be delightful. Where shall we go?"

Duroy, rather perplexed, did not know what to say; at length he made up his mind. "I have never been in the Folies Bergère. I should not mind taking a look round there," he said.

"The Folies Bergère," exclaimed his companion, "the deuce; we shall roast there as in an oven. But, very well, then, it is always funny there."

And they turned on their heels to make their way to the Rue du Faubourg Montmartre.

The lit-up front of the establishment threw a bright light into the four streets which met in front of it. A string of cabs were waiting for the close of the performance.

Forestier was walking in when Duroy checked him.

"You are passing the pay-box," said he.

"I never pay," was the reply, in a tone of importance.

When he approached the check-takers they bowed, and one of them held out his hand. The journalist asked: "Have you a good box?"

"Certainly, Monsieur Forestier."

He took the ticket held out to him, pushed the padded door with its leather borders, and they found themselves in the auditorium.

Tobacco smoke slightly veiled like a faint mist the stage and the further side of the theater. Rising incessantly in thin white spirals from the cigars and pipes, this light fog ascended to the ceiling, and there, accumulating, formed under the dome above the crowded gallery a cloudy sky.

In the broad corridor leading to the circular promenade a group of women were awaiting new-comers in front of one of the bars, at which sat enthroned three painted and faded vendors of love and liquor.

The tall mirrors behind them reflected their backs and the faces of passers-by.

Forestier pushed his way through the groups, advancing quickly with the air of a man entitled to consideration.

He went up to a box-keeper. "Box seventeen," said he.

"This way, sir."

And they were shut up in a little open box draped with red, and holding four chairs of the same color, so near to one another that one could scarcely slip between them. The two friends sat down. To the right, as to the left, following a long curved line, the two ends of which joined the proscenium, a row of similar cribs held people seated in like fashion, with only their heads and chests visible.

On the stage, three young fellows in fleshings, one tall, one of middle size, and one small, were executing feats in turn upon a trapeze.

The tall one first advanced with short, quick steps, smiling and waving his hand as though wafting a kiss.

The muscles of his arms and legs stood out under his tights. He expanded his chest to take off the effect of his too prominent stomach, and his face resembled that of a barber's block, for a careful parting divided his locks equally on the center of the skull. He gained the trapeze by a graceful bound, and, hanging by the hands, whirled round it like a wheel at full speed, or, with stiff arms and straightened body, held himself out horizontally in space.

Then he jumped down, saluted the audience again with a smile amidst the applause of the stalls, and went and leaned against the scenery, showing off the muscles of his legs at every step.

The second, shorter and more squarely built, advanced in turn, and went through the same performance, which the third also recommenced amidst most marked expressions of approval from the public.

But Duroy scarcely noticed the performance, and, with head averted, kept his eyes on the promenade behind him, full of men and prostitutes.

Said Forestier to him: "Look at the stalls; nothing but middle-class folk with their wives and children, good noodlepates who come to see the show. In the boxes, men about town, some artistes, some girls, good second-raters; and behind us, the strangest mixture in Paris. Who are these men? Watch them. There is something of everything, of every profession, and every caste; but blackguardism predominates. There are clerks of all kinds—bankers' clerks, government clerks, shopmen, reporters, ponces, officers in plain clothes, swells in evening dress, who have dined out, and have dropped in here on their way from the Opera to the Théatre des Italiens; and then again, too, quite a crowd of suspicious folk who defy analysis. As to the women, only one type, the girl who sups at the American *café*, the girl at one or two louis who looks out for foreigners at five louis, and lets her regular customers know when she is disengaged. We have known them for the last ten years; we see them every evening all the year round in the same places, except when they are making a hygienic sojourn at Saint Lazare or at Lourcine."

Duroy no longer heard him. One of these women was leaning against their box and looking at him. She was a stout brunette, her skin whitened with paint, her black eyes lengthened at the corners with pencil and shaded by enormous and artificial eyebrows. Her too exuberant bosom stretched the dark silk of her dress almost to bursting; and her painted lips, red as a fresh wound, gave her an aspect bestial, ardent, unnatural, but which, nevertheless, aroused desire.

She beckoned with her head one of the friends who was passing, a blonde with red hair, and stout, like herself, and said to her, in a voice loud enough to be heard: "There is a pretty fellow; if he would like to have me for ten louis I should not say no."

Forestier turned and tapped Duroy on the knee, with a smile. "That is meant for you; you are a success, my dear fellow. I congratulate you."

The ex-sub-officer blushed, and mechanically fingered the two pieces of gold in his waistcoat pocket.

The curtain had dropped, and the orchestra was now playing a waltz.

Duroy said: "Suppose we take a turn round the promenade."

"Just as you like."

They left their box, and were at once swept away by the throng of promenaders. Pushed, pressed, squeezed, shaken, they went on, having before their eyes a crowd of hats. The girls, in pairs, passed amidst this crowd of men, traversing it with facility, gliding between elbows, chests, and backs as if quite at home, perfectly at their ease, like fish in water, amidst this masculine flood.

Duroy, charmed, let himself be swept along, drinking in with intoxication the air vitiated by tobacco, the odor of humanity, and the perfumes of the hussies. But Forestier sweated, puffed, and coughed.

"Let us go into the garden," said he.

And turning to the left, they entered a kind of covered garden, cooled by two large and ugly fountains. Men and women were drinking at zinc tables placed beneath evergreen trees growing in boxes.

"Another bock, eh?" said Forestier.

"Willingly."

They sat down and watched the passing throng.

From time to time a woman would stop and ask, with stereotyped smile: "Are you going to stand me anything?"

And as Forestier answered: "A glass of water from the fountain," she would turn away, muttering: "Go on, you duffer."

But the stout brunette, who had been leaning, just before, against the box occupied by the two comrades, reappeared, walking proudly arm-in-arm with the stout blonde. They were really a fine pair of women, well matched.

She smiled on perceiving Duroy, as though their eyes had already told secrets, and, taking a chair, sat down quietly in face of him, and making her friend sit down, too, gave the order in a clear voice: "Waiter, two grenadines!"

Forestier, rather surprised, said: "You make yourself at home."

She replied: "It is your friend that captivates me. He is really a pretty fellow. I believe that I could make a fool of myself for his sake."

Duroy, intimidated, could find nothing to say. He twisted his curly moustache, smiling in a silly fashion. The waiter brought the drinks, which the women drank off at a draught; then they rose, and the brunette, with a friendly nod of the head, and a tap on the arm with her fan, said to Duroy: "Thanks, dear, you are not very talkative."

And they went off swaying their trains.

Forestier laughed. "I say, old fellow, you are very successful with the women. You must look after it. It may lead to something." He was silent for a moment, and then continued in the dreamy tone of men who think aloud: "It is through them, too, that one gets on quickest."

And as Duroy still smiled without replying, he asked: "Are you going to stop any longer? I have had enough of it. I am going home."

The other murmured: "Yes, I shall stay a little longer. It is not late."

Forestier rose. "Well, good-night, then. Till to-morrow. Don't forget. Seventeen Rue Fontaine, at half-past seven."

"That is settled. Till to-morrow. Thanks."

They shook hands, and the journalist walked away.

As soon as he had disappeared Duroy felt himself free, and again he joyfully felt the two pieces of gold in his pocket; then rising, he began to traverse the crowd, which he followed with his eyes.

He soon caught sight of the two women, the blonde and the brunette, who were still making their way, with their proud bearing of beggars, through the throng of men.

He went straight up to them, and when he was quite close he no longer dared to do anything.

The brunette said: "Have you found your tongue again?"

He stammered "By Jove!" without being able to say anything else.

The three stood together, checking the movement, the current of which swept round them.

All at once she asked: "Will you come home with me?"

And he, quivering with desire, answered roughly: "Yes, but I have only a louis in my pocket."

She smiled indifferently. "It is all the same to me,'" and took his arm in token of possession.

As they went out he thought that with the other louis he could easily hire a suit of dress clothes for the next evening.

II

"Monsieur Forestier, if you please?"

"Third floor, the door on the left," the concierge had replied, in a voice the amiable tone of which betokened a certain consideration for the tenant, and George Duroy ascended the stairs.

He felt somewhat abashed, awkward, and ill at ease. He was wearing a dress suit for the first time in his life, and was uneasy about the general effect of his toilet. He felt it was altogether defective, from his boots, which were not of patent leather, though neat, for he was naturally smart about his foot-gear, to his shirt, which he had bought that very morning for four franc fifty centimes at the Masgasin du Louvre, and the limp front of which was already rumpled. His everyday shirts were all more or less damaged, so that he had not been able to make use of even the least worn of them.

His trousers, rather too loose, set off his leg badly, seeming to flap about the calf with that creased appearance which second-hand clothes present. The coat alone did not look bad, being by chance almost a perfect fit.

He was slowly ascending the stairs with beating heart and anxious mind, tortured above all by the fear of appearing ridiculous, when suddenly he saw in front of him a gentleman in full dress looking at him. They were so close to one another that Duroy took a step back and then remained stupefied; it was himself, reflected by a tall mirror on the first-floor landing. A thrill of pleasure shot through him to find himself so much more presentable than he had imagined.

Only having a small shaving-glass in his room, he had not been able to see himself all at once, and as he had only an imperfect glimpse of the various items of his improvised toilet, he had mentally exaggerated its imperfections, and harped to himself on the idea of appearing grotesque.

But on suddenly coming upon his reflection in the mirror, he had not even recognized himself; he had taken himself for someone else, for a gentleman whom at the first glance he had thought very well dressed and fashionable looking. And now, looking at himself carefully, he recognized that really the general effect was satisfactory.

He studied himself as actors do when learning their parts. He smiled, held out his hand, made gestures, expressed sentiments of astonishment, pleasure, and approbation, and essayed smiles and glances, with a view of displaying his gallantry towards the ladies, and making them understand that they were admired and desired.

A door opened somewhere. He was afraid of being caught, and hurried upstairs, filled with the fear of having been seen grimacing thus by one of his friend's guests.

On reaching the second story he noticed another mirror, and slackened his pace to view himself in it as he went by. His bearing seemed to him really graceful. He walked well. And now he was filled with an unbounded confidence in himself. Certainly he must be successful with such an appearance, his wish to succeed, his native resolution, and his independence of mind. He wanted to run, to jump, as he ascended the last flight of stairs. He stopped in front of the third mirror, twirled his moustache as he had a trick of doing, took off his hat to run his fingers through his hair, and muttered half-aloud as he often did: "What a capital notion." Then raising his hand to the bell handle, he rang.

The door opened almost at once, and he found himself face to face with a man-servant out of livery, serious, clean-shaven, and so perfect in his get-up that Duroy became uneasy again without understanding the reason of his vague emotion, due, perhaps, to an unwitting comparison of the cut of their respective garments. The man-servant, who had patent-leather shoes, asked, as he took the overcoat which Duroy had carried on his arm, to avoid exposing the stains on it: "Whom shall I announce?"

And he announced the name through a door with a looped-back draping leading into a drawing-room.

But Duroy, suddenly losing his assurance, felt himself breathless and paralyzed by terror. He was about to take his first step in the world he had looked forward to and longed for. He advanced, nevertheless. A fair young woman, quite alone, was standing awaiting him in a large room, well lit up and full of plants as a greenhouse.

He stopped short, quite disconcerted. Who was this lady who was smiling at him? Then he remembered that Forestier was married, and the thought that this pretty and elegant blonde must be his friend's wife completed his alarm.

He stammered: "Madame, I am—"

She held out her hand, saying: "I know, sir; Charles has told me of your meeting last evening, and I am very pleased that he had the idea of asking you to dine with us to-day."

He blushed up to his ears, not knowing what to say, and felt himself examined from head to foot, reckoned up, and judged.

He longed to excuse himself, to invent some pretext for explaining the deficiencies of his toilet, but he could not think of one, and did not dare touch on this difficult subject.

He sat down on an armchair she pointed out to him, and as he felt the soft and springy velvet-covered seat yield beneath his weight, as he felt himself, as it were, supported and clasped by the padded back and arms, it seemed to him that he was entering upon a new and enchanting life, that he was taking possession of something delightful, that he was becoming somebody, that he was saved, and he looked at Madame Forestier, whose eyes had not quitted him.

She was attired in a dress of pale blue cashmere, which set off the outline of her slender waist and full bust. Her arms and neck issued from a cloud of white lace, with which the bodice and short sleeves were trimmed, and her fair hair, dressed high, left a fringe of tiny curls at the nape of her neck.

Duroy recovered his assurance beneath her glance, which reminded him, without his knowing why, of that of the girl met overnight at the Folies Bergére. She had gray eyes, of a bluish gray, which imparted to them a strange expression; a thin nose, full lips, a rather fleshy chin, and irregular but inviting features, full of archness and charm. It was one of those faces, every trait of which reveals a special grace, and seems to have its meaning—every movement to say or to hide something. After a brief silence she asked: "Have you been long in Paris?"

He replied slowly, recovering his self-possession: "A few months only, Madame. I have a berth in one of the railway companies, but Forestier holds out the hope that I may, thanks to him, enter journalism."

She smiled more plainly and kindly, and murmured, lowering her voice: "Yes, I know."

The bell had rung again. The servant announced "Madame de Marelle."

This was a little brunette, who entered briskly, and seemed to be outlined—modeled, as it were—from head to foot in a dark dress made quite plainly. A red rose placed in her black hair caught the eye at once, and seemed to stamp her physiognomy, accentuate her character, and strike the sharp and lively note needed.

A little girl in short frocks followed her.

Madame Forestier darted forward, exclaiming: "Good evening, Clotilde."

"Good evening, Madeleine." They kissed one another, and then the child offered her forehead, with the assurance of a grown-up person, saying: "Good evening, cousin."

Madame Forestier kissed her, and then introduced them, saying: "Monsieur George Duroy, an old friend of Charles; Madame de Marelle, my friend, and in some degree my relation." She added: "You know we have no ceremonious affectation here. You quite understand, eh?"

The young man bowed.

The door opened again, and a short, stout gentleman appeared, having on his arm a tall, handsome woman, much younger than himself, and of distinguished appearance and grave bearing. They were Monsieur Walter, a Jew from the South of France, deputy, financier, capitalist, and manager of the *Vie Francaise*, and his wife, the daughter of Monsieur Basile-Ravalau, the banker.

Then came, one immediately after the other, Jacques Rival, very elegantly got up, and Norbert de Varenne, whose coat collar shone somewhat from the friction of the long locks falling on his shoulders and scattering over them a few specks of white scurf. His badly-tied cravat looked as if it had already done duty. He advanced with the air and graces of an old beau, and taking Madame Forestier's hand, printed a kiss on her wrist. As he bent forward his long hair spread like water over her bare arm.

Forestier entered in his turn, offering excuses for being late. He had been detained at the office of the paper by the Morel affair. Monsieur Morel, a Radical deputy, had just addressed a question to the Ministry respecting a vote of credit for the colonization of Algeria.

The servant announced: "Dinner is served, Madame," and they passed into the dining-room.

Duroy found himself seated between Madame de Marelle and her daughter. He again felt ill at ease, being afraid of making some mistake in the conventional handling of forks, spoons, and glasses. There were four of these, one of a faint blue tint. What could be meant to be drunk out of that?

Nothing was said while the soup was being consumed, and then Norbert de Varenne asked: "Have you read the Gauthier case? What a funny business it is."

After a discussion on this case of adultery, complicated with blackmailing, followed. They did not speak of it as the events recorded in newspapers are spoken of in private families, but as a disease is spoken of among doctors, or vegetables among market gardeners. They were neither shocked nor astonished at the facts, but sought out their hidden and secret motives with professional curiosity, and an utter indifference for the crime itself. They sought to clearly explain the origin of certain acts, to determine all the cerebral phenomena which had given birth to the drama, the scientific result due to an especial condition of mind. The women, too, were interested in this investigation. And other recent events were examined, commented upon, turned so as to show every side of them, and weighed correctly, with the practical glance, and from the especial standpoint of dealers in news, and vendors of the drama of life at so much a line, just as articles destined for sale are examined, turned over, and weighed by tradesmen.

Then it was a question of a duel, and Jacques Rival spoke. This was his business; no one else could handle it.

Duroy dared not put in a word. He glanced from time to time at his neighbor, whose full bosom captivated him. A diamond, suspended by a thread of gold, dangled from her ear like a drop of water that had rolled down it. From time to time she made an observation which always brought a smile to her hearers' lips. She had a quaint, pleasant wit, that of an experienced tomboy who views things with indifference and judges them with frivolous and benevolent skepticism.

Duroy sought in vain for some compliment to pay her, and, not finding one, occupied himself with her daughter, filling her glass, holding her plate, and helping her. The child, graver than her mother, thanked him in a serious tone and with a slight bow, saying: "You are very good, sir," and listened to her elders with an air of reflection.

The dinner was very good, and everyone was enraptured. Monsieur Walter ate like an ogre, hardly spoke, and glanced obliquely under his glasses at the dishes offered to him. Norbert de Varenne kept him company, and from time to time let drops of gravy fall on his shirt front. Forestier, silent and serious, watched everything, exchanging glances of intelligence with his wife, like confederates engaged together on a difficult task which is going on swimmingly.

Faces grew red, and voices rose, as from time to time the man-servant murmured in the guests' ears: "Corton or Chateau-Laroze."

Duroy had found the Corton to his liking, and let his glass be filled every time. A delicious liveliness stole over him, a warm cheerfulness, that mounted from the stomach to the head, flowed through his limbs and penetrated him throughout. He felt himself wrapped in perfect comfort of life and thought, body and soul.

A longing to speak assailed him, to bring himself into notice, to be appreciated like these men, whose slightest words were relished.

But the conversation, which had been going on unchecked, linking ideas one to another, jumping from one topic to another at a chance word, a mere trifle, and skimming over a thousand matters, turned again on the great question put by Monsieur Morel in the Chamber respecting the colonization of Algeria.

Monsieur Walter, between two courses, made a few jests, for his wit was skeptical and broad. Forestier recited his next day's leader. Jacques Rival insisted on a military government with land grants to all officers after thirty years of colonial service.

"By this plan," he said, "you will create an energetic class of colonists, who will have already learned to love and understand the country, and will be acquainted with its language, and with all those grave local questions against which new-comers invariably run their heads."

Norbert de Varenne interrupted him with: "Yes; they will be acquainted with everything except agriculture. They will speak Arabic, but they will be ignorant how beet-root is planted out and wheat sown. They will be good at fencing, but very shaky as regards manures. On the contrary, this new land should be thrown entirely open to everyone. Intelligent men will achieve a position there; the others will go under. It is the social law."

A brief silence followed, and the listeners smiled at one another.

George Duroy opened his mouth, and said, feeling as much surprised at the sound of his own voice as if he had never heard himself speak: "What is most lacking there is good land. The really fertile estates cost as much as in France, and are bought up as investments by rich Parisians. The real colonists, the poor fellows who leave home for lack of bread, are forced into the desert, where nothing will grow for want of water."

Everyone looked at him, and he felt himself blushing.

Monsieur Walter asked: "Do you know Algeria, sir?"

George replied: "Yes, sir; I was there nearly two years and a half, and I was quartered in all three provinces."

Suddenly unmindful of the Morel question, Norbert de Varenne interrogated him respecting a detail of manners and customs of which he had been informed by an officer. It was with respect to the Mzab, that strange little Arab republic sprung up in the midst of the Sahara, in the driest part of that burning region.

Duroy had twice visited the Mzab, and he narrated some of the customs of this singular country, where drops of water are valued as gold; where every inhabitant is bound to discharge all public duties; and where commercial honesty is carried further than among civilized nations.

He spoke with a certain raciness excited by the wine and the desire to please, and told regimental yarns, incidents of Arab life and military adventure. He even hit on some telling phrases to depict these bare and yellow lands, eternally laid waste by the devouring fire of the sun.

All the women had their eyes turned upon him, and Madame Walter said, in her deliberate tones: "You could make a charming series of articles out of your recollections."

Then Walter looked at the young fellow over the glasses of his spectacles, as was his custom when he wanted to see anyone's face distinctly. He looked at the dishes underneath them.

Forestier seized the opportunity. "My dear sir, I had already spoken to you about Monsieur George Duroy, asking you to let me have him for my assistant in gleaning political topics. Since Marambot left us, I have no one to send in quest of urgent and confidential information, and the paper suffers from it."

Daddy Walter became serious, and pushed his spectacles upon his forehead, in order to look Duroy well in the face. Then he said: "It is true that Monsieur Duroy has evidently an original turn of thought. If he will come and have a chat with us to-morrow at three o'clock, we will settle the matter." Then, after a short silence, turning right round towards George, he added: "But write us a little fancy series of articles on Algeria at once. Relate your experiences, and mix up the colonization question with them as you did just now. They are facts, genuine facts, and I am sure they will greatly please our readers. But be quick. I must have the first article to-morrow or the day after, while the subject is being discussed in the Chamber, in order to catch the public."

Madame Walter added, with that serious grace which characterized everything she did, and which lent an air of favor to her words: "And you have a charming title, 'Recollections of a Chasseur d'Afrique.' Is it not so, Monsieur Norbert?"

The old poet, who had worn renown late in life, feared and hated newcomers. He replied dryly: "Yes, excellent, provided that the keynote be followed, for that is the great difficulty; the exact note, what in music is called the pitch."

Madame Forestier cast on Duroy a smiling and protective glance, the glance of a connoisseur, which seemed to say: "Yes, you will get on." Madame de

Marelle had turned towards him several times, and the diamond in her ear quivered incessantly as though the drop of water was about to fall.

The little girl remained quiet and serious, her head bent over her plate.

But the servant passed round the table, filling the blue glasses with Johannisberg, and Forestier proposed a toast, drinking with a bow to Monsieur Walter: "Prosperity to the *Vie Francaise*."

Everyone bowed towards the proprietor, who smiled, and Duroy, intoxicated with success, emptied his glass at a draught. He would have emptied a whole barrel after the same fashion; it seemed to him that he could have eaten a bullock or strangled a lion. He felt a superhuman strength in his limbs, unconquerable resolution and unbounded hope in his mind. He was now at home among these people; he had just taken his position, won his place. His glance rested on their faces with a new-born assurance, and he ventured for the first time to address his neighbor. "You have the prettiest earrings I have ever seen, Madame."

She turned towards him with a smile. "It was an idea of my own to have the diamonds hung like that, just at the end of a thread. They really look like dew-drops, do they not?"

He murmured, ashamed of his own daring, and afraid of making a fool of himself:

"It is charming; but the ear, too, helps to set it off."

She thanked him with a look, one of those woman's looks that go straight to the heart. And as he turned his head he again met Madame Forestier's eye, always kindly, but now he thought sparkling with a livelier mirth, an archness, an encouragement.

All the men were now talking at once with gesticulations and raised voices. They were discussing the great project of the metropolitan railway. The subject was not exhausted till dessert was finished, everyone having a deal to say about the slowness of the methods of communication in Paris, the inconvenience of the tramway, the delays of omnibus traveling, and the rudeness of cabmen.

Then they left the dining-room to take coffee. Duroy, in jest, offered his arm to the little girl. She gravely thanked him, and rose on tiptoe in order to rest her hand on it.

On returning to the drawing-room he again experienced the sensation of entering a greenhouse. In each of the four corners of the room tall palms unfolded their elegantly shaped leaves, rising to the ceiling, and there spreading fountain-wise.

On each side of the fireplace were india-rubber plants like round columns, with their dark green leaves tapering one above the other; and on the piano two unknown shrubs covered with flowers, those of one all crimson and those of the other all white, had the appearance of artificial plants, looking too beautiful to be real.

The air was cool, and laden with a soft, vague perfume that could scarcely be defined. The young fellow, now more himself, considered the room more attentively. It was not large; nothing attracted attention with the exception of the shrubs, no bright color struck one, but one felt at one's ease in it; one felt soothed and refreshed, and, as it were, caressed by one's surroundings. The walls were covered with an old-fashioned stuff of faded violet, spotted with little flowers in yellow silk about the size of flies. Hangings of grayish-blue cloth, embroidered here and there with crimson poppies, draped the doorways, and the chairs of all shapes and sizes, scattered about the room, lounging chairs, easy chairs, ottomans, and stools, were upholstered in Louise Seize silk or Utrecht velvet, with a crimson pattern on a cream-colored ground.

"Do you take coffee, Monsieur Duroy?" and Madame Forestier held out a cup towards him with that smile which never left her lips.

"Thank you, Madame." He took the cup, and as he bent forward to take a lump of sugar from the sugar-basin carried by the little girl, Madame Forestier said to him in a low voice: "Pay attention to Madame Walter."

Then she drew back before he had time to answer a word.

He first drank off his coffee, which he was afraid of dropping onto the carpet; then, his mind more at ease, he sought for some excuse to approach the wife of his new governor, and begin a conversation. All at once he noticed that she was holding an empty cup in her hand, and as she was at some distance from a table, did not know where to put it. He darted forward with, "Allow me, Madame?"

"Thank you, sir."

He took away the cup and then returned.

"If you knew, Madame," he began, "the happy hours the *Vie Francaise* helped me to pass when I was away in the desert. It is really the only paper that is readable out of France, for it is more literary, wittier, and less monotonous than the others. There is something of everything in it."

She smiled with amiable indifference, and answered, seriously:

"Monsieur Walter has had a great deal of trouble to create a type of newspaper supplying the want of the day."

And they began to chat. He had an easy flow of commonplace conversation, a charm in his voice and look, and an irresistible seductiveness about his moustache. It curled coquettishly about his lips, reddish brown, with a paler tint about the ends. They chatted about Paris, its suburbs, the banks of the Seine, watering places, summer amusements, all the current topics on which one can prate to infinity without wearying oneself.

Then as Monsieur Norbert de Varenne approached with a liqueur glass in his hand, Duroy discreetly withdrew.

Madame de Marelle, who had been speaking with Madame Forestier, summoned him.

"Well, sir," she said, abruptly, "so you want to try your hand at journalism?"

He spoke vaguely of his prospects, and there recommenced with her the conversation he had just had with Madame Walter, but as he was now a better master of his subject, he showed his superiority in it, repeating as his own the things he had just heard. And he continually looked his companion in the eyes, as though to give deep meaning to what he was saying.

She, in her turn, related anecdotes with the easy flow of spirits of a woman who knows she is witty, and is always seeking to appear so, and becoming familiar, she laid her hand from time to time on his arm, and lowered her voice to make trifling remarks which thus assumed a character of intimacy. He was inwardly excited by her contact. He would have liked to have shown his devotion for her on the spot, to have defended her, shown her what he was worth, and his delay in his replies to her showed the preoccupation of his mind.

But suddenly, without any reason, Madame de Marelle called, "Laurine!" and the little girl came.

"Sit down here, child; you will catch cold near the window."

Duroy was seized with a wild longing to kiss the child. It was as though some part of the kiss would reach the mother.

He asked in a gallant, and at the same time fatherly, tone: "Will you allow me to kiss you, Mademoiselle?"

The child looked up at him in surprise.

"Answer, my dear," said Madame de Marelle, laughingly.

"Yes, sir, this time; but it will not do always."

Duroy, sitting down, lifted Laurine onto his knees and brushed the fine curly hair above her forehead with his lips.

Her mother was surprised. "What! she has not run away; it is astounding. Usually she will only let ladies kiss her. You are irresistible, Monsieur Duroy."

He blushed without answering, and gently jogged the little girl on his knee.

Madame Forestier drew near, and exclaimed, with astonishment: "What, Laurine tamed! What a miracle!"

Jacques Rival also came up, cigar in mouth, and Duroy rose to take leave, afraid of spoiling, by some unlucky remark, the work done, his task of conquest begun.

He bowed, softly pressed the little outstretched hands of the women, and then heartily shook those of the men. He noted that the hand of Jacques Rival, warm and dry, answered cordially to his grip; that of Norbert de Varenne, damp and cold, slipped through his fingers; that of Daddy Walter, cold and flabby, was without expression or energy; and that of Forestier was plump and moist. His friend said to him in a low tone, "To-morrow, at three o'clock; do not forget."

"Oh! no; don't be afraid of that."

When he found himself once more on the stairs he felt a longing to run down them, so great was his joy, and he darted forward, going down two steps at a time, but suddenly he caught sight in a large mirror on the second-floor landing of a gentleman in a hurry, who was advancing briskly to meet him, and he stopped short, ashamed, as if he had been caught tripping. Then he looked at himself in the glass for some time, astonished at being really such a handsome fellow, smiled complacently, and taking leave of his reflection, bowed low to it as one bows to a personage of importance.

III

When George Duroy found himself in the street he hesitated as to what he should do. He wanted to run, to dream, to walk about thinking of the future as he breathed the soft night air, but the thought of the series of articles asked for by Daddy Walter haunted him, and he decided to go home at once and set to work.

He walked along quickly, reached the outer boulevards, and followed their line as far as the Rue Boursault, where he dwelt. The house, six stories high, was inhabited by a score of small households, trades-people or workmen, and he experienced a sickening sensation of disgust, a longing to leave the place and live like well-to-do people in a clean dwelling, as he ascended the stairs, lighting himself with wax matches on his way up the dirty steps, littered with bits of paper, cigarette ends, and scraps of kitchen refuse. A stagnant stench of cooking, cesspools and humanity, a close smell of dirt and old walls, which no rush of air could have driven out of the building, filled it from top to bottom.

The young fellow's room, on the fifth floor, looked into a kind of abyss, the huge cutting of the Western Railway just above the outlet by the tunnel of the Batignolles station. Duroy opened his window and leaned against the rusty iron cross-bar.

Below him, at the bottom of the dark hole, three motionless red lights resembled the eyes of huge wild animals, and further on a glimpse could be caught of others, and others again still further. Every moment whistles, prolonged or brief, pierced the silence of the night, some near at hand, others scarcely discernible, coming from a distance from the direction of Asnières. Their modulations were akin to those of the human voice. One of them came nearer and nearer, with its plaintive appeal growing louder and louder every moment, and soon a big yellow light appeared advancing with a loud noise, and Duroy watched the string of railway carriages swallowed up by the tunnel.

Then he said to himself: "Come, let's go to work."

He placed his light upon the table, but at the moment of commencing he found that he had only a quire of letter paper in the place. More the pity, but he would make use of it by opening out each sheet to its full extent. He dipped his pen in ink, and wrote at the head of the page, in his best hand, "Recollections of a Chasseur d'Afrique."

Then he tried to frame the opening sentence. He remained with his head on his hands and his eyes fixed on the white sheet spread out before him. What should he say? He could no longer recall anything of what he had been relating a little while back; not an anecdote, not a fact, nothing.

All at once the thought struck him: "I must begin with my departure."

And he wrote: "It was in 1874, about the middle of May, when France, in her exhaustion, was reposing after the catastrophe of the terrible year."

He stopped short, not knowing how to lead up to what should follow—his embarkation, his voyage, his first impressions.

After ten minutes' reflection, he resolved to put off the introductory slip till to-morrow, and to set to work at once to describe Algiers.

And he traced on his paper the words: "Algiers is a white city," without being able to state anything further. He recalled in his mind the pretty white city flowing down in a cascade of flat-roofed dwellings from the summit of its hills to the sea, but he could no longer find a word to express what he had seen and felt.

After a violent effort, he added: "It is partly inhabited by Arabs."

Then he threw down his pen and rose from his chair.

On his little iron bedstead, hollowed in the center by the pressure of his body, he saw his everyday garments cast down there, empty, worn, limp, ugly as the clothing at the morgue. On a straw-bottomed chair his tall hat, his only one, brim uppermost, seemed to be awaiting an alms.

The wall paper, gray with blue bouquets, showed as many stains as flowers, old suspicious-looking stains, the origin of which could not be defined; crushed insects or drops of oil; finger tips smeared with pomatum or soapy water scattered while washing. It smacked of shabby, genteel poverty, the poverty of a Paris lodging-house. Anger rose within him at the wretchedness of his mode of living. He said to himself that he must get out of it at once; that he must finish with this irksome existence the very next day.

A frantic desire of working having suddenly seized on him again, he sat down once more at the table, and began anew to seek for phrases to describe the strange and charming physiognomy of Algiers, that ante-room of vast and mysterious Africa; the Africa of wandering Arabs and unknown tribes of negroes; that unexplored Africa of which we are sometimes shown in public gardens the improbable-looking animals seemingly made to figure in fairy tales; the ostriches, those exaggerated fowls; the gazelles, those divine goats; the surprising and grotesque giraffes; the grave-looking camels, the monstrous hippopotomi, the shapeless rhinosceri, and the gorillas, those frightful-looking brothers of mankind.

He vaguely felt ideas occurring to him; he might perhaps have uttered them, but he could not put them into writing. And his impotence exasperated him, he got up again, his hands damp with perspiration, and his temples throbbing.

His eyes falling on his washing bill, brought up that evening by the concierge, he was suddenly seized with wild despair. All his joy vanishing in a twinkling, with his confidence in himself and his faith in the future. It was all up; he could not do anything, he would never be anybody; he felt played out, incapable, good for nothing, damned.

And he went and leaned out of the window again, just as a train issued from the tunnel with a loud and violent noise. It was going away, afar off, across the fields and plains towards the sea. And the recollection of his parents stirred in Duroy's breast. It would pass near them, that train, within a few leagues of their house. He saw it again, the little house at the entrance to the village of Canteleu, on the summit of the slope overlooking Rouen and the immense valley of the Seine.

His father and mother kept a little inn, a place where the tradesfolk of the suburbs of Rouen came out to lunch on Sunday at the sign of the Belle Vue. They had wanted to make a gentleman of their son, and had sent him to college. Having finished his studies, and been plowed for his bachelor's degree, he had entered on his military service with the intention of becoming an officer, a colonel, a general. But, disgusted with military life long before the completion of his five years' term of service, he had dreamed of making a fortune at Paris.

He came there at the expiration of his term of service, despite the entreaties of his father and mother, whose visions having evaporated, wanted now to have him at home with them. In his turn he hoped to achieve a future; he foresaw a triumph by means as yet vaguely defined in his mind, but which he felt sure he could scheme out and further.

He had had some successful love affairs in the regiment, some easy conquests, and even some adventures in a better class of society, having seduced a tax collector's daughter, who wanted to leave her home for his sake, and a lawyer's wife, who had tried to drown herself in despair at being abandoned.

His comrades used to say of him: "He is a sharp fellow, a deep one to get out of a scrape, a chap who knows which side his bread is buttered," and he had promised himself to act up to this character.

His conscience, Norman by birth, worn by the daily dealings of garrison life, rendered elastic by the examples of pillaging in Africa, illicit commissions, shaky dodges; spurred, too, by the notions of honor current in the army, military bravadoes, patriotic sentiments, the fine-sounding tales current among sub-officers, and the vain glory of the profession of arms, had become a kind of box of tricks in which something of everything was to be found.

But the wish to succeed reigned sovereign in it.

He had, without noticing it, began to dream again as he did every evening. He pictured to himself some splendid love adventure which should bring about all at once the realization of his hopes. He married the daughter of some banker or nobleman met with in the street, and captivated at the first glance.

The shrill whistle of a locomotive which, issuing from the tunnel like a big rabbit bolting out of its hole, and tearing at full speed along the rails towards the machine shed where it was to take its rest, awoke him from his dream.

Then, repossessed by the vague and joyful hope which ever haunted his mind, he wafted a kiss into the night, a kiss of love addressed to the vision of the woman he was awaiting, a kiss of desire addressed to the fortune he coveted. Then he closed his window and began to undress, murmuring:

"I shall feel in a better mood for it to-morrow. My thoughts are not clear to-night. Perhaps, too, I have had just a little too much to drink. One can't work well under those circumstances."

He got into bed, blew out his light, and went off to sleep almost immediately.

He awoke early, as one awakes on mornings of hope and trouble, and jumping out of bed, opened his window to drink a cup of fresh air, as he phrased it.

The houses of the Rue de Rome opposite, on the other side of the broad railway cutting, glittering in the rays of the rising sun, seemed to be painted with white light. Afar off on the right a glimpse was caught of the slopes of Argenteuil, the hills of Sannois, and the windmills of Orgemont through a light bluish mist; like a floating and transparent veil cast onto the horizon.

Duroy remained for some minutes gazing at the distant country side, and he murmured: "It would be devilish nice out there a day like this." Then he bethought himself that he must set to work, and that at once, and also send his concierge's lad, at a cost of ten sous, to the office to say that he was ill.

He sat down at his table, dipped his pen in the ink, leaned his forehead on his hand, and sought for ideas. All in vain, nothing came.

He was not discouraged, however. He thought, "Bah! I am not accustomed to it. It is a trade to be learned like all other trades. I must have some help the first time. I will go and find Forestier, who will give me a start for my article in ten minutes."

And he dressed himself.

When he got into the street he came to the conclusion that it was still too early to present himself at the residence of his friend, who must be a late sleeper. He therefore walked slowly along beneath the trees of the outer boulevards. It was not yet nine o'clock when he reached the Parc Monceau, fresh from its morning watering. Sitting down upon a bench he began to dream again. A well-dressed young man was walking up and down at a short distance, awaiting a woman, no doubt. Yes, she appeared, close veiled and quick stepping, and taking his arm, after a brief clasp of the hand, they walked away together.

A riotous need of love broke out in Duroy's heart, a need of amours at once distinguished and delicate. He rose and resumed his journey, thinking of Forestier. What luck the fellow had!

He reached the door at the moment his friend was coming out of it. "You here at this time of day. What do you want of me?"

Duroy, taken aback at meeting him thus, just as he was starting off, stammered: "You see, you see, I can't manage to write my article; you know the article Monsieur Walter asked me to write on Algeria. It is not very surprising, considering that I have never written anything. Practice is needed for that, as for everything else. I shall get used to it very quickly, I am sure, but I do not know how to set about beginning. I have plenty of ideas, but I cannot manage to express them."

He stopped, hesitatingly, and Forestier smiled somewhat slyly, saying: "I know what it is."

Duroy went on: "Yes, it must happen to everyone at the beginning. Well, I came, I came to ask you for a lift. In ten minutes you can give me a start, you can show me how to shape it. It will be a good lesson in style you will give me, and really without you I do not see how I can get on with it."

Forestier still smiled, and tapping his old comrade on the arm, said: "Go in and see my wife; she will settle your business quite as well as I could. I have trained her for that kind of work. I, myself, have not time this morning, or I would willingly have done it for you."

Duroy suddenly abashed, hesitated, feeling afraid.

"But I cannot call on her at this time of the day."

"Oh, yes; she is up. You will find her in my study arranging some notes for me."

Duroy refused to go upstairs, saying: "No, I can't think of such a thing."

Forestier took him by the shoulders, twisted him round on his heels, and pushing him towards the staircase, said: "Go along, you great donkey, when I tell you to. You are not going to oblige me to go up these flights of stairs again to introduce you and explain the fix you are in."

Then Duroy made up his mind. "Thanks, then, I will go up," he said. "I shall tell her that you forced me, positively forced me to come and see her."

"All right. She won't scratch your eyes out. Above all, do not forget our appointment for three o'clock."

"Oh! don't be afraid about that."

Forestier hastened off, and Duroy began to ascend the stairs slowly, step by step, thinking over what he should say, and feeling uneasy as to his probable reception.

The man servant, wearing a blue apron, and holding a broom in his hand, opened the door to him.

"Master is not at home," he said, without waiting to be spoken to.

Duroy persisted.

"Ask Madame Forestier," said he, "whether she will receive me, and tell her that I have come from her husband, whom I met in the street."

Then he waited while the man went away, returned, and opening the door on the right, said: "Madame will see you, sir."

She was seated in an office armchair in a small room, the walls of which were wholly hidden by books carefully ranged on shelves of black wood. The bindings, of various tints, red, yellow, green, violet, and blue, gave some color and liveliness to those monotonous lines of volumes.

She turned round, still smiling. She was wrapped in a white dressing gown, trimmed with lace, and as she held out her hand, displayed her bare arm in its wide sleeve.

"Already?" said she, and then added: "That is not meant for a reproach, but a simple question."

"Oh, madame, I did not want to come up, but your husband, whom I met at the bottom of the house, obliged me to. I am so confused that I dare not tell you what brings me."

She pointed to a chair, saying: "Sit down and tell me about it."

She was twirling a goose-quill between her fingers, and in front of her was a half-written page, interrupted by the young fellow's arrival. She seemed quite at home at this work table, as much at her ease as if in her drawing-room, engaged on everyday tasks. A faint perfume emanated from her dressing gown, the fresh perfume of a recent toilet. Duroy sought to divine, fancied he could trace, the outline of her plump, youthful figure through the soft material enveloping it.

She went on, as he did not reply: "Well, come tell me what is it."

He murmured, hesitatingly: "Well, you see—but I really dare not—I was working last night very late and quite early this morning on the article upon Algeria, upon which Monsieur Walter asked me to write, and I could not get on with it—I tore up all my attempts. I am not accustomed to this kind of work, and I came to ask Forestier to help me this once—"

She interrupted him, laughing heartily. "And he told you to come and see me? That is a nice thing."

"Yes, madame. He said that you will get me out of my difficulty better than himself, but I did not dare, I did not wish to—you understand."

She rose, saying: "It will be delightful to work in collaboration with you like that. I am charmed at the notion. Come, sit down in my place, for they know my hand-writing at the office. And we will knock you off an article; oh, but a good one."

He sat down, took a pen, spread a sheet of paper before him, and waited.

Madame Forestier, standing by, watched him make these preparations, then took a cigarette from the mantel-shelf, and lit it.

"I cannot work without smoking," said she. "Come, what are you going to say?"

He lifted his head towards her with astonishment.

"But that is just what I don't know, since it is that I came to see you about."

She replied: "Oh, I will put it in order for you. I will make the sauce, but then I want the materials of the dish."

He remained embarrassed before her. At length he said, hesitatingly: "I should like to relate my journey, then, from the beginning."

Then she sat down before him on the other side of the table, and looking him in the eyes:

"Well, tell it me first; for myself alone, you understand, slowly and without forgetting anything, and I will select what is to be used of it."

But as he did not know where to commence, she began to question him as a priest would have done in the confessional, putting precise questions which recalled to him forgotten details, people encountered and faces merely caught sight of.

When she had made him speak thus for about a quarter of an hour, she suddenly interrupted him with: "Now we will begin. In the first place, we will imagine that you are narrating your impressions to a friend, which will allow you to write a lot of tom-foolery, to make remarks of all kinds, to be natural and funny if we can. Begin:

"'My Dear Henry,—You want to know what Algeria is like, and you shall. I will send you, having nothing else to do in a little cabin of dried mud which serves me as a habitation, a kind of journal of my life, day by day, and hour by hour. It will be a little lively at times, more is the pity, but you are not obliged to show it to your lady friends.'"

She paused to re-light her cigarette, which had gone out, and the faint creaking of the quill on the paper stopped, too.

"Let us continue," said she.

"Algeria is a great French country on the frontiers of the great unknown countries called the Desert, the Sahara, central Africa, etc., etc.

"Algiers is the door, the pretty white door of this strange continent.

"But it is first necessary to get to it, which is not a rosy job for everyone. I am, you know, an excellent horseman, since I break in the colonel's horses; but a man may be a very good rider and a very bad sailor. That is my case.

"You remember Surgeon-Major Simbretras, whom we used to call Old Ipecacuanha, and how, when we thought ourselves ripe for a twenty-four hours' stay in the infirmary, that blessed sojourning place, we used to go up before him.

"How he used to sit in his chair, with his fat legs in his red trousers, wide apart, his hands on his knees, and his elbows stuck, rolling his great eyes and gnawing his white moustache.

"You remember his favorite mode of treatment: 'This man's stomach is out of order. Give him a dose of emetic number three, according to my prescription, and then twelve hours off duty, and he will be all right.'

"It was a sovereign remedy that emetic—sovereign and irresistible. One swallowed it because one had to. Then when one had undergone the effects of Old Ipecacuanha's prescription, one enjoyed twelve well-earned hours' rest.

"Well, my dear fellow, to reach Africa, it is necessary to undergo for forty hours the effects of another kind of irresistible emetic, according to the prescription of the Compagnie Transatlantique."

She rubbed her hands, delighted with the idea.

She got up and walked about, after having lit another cigarette, and dictated as she puffed out little whiffs of smoke, which, issuing at first through a little round hole in the midst of her compressed lips, slowly evaporated, leaving in the air faint gray lines, a kind of transparent mist, like a spider's web. Sometimes with her open hand she would brush these light traces aside; at others she would cut them asunder with her forefinger, and then watch with serious attention the two halves of the almost impenetrable vapor slowly disappear.

Duroy, with his eyes, followed all her gestures, her attitudes, the movements of her form and features—busied with this vague pastime which did not preoccupy her thoughts.

She now imagined the incidents of the journey, sketched traveling companions invented by herself, and a love affair with the wife of a captain of infantry on her way to join her husband.

Then, sitting down again, she questioned Duroy on the topography of Algeria, of which she was absolutely ignorant. In ten minutes she knew as much about it as he did, and she dictated a little chapter of political and colonial geography to coach the reader up in such matters and prepare him to understand the serious questions which were to be brought forward in the following articles. She continued by a trip into the provinces of Oran, a fantastic trip, in which it was, above all, a question of women, Moorish, Jewish, and Spanish.

"That is what interests most," she said.

She wound up by a sojourn at Saïda, at the foot of the great tablelands; and by a pretty little intrigue between the sub-officer, George Duroy, and a Spanish work-girl employed at the *alfa* factory at Ain el Hadjar. She described their rendezvous at night amidst the bare, stony hills, with jackals, hyenas, and Arab dogs yelling, barking and howling among the rocks.

And she gleefully uttered the words: "To be continued." Then rising, she added: "That is how one writes an article, my dear sir. Sign it, if you please."

He hesitated.

"But sign it, I tell you."

Then he began to laugh, and wrote at the bottom of the page, "George Duroy."

She went on smoking as she walked up and down; and he still kept looking at her, unable to find anything to say to thank her, happy to be with her, filled with gratitude, and with the sensual pleasure of this new-born intimacy. It seemed to him that everything surrounding him was part of her, everything down to the walls covered with books. The chairs, the furniture, the air in which the perfume of tobacco was floating, had something special, nice, sweet, and charming, which emanated from her.

Suddenly she asked: "What do you think of my friend, Madame de Marelle?"

He was surprised, and answered: "I think—I think—her very charming."

"Is it not so?"

"Yes, certainly."

He longed to add: "But not so much as yourself," but dared not.

She resumed: "And if you only knew how funny, original, and intelligent she is. She is a Bohemian—a true Bohemian. That is why her husband scarcely cares for her. He only sees her defects, and does not appreciate her good qualities."

Duroy felt stupefied at learning that Madame de Marelle was married, and yet it was only natural that she should be.

He said: "Oh, she is married, then! And what is her husband?"

Madame Forestier gently shrugged her shoulders, and raised her eyebrows, with a gesture of incomprehensible meaning.

"Oh! he is an inspector on the Northern Railway. He spends eight days out of the month in Paris. What his wife calls 'obligatory service,' or 'weekly duty,' or 'holy week.' When you know her better you will see how nice and bright she is. Go and call on her one of these days."

Duroy no longer thought of leaving. It seemed to him that he was going to stop for ever; that he was at home.

But the door opened noiselessly, and a tall gentleman entered without being announced. He stopped short on seeing a stranger. Madame Forestier seemed troubled for a moment; then she said in natural tones, though a slight rosy flush had risen to her cheeks:

"Come in, my dear sir. I must introduce one of Charles' old friends, Monsieur George Duroy, a future journalist." Then in another tone, she added: "Our best and most intimate friend, the Count de Vaudrec."

The two men bowed, looking each other in the eyes, and Duroy at once took his leave.

There was no attempt to detain him. He stammered a few thanks, grasped the outstretched hand of Madame Forestier, bowed again to the newcomer, who preserved the cold, grave air of a man of position, and went out quite disturbed, as if he had made a fool of himself.

On finding himself once more in the street, he felt sad and uneasy, haunted by the vague idea of some hidden vexation. He walked on, asking himself whence came this sudden melancholy. He could not tell, but the stern face of the Count de Vaudrec, already somewhat aged, with gray hair, and the calmly insolent look of a very wealthy man, constantly recurred to his recollection. He noted that the arrival of this unknown, breaking off a charming *tête-à-tête*, had produced in him that chilly, despairing sensation that a word overheard, a trifle noticed, the least thing suffices sometimes to bring about. It seemed to him, too, that this man, without his being able to guess why, had been displeased at finding him there.

He had nothing more to do till three o'clock, and it was not yet noon. He had still six francs fifty centimes in his pocket, and he went and lunched at a Bouillon Duval. Then he prowled about the boulevard, and as three o'clock struck, ascended the staircase, in itself an advertisement, of the *Vie Francaise*.

The messengers-in-waiting were seated with folded arms on a bench, while at a kind of desk a doorkeeper was sorting the correspondence that had just arrived. The entire get-up of the place, intended to impress visitors, was perfect. Everyone had the appearance, bearing, dignity, and smartness suitable to the ante-room of a large newspaper.

"Monsieur Walter, if you please?" inquired Duroy.

"The manager is engaged, sir," replied the doorkeeper. "Will you take a seat, sir?" and he indicated the waiting-room, already full of people.

There were men grave, important-looking, and decorated; and men without visible linen, whose frock-coats, buttoned up to the chin, bore upon the breast stains recalling the outlines of continents and seas on geographical maps. There were three women among them. One of them was pretty, smiling, and decked out, and had the air of a gay woman; her neighbor, with a wrinkled, tragic countenance, decked out also, but in more severe fashion, had about her something worn and artificial which old actresses generally have; a kind of false youth, like a scent of stale love. The third woman, in mourning, sat in a corner, with the air of a desolate widow. Duroy thought that she had come to ask for charity.

However, no one was ushered into the room beyond, and more than twenty minutes had elapsed.

Duroy was seized with an idea, and going back to the doorkeeper, said: "Monsieur Walter made an appointment for me to call on him here at three o'clock. At all events, see whether my friend, Monsieur Forestier, is here."

He was at once ushered along a lengthy passage, which brought him to a large room where four gentlemen were writing at a large green-covered table.

Forestier standing before the fireplace was smoking a cigarette and playing at cup and ball. He was very clever at this, and kept spiking the huge ball of yellow boxwood on the wooden point. He was counting "Twenty-two, twenty-three, twenty-four, twenty-five."

"Twenty-six," said Duroy.

His friend raised his eyes without interrupting the regular movement of his arm, saying: "Oh! here you are, then. Yesterday I landed the ball fifty-seven times right off. There is only Saint-Potin who can beat me at it among those here. Have you seen the governor? There is nothing funnier than to see that old tubby Norbert playing at cup and ball. He opens his mouth as if he was going to swallow the ball every time."

One of the others turned round towards him, saying: "I say, Forestier, I know of one for sale, a beauty in West Indian wood; it is said to have belonged to the Queen of Spain. They want sixty francs for it. Not dear."

Forestier asked: "Where does it hang out?"

And as he had missed his thirty-seventh shot, he opened a cupboard in which Duroy saw a score of magnificent cups and balls, arranged and numbered like a collection of art objects. Then having put back the one he had been using in its usual place, he repeated: "Where does this gem hang out?"

The journalist replied: "At a box-office keeper's of the Vaudeville. I will bring it you to-morrow, if you like."

"All right. If it is really a good one I will take it; one can never have too many." Then turning to Duroy he added: "Come with me. I will take you in to see the governor; otherwise you might be getting mouldy here till seven in the evening."

They re-crossed the waiting-room, in which the same people were waiting in the same order. As soon as Forestier appeared the young woman and the old actress, rising quickly, came up to him. He took them aside one after the other into the bay of the window, and although they took care to talk in low tones, Duroy noticed that they were on familiar terms.

Then, having passed through two padded doors, they entered the manager's room. The conference which had been going on for an hour or so was nothing more than a game at ecarté with some of the gentlemen with the flat brimmed hats whom Duroy had noticed the night before.

Monsieur Walter dealt and played with concentrated attention and crafty movements, while his adversary threw down, picked up, and handled the light bits of colored pasteboard with the swiftness, skill, and grace of a practiced player. Norbert de Varenne, seated in the managerial armchair, was writing an article. Jacques Rival, stretched at full length on a couch, was smoking a cigar with his eyes closed.

The room smelled close, with that blended odor of leather-covered furniture, stale tobacco, and printing-ink peculiar to editors' rooms and familiar to all journalists. Upon the black wood table, inlaid with brass, lay an incredible pile of papers, letters, cards, newspapers, magazines, bills, and printed matter of every description.

Forestier shook hands with the punters standing behind the card players, and without saying a word watched the progress of the game; then, as soon as Daddy Walter had won, he said: "Here is my friend, Duroy."

The manager glanced sharply at the young fellow over the glasses of his spectacles, and said:

"Have you brought my article? It would go very well to-day with the Morel debate."

Duroy took the sheets of paper folded in four from his pocket, saying: "Here it is sir."

The manager seemed pleased, and remarked, with a smile: "Very good, very good. You are a man of your word. You must look through this for me, Forestier."

But Forestier hastened to reply: "It is not worth while, Monsieur Walter. I did it with him to give him a lesson in the tricks of the trade. It is very well done."

And the manager, who was gathering up the cards dealt by a tall, thin gentleman, a deputy belonging to the Left Center, remarked with indifference: "All right, then."

Forestier, however, did not let him begin the new game, but stooping, murmured in his ear: "You know you promised me to take on Duroy to replace Marambot. Shall I engage him on the same terms?"

"Yes, certainly."

Taking his friend's arm, the journalist led him away, while Monsieur Walter resumed the game.

Norbert de Varenne had not lifted his head; he did not appear to have seen or recognized Duroy. Jacques Rival, on the contrary, had taken his hand with the marked and demonstrative energy of a comrade who may be reckoned upon in the case of any little difficulty.

They passed through the waiting-room again, and as everyone looked at them, Forestier said to the youngest of the women, in a tone loud enough to be heard by the rest: "The manager will see you directly. He is just now engaged with two members of the Budget Committee."

Then he passed swiftly on, with an air of hurry and importance, as though about to draft at once an article of the utmost weight.

As soon as they were back in the reporters' room Forestier at once took up his cup and ball, and as he began to play with it again, said to Duroy, breaking his sentences in order to count: "You will come here every day at three o'clock, and I will tell you the places you are to go to, either during the day or in the evening, or the next morning—one—I will give you, first of all, a letter of introduction to the head of the First Department of the Préfecture of Police—two—who will put you in communication with one of his clerks. You will settle with him about all the important information—three—from the Préfecture, official and quasi-official information, you know. In all matters of detail you will apply to Saint-Potin, who is up in the work—four—You can see him by-and-by, or to-morrow. You must, above all, cultivate the knack of dragging information out of men I send you to see—five—and to get in everywhere, in spite of closed doors—six—You will have for this a salary of two hundred francs a month, with two sous a line for the paragraphs you glean—seven—and two sous a line for all articles written by you to order on different subjects—eight."

Then he gave himself up entirely to his occupation, and went on slowly counting: "Nine, ten, eleven, twelve, thirteen." He missed the fourteenth, and swore, "Damn that thirteen, it always brings me bad luck. I shall die on the thirteenth of some month, I am certain."

One of his colleagues who had finished his work also took a cup and ball from the cupboard. He was a little man, who looked like a boy, although he was really five-and-thirty. Several other journalists having come in, went one after the other and got out the toy belonging to each of them. Soon there were six standing side by side, with their backs to the wall, swinging into the air, with even and regular motion, the balls of red, yellow, and black, according to the wood they were made of. And a match having begun, the two who were still working got up to act as umpires. Forestier won by eleven points. Then the little man, with the juvenile aspect, who had lost, rang for the messenger, and gave the order, "Nine bocks." And they began to play again pending the arrival of these refreshments.

Duroy drank a glass of beer with his new comrades, and then said to his friend: "What am I to do now?"

"I have nothing for you to-day. You can go if you want to."

"And our—our—article, will it go in to-night?"

"Yes, but do not bother yourself about it; I will correct the proofs. Write the continuation for to-morrow, and come here at three o'clock, the same as to-day."

Duroy having shaken hands with everyone, without even knowing their names, went down the magnificent staircase with a light heart and high spirits.

IV

George Duroy slept badly, so excited was he by the wish to see his article in print. He was up as soon as it was daylight, and was prowling about the streets long before the hour at which the porters from the newspaper offices run with their papers from kiosque to kiosque. He went on to the Saint Lazare terminus, knowing that the *Vie Francaise* would be delivered there before it reached his own district. As he was still too early, he wandered up and down on the footpath.

He witnessed the arrival of the newspaper vendor who opened her glass shop, and then saw a man bearing on his head a pile of papers. He rushed forward. There were the *Figaro*, the *Gil Blas*, the *Gaulois*, the *Evenement*, and two or three morning journals, but the *Vie Francaise* was not among them. Fear seized him. Suppose the "Recollections of a Chasseur d'Afrique" had been kept over for the next day, or that by chance they had not at the last moment seemed suitable to Daddy Walter.

Turning back to the kiosque, he saw that the paper was on sale without his having seen it brought there. He darted forward, unfolded it, after having thrown down the three sous, and ran through the headings of the articles on the first page. Nothing. His heart began to beat, and he experienced strong emotion on reading at the foot of a column in large letters, "George Duroy." It was in; what happiness!

He began to walk along unconsciously, the paper in his hand and his hat on one side of his head, with a longing to stop the passers-by in order to say to them: "Buy this, buy this, there is an article by me in it." He would have liked to have bellowed with all the power of his lungs, like some vendors of papers at night on the boulevards, "Read the *Vie Francaise*; read George Duroy's article, 'Recollections of a Chasseur d'Afrique.'" And suddenly he felt a wish to read this article himself, read it in a public place, a *café*, in sight of all. He looked about for some establishment already filled with customers. He had to walk in search of one for some time. He sat down at last in front of a kind of wine shop, where several customers were already installed, and asked for a glass of rum, as he would have asked for one of absinthe, without thinking of the time. Then he cried: "Waiter, bring me the *Vie Francaise*."

A man in a white apron stepped up, saying: "We have not got it, sir; we only take in the *Rappel*, the *Siecle*, the *Lanierne*, and the *Petit Parisien*."

"What a den!" exclaimed Duroy, in a tone of anger and disgust. "Here, go and buy it for me."

The waiter hastened to do so, and brought back the paper. Duroy began to read his article, and several times said aloud: "Very good, very well put," to attract the attention of his neighbors, and inspire them with the wish to know what there was in this sheet. Then, on going away, he left it on the table. The master of the place, noticing this, called him back, saying: "Sir, sir, you are forgetting your paper."

And Duroy replied: "I will leave it to you. I have finished with it. There is a very interesting article in it this morning."

He did not indicate the article, but he noticed as he went away one of his neighbors take the *Vie Francaise* up from the table on which he had left it.

He thought: "What shall I do now?" And he decided to go to his office, take his month's salary, and tender his resignation. He felt a thrill of anticipatory pleasure at the thought of the faces that would be pulled up by the chief of his room and his colleagues. The notion of the bewilderment of the chief above all charmed him.

He walked slowly, so as not to get there too early, the cashier's office not opening before ten o'clock.

His office was a large, gloomy room, in which gas had to be kept burning almost all day long in winter. It looked into a narrow court-yard, with other offices on the further side of it. There were eight clerks there, besides a sub-chief hidden behind a screen in one corner.

Duroy first went to get the hundred and eighteen francs twenty-five centimes enclosed in a yellow envelope, and placed in the drawer of the clerk entrusted with such payments, and then, with a conquering air, entered the large room in which he had already spent so many days.

As soon as he came in the sub-chief, Monsieur Potel, called out to him: "Ah! it is you, Monsieur Duroy? The chief has already asked for you several times. You know that he will not allow anyone to plead illness two days running without a doctor's certificate."

Duroy, who was standing in the middle of the room preparing his sensational effect, replied in a loud voice:

"I don't care a damn whether he does or not."

There was a movement of stupefaction among the clerks, and Monsieur Potel's features showed affrightedly over the screen which shut him up as in a box. He barricaded himself behind it for fear of draughts, for he was rheumatic, but had pierced a couple of holes through the paper to keep an eye on his staff. A pin might have been heard to fall. At length the sub-chief said, hesitatingly: "You said?"

"I said that I don't care a damn about it. I have only called to-day to tender my resignation. I am engaged on the staff of the *Vie Francaise* at five hundred francs a month, and extra pay for all I write. Indeed, I made my *début* this morning."

He had promised himself to spin out his enjoyment, but had not been able to resist the temptation of letting it all out at once.

The effect, too, was overwhelming. No one stirred.

Duroy went on: "I will go and inform Monsieur Perthuis, and then come and wish you good-bye."

And he went out in search of the chief, who exclaimed, on seeing him: "Ah, here you are. You know that I won't have—"

His late subordinate cut him short with: "It's not worth while yelling like that."

Monsieur Perthuis, a stout man, as red as a turkey cock, was choked with bewilderment.

Duroy continued: "I have had enough of this crib. I made my *début* this morning in journalism, where I am assured of a very good position. I have the honor to bid you good-day." And he went out. He was avenged.

As he promised, he went and shook hands with his old colleagues, who scarcely dared to speak to him, for fear of compromising themselves, for they had overheard his conversation with the chief, the door having remained open.

He found himself in the street again, with his salary in his pocket. He stood himself a substantial breakfast at a good but cheap restaurant he was acquainted with, and having again purchased the *Vie Francaise*, and left it on the table, went into several shops, where he bought some trifles, solely for the sake of ordering them to be sent home, and giving his name: "George Duroy," with the addition, "I am the editor of the *Vie Francaise*."

Then he gave the name of the street and the number, taking care to add: "Leave it with the doorkeeper."

As he had still some time to spare he went into the shop of a lithographer, who executed visiting cards at a moment's notice before the eyes of passers-by, and had a hundred, bearing his new occupation under his name, printed off while he waited.

Then he went to the office of the paper.

Forestier received him loftily, as one receives a subordinate. "Ah! here you are. Good. I have several things for you to attend to. Just wait ten minutes. I will just finish what I am about."

And he went on with a letter he was writing.

At the other end of the large table a fat, bald little man, with a very pale, puffy face, and a white and shining head, was writing, with his nose on the paper owing to extreme shortsightedness. Forestier said to him: "I say, Saint-Potin, when are you going to interview those people?"

"At four o'clock."

"Will you take young Duroy here with you, and let him into the way of doing it?"

"All right."

Then turning to his friend, Forestier added: "Have you brought the continuation of the Algerian article? The opening this morning was very successful."

Duroy, taken aback, stammered: "No. I thought I should have time this afternoon. I had heaps of things to do. I was not able."

The other shrugged his shoulders with a dissatisfied air. "If you are not more exact than that you will spoil your future. Daddy Walter was reckoning on your copy. I will tell him it will be ready to-morrow. If you think you are to be paid for doing nothing you are mistaken."

Then, after a short silence, he added: "One must strike the iron while it is hot, or the deuce is in it."

Saint-Potin rose, saying: "I am ready."

Then Forestier, leaning back in his chair, assumed a serious attitude in order to give his instructions, and turning to Duroy, said: "This is what it is. Within the last two days the Chinese General, Li Theng Fao, has arrived at the Hotel Continental, and the Rajah Taposahib Ramaderao Pali at the Hotel Bristol. You will go and interview them." Turning to Saint-Potin, he continued: "Don't forget the main points I told you of. Ask the General and the Rajah their opinion upon the action of England in the East, their ideas upon her system of colonization and domination, and their hopes respecting the intervention of Europe, and especially of France." He was silent for a moment, and then added in a theatrical aside: "It will be most interesting to our readers to learn at the same time what is thought in China and India upon these matters which so forcibly occupy public attention at this moment." He continued, for the benefit of Duroy: "Watch how Saint-

Potin sets to work; he is a capital reporter; and try to learn the trick of pumping a man in five minutes."

Then he gravely resumed his writing, with the evident intention of defining their relative positions, and putting his old comrade and present colleague in his proper place.

As soon as they had crossed the threshold Saint-Potin began to laugh, and said to Duroy: "There's a fluffer for you. He tried to fluff even us. One would really think he took us for his readers."

They reached the boulevard, and the reporter observed: "Will you have a drink?"

"Certainly. It is awfully hot."

They turned into a *café* and ordered cooling drinks. Saint-Potin began to talk. He talked about the paper and everyone connected with it with an abundance of astonishing details.

"The governor? A regular Jew? And you know, nothing can alter a Jew. What a breed!" And he instanced some astounding traits of avariciousness peculiar to the children of Israel, economies of ten centimes, petty bargaining, shameful reductions asked for and obtained, all the ways of a usurer and pawnbroker.

"And yet with all this, a good fellow who believes in nothing and does everyone. His paper, which is Governmental, Catholic, Liberal, Republican, Orleanist, pay your money and take your choice, was only started to help him in his speculations on the Bourse, and bolster up his other schemes. At that game he is very clever, and nets millions through companies without four sous of genuine capital."

He went on, addressing Duroy as "My dear fellow."

"And he says things worthy of Balzac, the old shark. Fancy, the other day I was in his room with that old tub Norbert, and that Don Quixote Rival, when Montelin, our business manager, came in with his morocco bill-case, that bill-case that everyone in Paris knows, under his arm. Walter raised his head and asked: 'What news?' Montelin answered simply: 'I have just paid the sixteen thousand francs we owed the paper maker.' The governor gave a jump, an astonishing jump. 'What do you mean?' said he. 'I have just paid Monsieur Privas,' replied Montelin. 'But you are mad.' 'Why?' 'Why—why—why—' he took off his spectacles and wiped them. Then he smiled with that queer smile that flits across his fat cheeks whenever he is going to say something deep or smart, and went on in a mocking and derisive tone, 'Why? Because we could have obtained a reduction of from four to five thousand francs.' Montelin replied, in astonishment: 'But, sir, all the accounts were correct, checked by me and passed by yourself.' Then the governor, quite serious again, observed: 'What a fool you are. Don't you know, Monsieur Montelin, that one should always let one's debts mount up, in order to offer a composition?'"

And Saint-Potin added, with a knowing shake of his head, "Eh! isn't that worthy of Balzac?"

Duroy had not read Balzac, but he replied, "By Jove! yes."

Then the reporter spoke of Madame Walter, an old goose; of Norbert de Varenne, an old failure; of Rival, a copy of Fervacques. Next he came to Forestier. "As to him, he has been lucky in marrying his wife, that is all."

Duroy asked: "What is his wife, really?"

Saint-Potin rubbed his hands. "Oh! a deep one, a smart woman. She was the mistress of an old rake named Vaudrec, the Count de Vaudrec, who gave her a dowry and married her off."

Duroy suddenly felt a cold shiver run through him, a tingling of the nerves, a longing to smack this gabbler on the face. But he merely interrupted him by asking:

"And your name is Saint-Potin?"

The other replied, simply enough:

"No, my name is Thomas. It is in the office that they have nicknamed me Saint-Potin."

Duroy, as he paid for the drinks, observed: "But it seems to me that time is getting on, and that we have two noble foreigners to call on."

Saint-Potin began to laugh. "You are still green. So you fancy I am going to ask the Chinese and the Hindoo what they think of England? As if I did not know better than themselves what they ought to think in order to please the readers of the *Vie Francaise*. I have already interviewed five hundred of these Chinese, Persians, Hindoos, Chilians, Japanese, and others. They all reply the same, according to me. I have only to take my article on the last comer and copy it word for word. What has to be changed, though, is their appearance, their name, their title, their age, and their suite. Oh! on that point it does not do to make a mistake, for I should be snapped up sharp by the *Figaro* or the *Gaulois*. But on these matters the hall porters at the Hotel Bristol and the Hotel Continental will put me right in five minutes. We will smoke a cigar as we walk there. Five francs cab hire to charge to the paper. That is how one sets about it, my dear fellow, when one is practically inclined."

"It must be worth something decent to be a reporter under these circumstances," said Duroy.

The journalist replied mysteriously: "Yes, but nothing pays so well as paragraphs, on account of the veiled advertisements."

They had got up and were passing down the boulevards towards the Madeleine. Saint-Potin suddenly observed to his companion: "You know if you have anything else to do, I shall not need you in any way."

Duroy shook hands and left him. The notion of the article to be written that evening worried him, and he began to think. He stored his mind with ideas, reflections, opinions, and anecdotes as he walked along, and went as far as the end of the Avenue des Champs Elysées, where only a few strollers were to be seen, the heat having caused Paris to be evacuated.

Having dined at a wine shop near the Arc de Triomphe, he walked slowly home along the outer boulevards and sat down at his table to work. But as soon as he had the sheet of blank paper before his eyes, all the materials that he had accumulated fled from his mind as though his brain had evaporated. He tried to seize on fragments of his recollections and to retain them, but they escaped him as fast as he laid hold of them, or else they rushed on him altogether pell-mell, and he did not know how to clothe and present them, nor which one to begin with.

After an hour of attempts and five sheets of paper blackened by opening phrases that had no continuation, he said to himself: "I am not yet well enough up in the business. I must have another lesson." And all at once the prospect of another morning's work with Madame Forestier, the hope of another long and intimate *tête-à-tête* so cordial and so pleasant, made him quiver with desire. He went to bed in a hurry, almost afraid now of setting to work again and succeeding all at once.

He did not get up the next day till somewhat late, putting off and tasting in advance the pleasure of this visit.

It was past ten when he rang his friend's bell.

The man-servant replied: "Master is engaged at his work."

Duroy had not thought that the husband might be at home. He insisted, however, saying: "Tell him that I have called on a matter requiring immediate attention."

After waiting five minutes he was shown into the study in which he had passed such a pleasant morning. In the chair he had occupied Forestier was now seated writing, in a dressing-gown and slippers and with a little Scotch bonnet on his head, while his wife in the same white gown leant against the mantelpiece and dictated, cigarette in mouth.

Duroy, halting on the threshold, murmured: "I really beg your pardon; I am afraid I am disturbing you."

His friend, turning his face towards him—an angry face, too—growled: "What is it you want now? Be quick; we are pressed for time."

The intruder, taken back, stammered: "It is nothing; I beg your pardon."

But Forestier, growing angry, exclaimed: "Come, hang it all, don't waste time about it; you have not forced your way in just for the sake of wishing us good-morning, I suppose?"

Then Duroy, greatly perturbed, made up his mind. "No—you see—the fact is—I can't quite manage my article—and you were—so—so kind last time—that I hoped—that I ventured to come—"

Forestier cut him short. "You have a pretty cheek. So you think I am going to do your work, and that all you have to do is to call on the cashier at the end of the month to draw your screw? No, that is too good."

The young woman went on smoking without saying a word, smiling with a vague smile, which seemed like an amiable mask, concealing the irony of her thoughts.

Duroy, colored up, stammered: "Excuse me—I fancied—I thought—" then suddenly, and in a clear voice, he went on: "I beg your pardon a thousand times, Madame, while again thanking you most sincerely for the charming article you produced for me yesterday." He bowed, remarked to Charles: "I shall be at the office at three," and went out.

He walked home rapidly, grumbling: "Well, I will do it all alone, and they shall see—"

Scarcely had he got in than, excited by anger, he began to write. He continued the adventure began by Madame Forestier, heaping up details of catch-penny romance, surprising incidents, and inflated descriptions, with the style of a schoolboy and the phraseology of the barrack-room. Within an hour he had finished an article which was a chaos of nonsense, and took it with every assurance to the *Vie Française*.

The first person he met was Saint-Potin, who, grasping his hand with the energy of an accomplice, said: "You have read my interview with the Chinese and the Hindoo? Isn't it funny? It has amused everyone. And I did not even get a glimpse of them."

Duroy, who had not read anything, at once took up the paper and ran his eye over a long article headed: "India and China," while the reporter pointed out the most interesting passages.

Forestier came in puffing, in a hurry, with a busy air, saying:

"Good; I want both of you."

And he mentioned a number of items of political information that would have to be obtained that very afternoon.

Duroy held out his article.

"Here is the continuation about Algeria."

"Very good; hand it over; and I will give it to the governor."

That was all.

Saint-Potin led away his new colleague, and when they were in the passage, he said to him: "Have you seen the cashier?"

"No; why?"

"Why? To draw your money. You see you should always draw a month in advance. One never knows what may happen."

"But—I ask for nothing better."

"I will introduce you to the cashier. He will make no difficulty about it. They pay up well here."

Duroy went and drew his two hundred francs, with twenty-eight more for his article of the day before, which, added to what remained of his salary from the railway company, gave him three hundred and forty francs in his pocket. He had never owned such a sum, and thought himself possessed of wealth for an indefinite period.

Saint-Potin then took him to have a gossip in the offices of four or five rival papers, hoping that the news he was entrusted to obtain had already been gleaned by others, and that he should be able to draw it out of them—thanks to the flow and artfulness of his conversation.

When evening had come, Duroy, who had nothing more to do, thought of going again to the Folies Bergères, and putting a bold face on, he went up to the box office.

"I am George Duroy, on the staff of the *Vie Francaise*. I came here the other day with Monsieur Forestier, who promised me to see about my being put on the free list; I do not know whether he has thought of it."

The list was referred to. His name was not entered.

However, the box office-keeper, a very affable man, at once said: "Pray, go in all the same, sir, and write yourself to the manager, who, I am sure, will pay attention to your letter."

He went in and almost immediately met Rachel, the woman he had gone off with the first evening. She came up to him, saying: "Good evening, ducky. Are you quite well?"

"Very well, thanks—and you?"

"I am all right. Do you know, I have dreamed of you twice since last time?"

Duroy smiled, feeling flattered. "Ah! and what does that mean?"

"It means that you pleased me, you old dear, and that we will begin again whenever you please."

"To-day, if you like."

"Yes, I am quite willing."

"Good, but—" He hesitated, a little ashamed of what he was going to do. "The fact is that this time I have not a penny; I have just come from the club, where I have dropped everything."

She looked him full in the eyes, scenting a lie with the instinct and habit of a girl accustomed to the tricks and bargainings of men, and remarked: "Bosh! That is not a nice sort of thing to try on me."

He smiled in an embarrassed way. "If you will take ten francs, it is all I have left."

She murmured, with the disinterestedness of a courtesan gratifying a fancy: "What you please, my lady; I only want you."

And lifting her charming eyes towards the young man's moustache, she took his arm and leant lovingly upon it.

"Let us go and have a grenadine first of all," she remarked. "And then we will take a stroll together. I should like to go to the opera like this, with you, to show you off. And we will go home early, eh?"

He lay late at this girl's place. It was broad day when he left, and the notion occurred to him to buy the *Vie Francaise*. He opened the paper with feverish hand. His article was not there, and he stood on the footpath, anxiously running his eye down the printed columns with the hope of at length finding what he was in search of. A weight suddenly oppressed his heart, for after the fatigue of a night of love, this vexation came upon him with the weight of a disaster.

He reached home and went to sleep in his clothes on the bed.

Entering the office some hours later, he went on to see Monsieur Walter.

"I was surprised at not seeing my second article on Algeria in the paper this morning, sir," said he.

The manager raised his head, and replied in a dry tone: "I gave it to your friend Forestier, and asked him to read it through. He did not think it up to the mark; you must rewrite it."

Duroy, in a rage, went out without saying a word, and abruptly entering his old comrade's room, said:

"Why didn't you let my article go in this morning?"

The journalist was smoking a cigarette with his back almost on the seat of his armchair and his feet on the table, his heels soiling an article already commenced. He said slowly, in a bored and distant voice, as though speaking from the depths of a hole: "The governor thought it poor, and told me to give it back to you to do over again. There it is." And he pointed out the slips flattened out under a paperweight.

Duroy, abashed, could find nothing to say in reply, and as he was putting his prose into his pocket, Forestier went on: "To-day you must first of all go to the Préfecture." And he proceeded to give a list of business errands and items of news to be attended to.

Duroy went off without having been able to find the cutting remark he wanted to. He brought back his article the next day. It was returned to him again. Having rewritten it a third time, and finding it still refused, he understood that he was trying to go ahead too fast, and that Forestier's hand alone could help him on his way. He did not therefore say anything more about the "Recollections of a Chasseur d'Afrique," promising himself to be supple and cunning since it was needful, and while awaiting something better to zealously discharge his duties as a reporter.

He learned to know the way behind the scenes in theatrical and political life; the waiting-rooms of statesmen and the lobby of the Chamber of Deputies; the important countenances of permanent secretaries, and the grim looks of sleepy ushers. He had continual relations with ministers, doorkeepers, generals, police agents, princes, bullies, courtesans, ambassadors, bishops, panders, adventurers, men of fashion, card-sharpers, cab drivers, waiters, and many others, having become the interested yet indifferent friend of all these; confounding them together in his estimation, measuring them with the same measure, judging them with the same eye, though having to see them every day at every hour, without any transition, and to speak with them all on the same business of his own. He compared himself to a man who had to drink off samples of every kind of wine one after the other, and who would soon be unable to tell Château Margaux from Argenteuil.

He became in a short time a remarkable reporter, certain of his information, artful, swift, subtle, a real find for the paper, as was observed by Daddy Walter, who knew what newspaper men were. However, as he got only centimes a line in addition to his monthly screw of two hundred francs, and as life on the boulevards and in *cafés* and restaurants is costly, he never had a halfpenny, and was disgusted with his poverty. There is some knack to be got hold of, he thought, seeing some of his fellows with their pockets full of money without ever being able to understand what secret methods they could make use of to procure this abundance. He enviously suspected unknown and suspicious transactions, services rendered, a whole system of contraband accepted and agreed to. But it was necessary that he should penetrate the mystery, enter into the tacit partnership, make himself one with the comrades who were sharing without him.

And he often thought of an evening, as he watched the trains go by from his window, of the steps he ought to take.

V

Two months had gone by, September was at hand, and the rapid fortune which Duroy had hoped for seemed to him slow in coming. He was, above all, uneasy at the mediocrity of his position, and did not see by what path he could scale the heights on the summit of which one finds respect, power, and money. He felt shut up in the mediocre calling of a reporter, so walled in as to be unable to get out of it. He was appreciated, but estimated in accordance with his position. Even Forestier, to whom he rendered a thousand services, no longer invited him to dinner, and treated him in every way as an inferior, though still accosting him as a friend.

From time to time, it is true, Duroy, seizing an opportunity, got in a short article, and having acquired through his paragraphs a mastery over his pen, and a tact which was lacking to him when he wrote his second article on Algeria, no longer ran any risk of having his descriptive efforts refused. But from this to writing leaders according to his fancy, or dealing with political questions with authority, there was as great a difference as driving in the Bois de Boulogne as a coachman, and as the owner of an equipage. That which humiliated him above everything was to see the door of society closed to him, to have no equal relations with it, not to be able to penetrate into the intimacy of its women, although several well-known actresses had occasionally received him with an interested familiarity.

He knew, moreover, from experience that all the sex, ladies or actresses, felt a singular attraction towards him, an instantaneous sympathy, and he experienced the impatience of a hobbled horse at not knowing those whom his future may depend on.

He had often thought of calling on Madame Forestier, but the recollection of their last meeting checked and humiliated him; and besides, he was awaiting an invitation to do so from her husband. Then the recollection of Madame de Marelle occurred to him, and recalling that she had asked him to come and see her, he called one afternoon when he had nothing to do.

"I am always at home till three o'clock," she had said.

He rang at the bell of her residence, a fourth floor in the Rue de Verneuil, at half-past two.

At the sound of the bell a servant opened the door, an untidy girl, who tied her cap strings as she replied: "Yes, Madame is at home, but I don't know whether she is up."

And she pushed open the drawing-room door, which was ajar. Duroy went in. The room was fairly large, scantily furnished and neglected looking. The chairs, worn and old, were arranged along the walls, as placed by the servant, for there was nothing to reveal the tasty care of the woman who loves her home. Four indifferent pictures, representing a boat on a stream, a ship at sea, a mill on a plain, and a wood-cutter in a wood, hung in the center of the four walls by cords of unequal length, and all four on one side. It could be divined that they had been dangling thus askew ever so long before indifferent eyes.

Duroy sat down immediately. He waited a long time. Then a door opened, and Madame de Marelle hastened in, wearing a Japanese morning gown of rose-colored silk embroidered with yellow landscapes, blue flowers, and white birds.

"Fancy! I was still in bed!" she exclaimed. "How good of you to come and see me! I had made up my mind that you had forgotten me."

She held out both her hands with a delighted air, and Duroy, whom the commonplace appearance of the room had put at his ease, kissed one, as he had seen Norbert de Varenne do.

She begged him to sit down, and then scanning him from head to foot, said: "How you have altered! You have improved in looks. Paris has done you good. Come, tell me the news."

And they began to gossip at once, as if they had been old acquaintances, feeling an instantaneous familiarity spring up between them; feeling one of those mutual currents of confidence, intimacy, and affection, which, in five minutes, make two beings of the same breed and character good friends.

Suddenly, Madame de Marelle exclaimed in astonishment: "It is funny how I get on with you. It seems to me as though I had known you for ten years. We shall become good friends, no doubt. Would you like it?"

He answered: "Certainly," with a smile which said still more.

He thought her very tempting in her soft and bright-hued gown, less refined and delicate than the other in her white one, but more exciting and spicy. When he was beside Madame Forestier, with her continual and gracious smile which attracted and checked at the same time; which seemed to say: "You please me," and also "Take care," and of which the real meaning was never clear, he felt above all the wish to lie down at her feet, or to kiss the lace bordering of her bodice, and slowly inhale the warm and perfumed atmosphere that must issue from it. With Madame de Marelle he felt within him a more definite, a more brutal desire—a desire that made his fingers quiver in presence of the rounded outlines of the light silk.

She went on talking, scattering in each phrase that ready wit of which she had acquired the habit just as a workman acquires the knack needed to accomplish a task reputed difficult, and at which other folk are astonished. He listened, thinking: "All this is worth remembering. A man could write charming articles of Paris gossip by getting her to chat over the events of the day."

Some one tapped softly, very softly, at the door by which she had entered, and she called out: "You can come in, pet."

Her little girl made her appearance, walked straight up to Duroy, and held out her hand to him. The astonished mother murmured: "But this is a complete conquest. I no longer recognize her."

The young fellow, having kissed the child, made her sit down beside him, and with a serious manner asked her pleasant questions as to what she had been doing since they last met. She replied, in her little flute-like voice, with her grave and grown-up air.

The clock struck three, and the journalist arose.

"Come often," said Madame de Marelle, "and we will chat as we have done to-day; it will always give me pleasure. But how is it one no longer sees you at the Forestiers?" He replied: "Oh! for no reason. I have been very busy. I hope to meet you there again one of these days."

He went out, his heart full of hope, though without knowing why.

He did not speak to Forestier of this visit. But he retained the recollection of it the following days, and more than the recollection—a sensation of the unreal yet persistent presence of this woman. It seemed to him that he had carried away something of her, the reflection of her form in his eyes, and the smack of her moral self in his heart. He remained under the haunted influence of her image, as it happens sometimes when we have passed pleasant hours with some one.

He paid a second visit a few days later.

The maid ushered him into the drawing-room, and Laurine at once appeared. She held out no longer her hand, but her forehead, and said: "Mamma has told me to request you to wait for her. She will be a quarter-of-an-hour, because she is not dressed yet. I will keep you company."

Duroy, who was amused by the ceremonious manners of the little girl, replied: "Certainly, Mademoiselle. I shall be delighted to pass a quarter-of-an-hour with you, but I warn you that for my part I am not at all serious, and that I play all day long, so I suggest a game at touch."

The girl was astonished; then she smiled as a woman would have done at this idea, which shocked her a little as well as astonished her, and murmured: "Rooms are not meant to be played in."

He said: "It is all the same to me. I play everywhere. Come, catch me."

And he began to go round the table, exciting her to pursue him, while she came after him, smiling with a species of polite condescension, and sometimes extending her hand to touch him, but without ever giving way so far as to run. He stopped, stooped down, and when she drew near with her little hesitating steps, sprung up in the air like a jack-in-the-box, and then bounded with a single stride to the other end of the dining-room. She thought it funny, ended by laughing, and becoming aroused, began to trot after him, giving little gleeful yet timid cries when she thought she had him. He shifted the chairs and used them as obstacles, forcing her to go round and round one of them for a minute at a time, and then leaving that one to seize upon another. Laurine ran now, giving herself wholly up to the charm of this new game, and with flushed face, rushed forward with the bound of a delighted child at each of the flights, the tricks, the feints of her companion. Suddenly, just as she thought she had got him, he seized her in his arms, and lifting her to the ceiling, exclaimed: "Touch."

The delighted girl wriggled her legs to escape, and laughed with all her heart.

Madame de Marelle came in at that moment, and was amazed. "What, Laurine, Laurine, playing! You are a sorcerer, sir."

He put down the little girl, kissed her mother's hand, and they sat down with the child between them. They began to chat, but Laurine, usually so silent, kept talking all the while, and had to be sent to her room. She obeyed without a word, but with tears in her eyes.

As soon as they were alone, Madame de Marelle lowered her voice. "You do not know, but I have a grand scheme, and I have thought of you. This is it. As I dine every week at the Forestiers, I return their hospitality from time to time at some restaurant. I do not like to entertain company at home, my household is not arranged for that, and besides, I do not understand anything about domestic affairs, anything about the kitchen, anything at all. I like to live anyhow. So I entertain them now and then at a restaurant, but it is not very lively when there are only three, and my own acquaintances scarcely go well with them. I tell you all this in order to explain a somewhat irregular invitation. You understand, do you not, that I want you to make one of us on Saturday at the Café Riche, at half-past seven. You know the place?"

He accepted with pleasure, and she went on: "There will be only us four. These little outings are very amusing to us women who are not accustomed to them."

She was wearing a dark brown dress, which showed off the lines of her waist, her hips, her bosom, and her arm in a coquettishly provocative way. Duroy felt confusedly astonished at the lack of harmony between this carefully refined elegance and her evident carelessness as regarded her dwelling. All that clothed her body, all that closely and directly touched her flesh was fine and delicate, but that which surrounded her did not matter to her.

He left her, retaining, as before, the sense of her continued presence in species of hallucination of the senses. And he awaited the day of the dinner with growing impatience.

Having hired, for the second time, a dress suit—his funds not yet allowing him to buy one—he arrived first at the rendezvous, a few minutes before the time. He was ushered up to the second story, and into a small private dining-room hung with red and white, its single window opening into the boulevard. A square table, laid for four, displaying its white cloth, so shining that it seemed to be varnished, and the glasses and the silver glittered brightly in the light of the twelve candles of two tall candelabra. Without was a broad patch of light green, due to the leaves of a tree lit up by the bright light from the dining-rooms.

Duroy sat down in a low armchair, upholstered in red to match the hangings on the walls. The worn springs yielding beneath him caused him to feel as though sinking into a hole. He heard throughout the huge house a confused murmur, the murmur of a large restaurant, made up of the clattering of glass and silver, the hurried steps of the waiters, deadened by the carpets in the passages, and the opening of doors letting out the sound of voices from the numerous private rooms in which people were dining. Forestier came in and shook hands with him, with a cordial familiarity which he never displayed at the offices of the *Vie Francaise*.

"The ladies are coming together," said he; "these little dinners are very pleasant."

Then he glanced at the table, turned a gas jet that was feebly burning completely off, closed one sash of the window on account of the draught, and chose a sheltered place for himself, with a remark: "I must be careful; I have been better for a month, and now I am queer again these last few days. I must have caught cold on Tuesday, coming out of the theater."

The door was opened, and, followed by a waiter, the two ladies appeared, veiled, muffled, reserved, with that charmingly mysterious bearing they assume in such places, where the surroundings are suspicious.

As Duroy bowed to Madame Forestier she scolded him for not having come to see her again; then she added with a smile, in the direction of her friend: "I know what it is; you prefer Madame de Marelle, you can find time to visit her."

They sat down to table, and the waiter having handed the wine card to Forestier, Madame de Marelle exclaimed: "Give these gentlemen whatever they like, but for us iced champagne, the best, sweet champagne, mind—nothing else." And the man having withdrawn, she added with an excited laugh: "I am going to get tipsy this evening; we will have a spree—a regular spree."

Forestier, who did not seem to have heard, said: "Would you mind the window being closed? My chest has been rather queer the last few days."

"No, not at all."

He pushed too the sash left open, and returned to his place with a reassured and tranquil countenance. His wife said nothing. Seemingly lost in thought, and with her eyes lowered towards the table, she smiled at the glasses with that vague smile which seemed always to promise and never to grant.

The Ostend oysters were brought in, tiny and plump like little ears enclosed in shells, and melting between the tongue and the palate like salt bon-bons. Then, after the soup, was served a trout as rose-tinted as a young girl, and the guests began to talk.

They spoke at first of a current scandal; the story of a lady of position, surprised by one of her husband's friends supping in a private room with a foreign prince. Forestier laughed a great deal at the adventure; the two ladies declared that the indiscreet gossip was nothing less than a blackguard and a coward. Duroy was of their opinion, and loudly proclaimed that it is the duty of a man in these matters, whether he be actor, confidant, or simple spectator, to be silent as the grave. He added: "How full life would be of pleasant things if we could reckon upon the absolute discretion of one another. That which often, almost always, checks women is the fear of the secret being revealed. Come, is it not true?" he continued. "How many are there who would yield to a sudden desire, the caprice of an hour, a passing fancy, did they not fear to pay for a short-lived and fleeting pleasure by an irremediable scandal and painful tears?"

He spoke with catching conviction, as though pleading a cause, his own cause, as though he had said: "It is not with me that one would have to dread such dangers. Try me and see."

They both looked at him approvingly, holding that he spoke rightly and justly, confessing by their friendly silence that their flexible morality as Parisians would not have held out long before the certainty of secrecy. And Forestier, leaning back in his place on the divan, one leg bent under him, and his napkin thrust into his waistcoat, suddenly said with the satisfied laugh of a skeptic: "The deuce! yes, they would all go in for it if they were certain of silence. Poor husbands!"

And they began to talk of love. Without admitting it to be eternal, Duroy understood it as lasting, creating a bond, a tender friendship, a confidence. The union of the senses was only a seal to the union of hearts. But he was angry at the outrageous jealousies, melodramatic scenes, and unpleasantness which almost always accompany ruptures.

When he ceased speaking, Madame de Marelle replied: "Yes, it is the only pleasant thing in life, and we often spoil it by preposterous unreasonableness."

Madame Forestier, who was toying with her knife, added: "Yes—yes—it is pleasant to be loved."

And she seemed to be carrying her dream further, to be thinking things that she dared not give words to.

As the first *entreé* was slow in coming, they sipped from time to time a mouthful of champagne, and nibbled bits of crust. And the idea of love, entering into them, slowly intoxicated their souls, as the bright wine, rolling drop by drop down their throats, fired their blood and perturbed their minds.

The waiter brought in some lamb cutlets, delicate and tender, upon a thick bed of asparagus tips.

"Ah! this is good," exclaimed Forestier; and they ate slowly, savoring the delicate meat and vegetables as smooth as cream.

Duroy resumed: "For my part, when I love a woman everything else in the world disappears." He said this in a tone of conviction.

Madame Forestier murmured, with her let-me-alone air:

"There is no happiness comparable to that of the first hand-clasp, when the one asks, 'Do you love me?' and the other replies, 'Yes.'"

Madame de Marelle, who had just tossed a fresh glass of champagne off at a draught, said gayly, as she put down her glass: "For my part, I am not so Platonic."

And all began to smile with kindling eyes at these words.

Forestier, stretched out in his seat on the divan, opened his arms, rested them on the cushions, and said in a serious tone: "This frankness does you honor, and proves that you are a practical woman. But may one ask you what is the opinion of Monsieur de Marelle?"

She shrugged her shoulders slightly, with infinite and prolonged disdain; and then in a decided tone remarked: "Monsieur de Marelle has no opinions on this point. He only has—abstentions."

And the conversation, descending from the elevated theories, concerning love, strayed into the flowery garden of polished blackguardism. It was the moment of clever double meanings; veils raised by words, as petticoats are lifted by the wind; tricks of language; clever disguised audacities; sentences which reveal nude images in covered phrases; which cause the vision of all that may not be said to flit rapidly before the eye and the mind, and allow the well-bred people the enjoyment of a kind of subtle and mysterious love, a species of impure mental contact, due to the simultaneous evocation of secret, shameful, and longed-for pleasures. The roast, consisting of partridges flanked by quails, had been served; then a dish of green peas, and then a terrine of foie gras, accompanied by a curly-leaved salad, filling a salad bowl as though with green foam. They had partaken of all these things without tasting them, without knowing, solely taken up by what they were talking of, plunged as it were in a bath of love.

The two ladies were now going it strongly in their remarks. Madame de Marelle, with a native audacity which resembled a direct provocation, and Madame Forestier with a charming reserve, a modesty in her tone, voice, smile, and bearing that underlined while seeming to soften the bold remarks falling from her lips. Forestier, leaning quite back on the cushions, laughed, drank and ate without leaving off, and sometimes threw in a word so risque or so crude that the ladies, somewhat shocked by its appearance, and for appearance sake, put on a little air of embarrassment that lasted two or three seconds. When he had given vent to something a little too coarse, he added: "You are going ahead nicely, my children. If you go on like that you will end by making fools of yourselves."

Dessert came, and then coffee; and the liquors poured a yet warmer dose of commotion into the excited minds.

As she had announced on sitting down to table, Madame de Marelle was intoxicated, and acknowledged it in the lively and graceful rabble of a woman emphasizing, in order to amuse her guests, a very real commencement of drunkenness.

Madame Forestier was silent now, perhaps out of prudence, and Duroy, feeling himself too much excited not to be in danger of compromising himself, maintained a prudent reserve.

Cigarettes were lit, and all at once Forestier began to cough. It was a terrible fit, that seemed to tear his chest, and with red face and forehead damp with perspiration, he choked behind his napkin. When the fit was over he growled angrily: "These feeds are very bad for me; they are ridiculous." All his good humor had vanished before his terror of the illness that haunted his thoughts. "Let us go home," said he.

Madame de Marelle rang for the waiter, and asked for the bill. It was brought almost immediately. She tried to read it, but the figures danced before her eyes, and she passed it to Duroy, saying: "Here, pay for me; I can't see, I am too tipsy."

And at the same time she threw him her purse. The bill amounted to one hundred and thirty francs. Duroy checked it, and then handed over two notes and received back the change, saying in a low tone: "What shall I give the waiter?"

"What you like; I do not know."

He put five francs on the salver, and handed back the purse, saying: "Shall I see you to your door?"

"Certainly. I am incapable of finding my way home."

They shook hands with the Forestiers, and Duroy found himself alone with Madame de Marelle in a cab. He felt her close to him, so close, in this dark box, suddenly lit up for a moment by the lamps on the sidewalk. He felt through his sleeve the warmth of her shoulder, and he could find nothing to say to her, absolutely nothing, his mind being paralyzed by the imperative desire to seize her in his arms.

"If I dared to, what would she do?" he thought. The recollection of all the things uttered during dinner emboldened him, but the fear of scandal restrained him at the same time.

Nor did she say anything either, but remained motionless in her corner. He would have thought that she was asleep if he had not seen her eyes glitter every time that a ray of light entered the carriage.

"What was she thinking?" He felt that he must not speak, that a word, a single word, breaking this silence would destroy his chance; yet courage failed him, the courage needed for abrupt and brutal action. All at once he felt her foot move. She had made a movement, a quick, nervous movement of impatience, perhaps of appeal. This almost imperceptible gesture caused a thrill to run through him from head to foot, and he threw himself upon her, seeking her mouth with his lips, her form with his hands.

But the cab having shortly stopped before the house in which she resided, Duroy, surprised, had no time to seek passionate phrases to thank her, and express his grateful love. However, stunned by what had taken place, she did not rise, she did not stir. Then he was afraid that the driver might suspect something, and got out first to help her to alight.

At length she got out of the cab, staggering and without saying a word. He rang the bell, and as the door opened, said, tremblingly: "When shall I see you again?"

She murmured so softly that he scarcely heard it: "Come and lunch with me to-morrow." And she disappeared in the entry, pushed to the heavy door, which closed with a noise like that of a cannon. He gave the driver five francs, and began to walk along with rapid and triumphant steps, and heart overflowing with joy.

He had won at last—a married woman, a lady. How easy and unexpected it had all been. He had fancied up till then that to assail and conquer one of these so greatly longed-for beings, infinite pains, interminable expectations, a skillful siege carried on by means of gallant attentions, words of love, sighs, and gifts were needed. And, lo! suddenly, at the faintest attack, the first whom he had encountered had yielded to him so quickly that he was stupefied at it.

"She was tipsy," he thought; "to-morrow it will be another story. She will meet me with tears." This notion disturbed him, but he added: "Well, so much the worse. Now I have her, I mean to keep her."

He was somewhat agitated the next day as he ascended Madame de Marelle's staircase. How would she receive him? And suppose she would not receive him at all? Suppose she had forbidden them to admit him? Suppose she had said—but, no, she could not have said anything without letting the whole truth be guessed. So he was master of the situation.

The little servant opened the door. She wore her usual expression. He felt reassured, as if he had anticipated her displaying a troubled countenance, and asked: "Is your mistress quite well?"

She replied: "Oh! yes, sir, the same as usual," and showed him into the drawing-room.

He went straight to the chimney-glass to ascertain the state of his hair and his toilet, and was arranging his necktie before it, when he saw in it the young woman watching him as she stood at the door leading from her room. He pretended not to have noticed her, and the pair looked at one another for a few moments in the glass, observing and watching before finding themselves face to face. He turned round. She had not moved, and seemed to be waiting. He darted forward, stammering: "My darling! my darling!"

She opened her arms and fell upon his breast; then having lifted her head towards him, their lips met in a long kiss.

He thought: "It is easier than I should have imagined. It is all going on very well."

And their lips separating, he smiled without saying a word, while striving to throw a world of love into his looks. She, too, smiled, with that smile by which women show their desire, their consent, their wish to yield themselves, and murmured: "We are alone. I have sent Laurine to lunch with one of her young friends."

He sighed as he kissed her. "Thanks, I will worship you."

Then she took his arm, as if he had been her husband, to go to the sofa, on which they sat down side by side. He wanted to start a clever and attractive chat, but not being able to do so to his liking, stammered: "Then you are not too angry with me?"

She put her hand on his mouth, saying "Be quiet."

They sat in silence, looking into one another's eyes, with burning fingers interlaced.

"How I did long for you!" said he.

She repeated: "Be quiet."

They heard the servant arranging the table in the adjoining dining-room, and he rose, saying: "I must not remain so close to you. I shall lose my head."

The door opened, and the servant announced that lunch was ready. Duroy gravely offered his arm.

They lunched face to face, looking at one another and constantly smiling, solely taken up by themselves, and enveloped in the sweet enchantment of a growing love. They ate, without knowing what. He felt a foot, a little foot, straying under the table. He took it between his own and kept it there, squeezing it with all his might. The servant came and went, bringing and taking away the dishes with a careless air, without seeming to notice anything.

When they had finished they returned to the drawing-room, and resumed their place on the sofa, side by side. Little by little he pressed up against her, striving to take her in his arms. But she calmly repulsed him, saying: "Take care; someone may come in."

He murmured: "When can I see you quite alone, to tell you how I love you?"

She leant over towards him and whispered: "I will come and pay you a visit one of these days."

He felt himself redden. "You know—you know—my place is very small."

She smiled: "That does not matter. It is you I shall call to see, and not your rooms."

Then he pressed her to know when she would come. She named a day in the latter half of the week. He begged of her to advance the date in broken sentences, playing with and squeezing her hands, with glittering eyes, and flushed face, heated and torn by desire, that imperious desire which follows *tête-à-tête* repasts. She was amazed to see him implore her with such ardor, and yielded a day from time to time. But he kept repeating: "To-morrow, only say to-morrow."

She consented at length. "Yes, to-morrow; at five o'clock."

He gave a long sigh of joy, and they then chatted almost quietly with an air of intimacy, as though they had known one another twenty years. The sound of the door bell made them start, and with a bound they separated to a distance. She murmured: "It must be Laurine."

The child made her appearance, stopped short in amazement, and then ran to Duroy, clapping her hands with pleasure at seeing him, and exclaiming: "Ah! pretty boy."

Madame de Marelle began to laugh. "What! Pretty boy! Laurine has baptized you. It's a nice little nickname for you, and I will call you Pretty-boy, too."

He had taken the little girl on his knee, and he had to play with her at all the games he had taught her. He rose to take his leave at twenty minutes to three to go to the office of the paper, and on the staircase, through the half-closed door, he still whispered: "To-morrow, at five."

She answered "Yes," with a smile, and disappeared.

As soon as he had got through his day's work, he speculated how he should arrange his room to receive his mistress, and hide as far as possible the poverty of the place. He was struck by the idea of pinning a lot of Japanese trifles on the walls, and he bought for five francs quite a collection of little fans and screens, with which he hid the most obvious of the marks on the wall paper. He pasted on the window panes transparent pictures representing boats floating down rivers, flocks of birds flying across rosy skies, multi-colored ladies on balconies, and processions of little black men over plains covered with snow. His room, just big enough to sleep and sit down in, soon looked like the inside of a Chinese lantern. He thought the effect satisfactory, and passed the evening in pasting on the ceiling birds that he had cut from the colored sheets remaining over. Then he went to bed, lulled by the whistle of the trains.

He went home early the next day, carrying a paper bag of cakes and a bottle of Madeira, purchased at the grocer's. He had to go out again to buy two plates and two glasses, and arranged this collation on his dressing-table, the dirty wood of which was covered by a napkin, the jug and basin being hidden away beneath it.

Then he waited.

She came at about a quarter-past five; and, attracted by the bright colors of the pictures, exclaimed: "Dear me, yours is a nice place. But there are a lot of people about on the staircase."

He had clasped her in his arms, and was eagerly kissing the hair between her forehead and her bonnet through her veil.

An hour and a half later he escorted her back to the cab-stand in the Rue de Rome. When she was in the carriage he murmured: "Tuesday at the same time?"

She replied: "Tuesday at the same time." And as it had grown dark, she drew his head into the carriage and kissed him on the lips. Then the driver, having whipped up his beast, she exclaimed: "Good-bye, Pretty-boy," and the old vehicle started at the weary trot of its old white horse.

For three weeks Duroy received Madame de Marelle in this way every two or three days, now in the evening and now in the morning. While he was expecting her one afternoon, a loud uproar on the stairs drew him to the door. A child was crying. A man's angry voice shouted: "What is that little devil howling about now?" The yelling and exasperated voice of a woman replied: "It is that dirty hussy who comes to see the penny-a-liner upstairs; she has upset Nicholas on the landing. As if dabs like that, who pay no attention to children on the staircase, should be allowed here."

Duroy drew back, distracted, for he could hear the rapid rustling of skirts and a hurried step ascending from the story just beneath him. There was soon a knock at the door, which he had reclosed. He opened it, and

Madame de Marelle rushed into the room, terrified and breathless, stammering: "Did you hear?"

He pretended to know nothing. "No; what?"

"How they have insulted me."

"Who? Who?"

"The blackguards who live down below."

"But, surely not; what does it all mean, tell me?"

She began to sob, without being able to utter a word. He had to take off her bonnet, undo her dress, lay her on the bed, moisten her forehead with a wet towel. She was choking, and then when her emotion was somewhat abated, all her wrathful indignation broke out. She wanted him to go down at once, to thrash them, to kill them.

He repeated: "But they are only work-people, low creatures. Just remember that it would lead to a police court, that you might be recognized, arrested, ruined. One cannot lower one's self to have anything to do with such people."

She passed on to another idea. "What shall we do now? For my part, I cannot come here again."

He replied: "It is very simple; I will move."

She murmured: "Yes, but that will take some time." Then all at once she framed a plan, and reassured, added softly: "No, listen, I know what to do; let me act, do not trouble yourself about anything. I will send you a telegram to-morrow morning."

She smiled now, delighted with her plan, which she would not reveal, and indulged in a thousand follies. She was very agitated, however, as she went downstairs, leaning with all her weight on her lover's arm, her legs trembled so beneath her. They did not meet anyone, though.

As he usually got up late, he was still in bed the next day, when, about eleven o'clock, the telegraph messenger brought him the promised telegram. He opened it and read:

"Meet me at five; 127, Rue de Constantinople. Rooms hired by Madame Duroy.—Clo."

At five o'clock to the minute he entered the doorkeeper's lodge of a large furnished house, and asked: "It is here that Madame Duroy has taken rooms, is it not?"

"Yes, sir."

"Will you show me to them, if you please."

The man, doubtless used to delicate situations in which prudence is necessary, looked him straight in the eyes, and then, selecting one of the long range of keys, said: "You are Monsieur Duroy?"

"Yes, certainly."

The man opened the door of a small suite of rooms on the ground floor in front of the lodge. The sitting-room, with a tolerably fresh wall-paper of floral design, and a carpet so thin that the boards of the floor could be felt through it, had mahogany furniture, upholstered in green rep with a yellow pattern. The bedroom was so small that the bed three-parts filled it. It occupied the further end, stretching from one wall to the other—the large bed of a furnished lodging-house, shrouded in heavy blue curtains also of rep, and covered with an eider-down quilt of red silk stained with suspicious-looking spots.

Duroy, uneasy and displeased, thought: "This place will cost, Lord knows how much. I shall have to borrow again. It is idiotic what she has done."

The door opened, and Clotilde came in like a whirlwind, with outstretched arms and rustling skirts. She was delighted. "Isn't it nice, eh, isn't it nice? And on the ground floor, too; no stairs to go up. One could get in and out of the windows without the doorkeeper seeing one. How we will love one another here!"

He kissed her coldly, not daring to put the question that rose to his lips. She had placed a large parcel on the little round table in the middle of the room. She opened it, and took out a cake of soap, a bottle of scent, a sponge, a box of hairpins, a buttonhook, and a small pair of curling tongs to set right her fringe, which she got out of curl every time. And she played at moving in, seeking a place for everything, and derived great amusement from it.

She kept on chattering as she opened the drawers. "I must bring a little linen, so as to be able to make a change if necessary. It will be very convenient. If I get wet, for instance, while I am out, I can run in here to dry myself. We shall each have one key, beside the one left with the doorkeeper in case we forget it. I have taken the place for three months, in your name, of course, since I could not give my own."

Then he said: "You will let me know when the rent is to be paid."

She replied, simply: "But it is paid, dear."

"Then I owe it to you."

"No, no, my dear; it does not concern you at all; this is a little fancy of my own."

He seemed annoyed: "Oh, no, indeed; I can't allow that."

She came to him in a supplicating way, and placing her hands on his shoulders, said: "I beg of you, George; it will give me so much pleasure to feel that our little nest here is mine—all my own. You cannot be annoyed at that. How can you? I wanted to contribute that much towards our loves. Say you agree, Georgy; say you agree."

She implored him with looks, lips, the whole of her being. He held out, refusing with an irritated air, and then he yielded, thinking that, after all, it was fair. And when she had gone, he murmured, rubbing his hands, and without seeking in the depths of his heart whence the opinion came on that occasion: "She is very nice."

He received, a few days later, another telegram running thus: "My husband returns to-night, after six weeks' inspection, so we shall have a week off. What a bore, darling.—Clo."

Duroy felt astounded. He had really lost all idea of her being married. But here was a man whose face he would have liked to see just once, in order to know him. He patiently awaited the husband's departure, but he passed two evenings at the Folies Bergère, which wound up with Rachel.

Then one morning came a fresh telegram: "To-day at five.—Clo."

They both arrived at the meeting-place before the time. She threw herself into his arms with an outburst of passion, and kissed him all over the face, and then said: "If you like, when we have loved one another a great deal, you shall take me to dinner somewhere. I have kept myself disengaged."

It was at the beginning of the month, and although his salary was long since drawn in advance, and he lived from day to day upon money gleaned on every side, Duroy happened to be in funds, and was pleased at the opportunity of spending something upon her, so he replied: "Yes, darling, wherever you like."

They started off, therefore, at about seven, and gained the outer boulevards. She leaned closely against him, and whispered in his ear: "If you only knew how pleased I am to walk out on your arm; how I love to feel you beside me."

He said: "Would you like to go to Père Lathuile's?"

"Oh, no, it is too swell. I should like something funny, out of the way! a restaurant that shopmen and work-girls go to. I adore dining at a country inn. Oh! if we only had been able to go into the country."

As he knew nothing of the kind in the neighborhood, they wandered along the boulevard, and ended by going into a wine-shop where there was a dining-room. She had seen through the window two bareheaded girls seated at tables with two soldiers. Three cab-drivers were dining at the further end of the long and narrow room, and an individual impossible to classify under any calling was smoking, stretched on a chair, with his legs stuck out in front of him, his hands in the waist-band of his trousers, and his head thrown back over the top bar. His jacket was a museum of stains, and in his swollen pockets could be noted the neck of a bottle, a piece of bread, a parcel wrapped up in a newspaper, and a dangling piece of string. He had thick, tangled, curly hair, gray with scurf, and his cap was on the floor under his chair.

The entrance of Clotilde created a sensation, due to the elegance of her toilet. The couples ceased whispering together, the three cab-drivers left off arguing, and the man who was smoking, having taken his pipe from his mouth and spat in front of him, turned his head slightly to look.

Madame de Marelle murmured: "It is very nice; we shall be very comfortable here. Another time I will dress like a work-girl." And she sat down, without embarrassment or disgust, before the wooden table, polished by the fat of dishes, washed by spilt liquors, and cleaned by a wisp of the waiter's napkin. Duroy, somewhat ill at ease, and slightly ashamed, sought a peg to hang his tall hat on. Not finding one, he put it on a chair.

They had a ragout, a slice of melon, and a salad. Clotilde repeated: "I delight in this. I have low tastes. I like this better than the Café Anglais." Then she added: "If you want to give me complete enjoyment, you will take me to a dancing place. I know a very funny one close by called the Reine Blanche."

Duroy, surprised at this, asked: "Whoever took you there?"

He looked at her and saw her blush, somewhat disturbed, as though this sudden question had aroused within her some delicate recollections. After one of these feminine hesitations, so short that they can scarcely be guessed, she replied: "A friend of mine," and then, after a brief silence, added, "who is dead." And she cast down her eyes with a very natural sadness.

Duroy, for the first time, thought of all that he did not know as regarded the past life of this woman. Certainly she already had lovers, but of what kind, in what class of society? A vague jealousy, a species of enmity awoke within him; an enmity against all that he did not know, all that had not belonged to him. He looked at her, irritated at the mystery wrapped up within that pretty, silent head, which was thinking, perhaps, at that very moment, of the other, the others, regretfully. How he would have liked to have looked into her recollections—to have known all.

She repeated: "Will you take me to the Reine Blanche? That will be a perfect treat."

He thought: "What matters the past? I am very foolish to bother about it," and smilingly replied: "Certainly, darling."

When they were in the street she resumed, in that low and mysterious tone in which confidences are made: "I dared not ask you this until now, but you cannot imagine how I love these escapades in places ladies do not go to. During the carnival I will dress up as a schoolboy. I make such a capital boy."

When they entered the ball-room she clung close to him, gazing with delighted eyes on the girls and the bullies, and from time to time, as though to reassure herself as regards any possible danger, saying, as she noticed some serious and motionless municipal guard: "That is a strong-looking fellow." In a quarter of an hour she had had enough of it and he escorted her home.

Then began quite a series of excursions in all the queer places where the common people amuse themselves, and Duroy discovered in his mistress quite a liking for this vagabondage of students bent on a spree. She came to their meeting-place in a cotton frock and with a servant's cap—a theatrical servant's cap—on her head; and despite the elegant and studied simplicity of her toilet, retained her rings, her bracelets, and her diamond earrings, saying, when he begged her to remove them: "Bah! they will think they are paste."

She thought she was admirably disguised, and although she was really only concealed after the fashion of an ostrich, she went into the most ill-famed drinking places. She wanted Duroy to dress himself like a workman, but he resisted, and retained his correct attire, without even consenting to exchange his tall hat for one of soft felt. She was consoled for this obstinacy on his part by the reflection that she would be taken for a chambermaid engaged in a love affair with a gentleman, and thought this delightful. In this guise they went into popular wine-shops, and sat down on rickety chairs at old wooden tables in smoke-filled rooms. A cloud of strong tobacco smoke, with which still blended the smell of fish fried at dinner time, filled the room; men in blouses shouted at one another as they tossed off nips of spirits; and the astonished waiter would stare at this strange couple as he placed before them two cherry brandies. She—trembling, fearsome, yet charmed—began to sip the red liquid, looking round her with uneasy and kindling eye. Each cherry swallowed gave her the sensation of a sin committed, each drop of burning liquor flowing down her throat gave her the pleasure of a naughty and forbidden joy.

Then she would say, "Let us go," and they would leave. She would pass rapidly, with bent head and the short steps of an actress leaving the stage, among the drinkers, who, with their elbows on the tables, watched her go by with suspicious and dissatisfied glances; and when she had crossed the threshold would give a deep sigh, as if she had just escaped some terrible danger.

Sometimes she asked Duroy, with a shudder: "If I were insulted in these places, what would you do?"

He would answer, with a swaggering air: "Take your part, by Jove!"

And she would clasp his arm with happiness, with, perhaps, a vague wish to be insulted and defended, to see men fight on her account, even such men as those, with her lover.

But these excursions taking place two or three times a week began to weary Duroy, who had great difficulty, besides, for some time past, in procuring the ten francs necessary for the cake and the drinks. He now lived very hardly and with more difficulty than when he was a clerk in the Northern Railway; for having spent lavishly during his first month of journalism, in the constant hope of gaining large sums of money in a day or two, he had exhausted all his resources and all means of procuring money. A very simple method, that of borrowing from the cashier, was very soon exhausted; and he already owed the paper four months' salary, besides six hundred francs advanced on his lineage account. He owed, besides, a hundred francs to Forestier, three hundred to Jacques Rival, who was free-handed with his money; and he was also eaten up by a number of small debts of from five francs to twenty. Saint-Potin, consulted as to the means of raising another hundred francs, had discovered no expedient, although a man of inventive mind, and Duroy was exasperated at this poverty, of which he was more sensible now than formerly, since he had more wants. A sullen rage against everyone smouldered within him, with an ever-increasing irritation, which manifested itself at every moment on the most futile pretexts. He sometimes asked himself how he could have spent an average of a thousand francs a month, without any excess and the gratification of any extravagant fancy, and he found that, by adding a lunch at eight francs to a dinner at twelve, partaken of in some large café on the boulevards, he at once came to a louis, which, added to ten francs pocket-money—that pocket-money that melts away, one does not know how—makes a total of thirty francs. But thirty francs a day is nine hundred francs at the end of the month. And he did not reckon in the cost of clothes, boots, linen, washing, etc.

So on the 14th December he found himself without a sou in his pocket, and without a notion in his mind how to get any money. He went, as he had often done of old, without lunch, and passed the afternoon working at the newspaper office, angry and preoccupied. About four o'clock he received a telegram from his mistress, running: "Shall we dine together, and have a lark afterwards?"

He at once replied: "Cannot dine." Then he reflected that he would be very stupid to deprive himself of the pleasant moments she might afford him, and added: "But will wait at nine at our place." And having sent one of the messengers with this, to save the cost of a telegram, he began to reflect what he should do to procure himself a dinner.

At seven o'clock he had not yet hit upon anything and a terrible hunger assailed him. Then he had recourse to the stratagem of a despairing man. He let all his colleagues depart, one after the other, and when he was alone rang sharply. Monsieur Walter's messenger, left in charge of the offices, came in. Duroy was standing feeling in his pockets, and said in an abrupt voice: "Foucart, I have left my purse at home, and I have to go and dine at the Luxembourg. Lend me fifty sous for my cab."

The man took three francs from his waistcoat pocket and said: "Do you want any more, sir?"

"No, no, that will be enough. Thanks."

And having seized on the coins, Duroy ran downstairs and dined at a slap-bank, to which he drifted on his days of poverty.

At nine o'clock he was awaiting his mistress, with his feet on the fender, in the little sitting-room. She came in, lively and animated, brisked up by the keen air of the street. "If you like," said she, "we will first go for a stroll, and then come home here at eleven. The weather is splendid for walking."

He replied, in a grumbling tone: "Why go out? We are very comfortable here."

She said, without taking off her bonnet: "If you knew, the moonlight is beautiful. It is splendid walking about to-night."

"Perhaps so, but I do not care for walking about!"

He had said this in an angry fashion. She was struck and hurt by it, and asked: "What is the matter with you? Why do you go on in this way? I should like to go for a stroll, and I don't see how that can vex you."

He got up in a rage. "It does not vex me. It is a bother, that is all."

She was one of those sort of women whom resistance irritates and impoliteness exasperates, and she said disdainfully and with angry calm: "I am not accustomed to be spoken to like that. I will go alone, then. Good-bye."

He understood that it was serious, and darting towards her, seized her hands and kissed them, saying: "Forgive me, darling, forgive me. I am very nervous this evening, very irritable. I have had vexations and annoyances, you know—matters of business."

She replied, somewhat softened, but not calmed down: "That does not concern me, and I will not bear the consequences of your ill-temper."

He took her in his arms, and drew her towards the couch.

"Listen, darling, I did not want to hurt you; I was not thinking of what I was saying."

He had forced her to sit down, and, kneeling before her, went on: "Have you forgiven me? Tell me you have forgiven me?"

She murmured, coldly: "Very well, but do not do so again;" and rising, she added: "Now let us go for a stroll."

He had remained at her feet, with his arms clasped about her hips, and stammered: "Stay here, I beg of you. Grant me this much. I should so like to keep you here this evening all to myself, here by the fire. Say yes, I beg of you, say yes."

She answered plainly and firmly: "No, I want to go out, and I am not going to give way to your fancies."

He persisted. "I beg of you, I have a reason, a very serious reason."

She said again: "No; and if you won't go out with me, I shall go. Good-bye."

She had freed herself with a jerk, and gained the door. He ran towards her, and clasped her in his arms, crying:

"Listen, Clo, my little Clo; listen, grant me this much."

She shook her head without replying, avoiding his kisses, and striving to escape from his grasp and go.

He stammered: "Clo, my little Clo, I have a reason."

She stopped, and looking him full in the face, said: "You are lying. What is it?"

He blushed not knowing what to say, and she went on in an indignant tone: "You see very well that you are lying, you low brute." And with an angry gesture and tears in her eyes, she escaped him.

He again caught her by the shoulders, and, in despair, ready to acknowledge anything in order to avoid a rupture, he said, in a despairing tone: "I have not a son. That's what it all means." She stopped short, and looking into his eyes to read the truth in them, said: "You say?"

He had flushed to the roots of his hair. "I say that I have not a sou. Do you understand? Not twenty sous, not ten, not enough to pay for a glass of cassis in the café we may go into. You force me to confess what I am ashamed of. It was, however, impossible for me to go out with you, and when we were seated with refreshments in front of us to tell you quietly that I could not pay for them."

She was still looking him in the face. "It is true, then?"

In a moment he had turned out all his pockets, those of his trousers, coat, and waistcoat, and murmured: "There, are you satisfied now?"

Suddenly opening her arms, in an outburst of passion, she threw them around his neck, crying: "Oh, my poor darling, my poor darling, if I had only known. How did it happen?"

She made him sit down, and sat down herself on his knees; then, with her arm round his neck, kissing him every moment on his moustache, his mouth, his eyes, she obliged him to tell her how this misfortune had come about.

He invented a touching story. He had been obliged to come to the assistance of his father, who found himself in difficulties. He had not only handed over to him all his savings, but had even incurred heavy debts on his behalf. He added: "I shall be pinched to the last degree for at least six months, for I have exhausted all my resources. So much the worse; there are crises in every life. Money, after all, is not worth troubling about."

She whispered: "I will lend you some; will you let me?"

He answered, with dignity: "You are very kind, pet; but do not think of that, I beg of you. You would hurt my feelings."

She was silent, and then clasping him in her arms, murmured: "You will never know how much I love you."

It was one of their most pleasant evenings.

As she was leaving, she remarked, smilingly: "How nice it is when one is in your position to find money you had forgotten in your pocket—a coin that had worked its way between the stuff and the lining."

He replied, in a tone of conviction: "Ah, yes, that it is."

She insisted on walking home, under the pretense that the moon was beautiful and went into ecstasies over it. It was a cold, still night at the beginning of winter. Pedestrians and horses went by quickly, spurred by a sharp frost. Heels rang on the pavement. As she left him she said: "Shall we meet again the day after to-morrow?"

"Certainly."

"At the same time?"

"The same time."

"Good-bye, dearest." And they kissed lovingly.

Then he walked home swiftly, asking himself what plan he could hit on the morrow to get out of his difficulty. But as he opened the door of his room, and fumbled in his waistcoat pocket for a match, he was stupefied to find a coin under his fingers. As soon as he had a light he hastened to examine it. It was a louis. He thought he must be mad. He turned it over and over, seeking by what miracle it could have found its way there. It could not, however, have fallen from heaven into his pocket.

Then all at once he guessed, and an angry indignation awoke within him. His mistress had spoken of money slipping into the lining, and being found in times of poverty. It was she who had tendered him this alms. How shameful! He swore: "Ah! I'll talk to her the day after to-morrow. She shall have a nice time over it."

And he went to bed, his heart filled with anger and humiliation.

He woke late. He was hungry. He tried to go to sleep again, in order not to get up till two o'clock, and then said to himself: "That will not forward matters. I must end by finding some money." Then he went out, hoping that an idea might occur to him in the street. It did not; but at every restaurant he passed a longing to eat made his mouth water. As by noon he had failed to hit on any plan, he suddenly made up his mind: "I will lunch out of Clotilde's twenty francs. That won't hinder me from paying them back to-morrow."

He, therefore, lunched for two francs fifty centimes. On reaching the office he also gave three francs to the messenger, saying: "Here, Foucart, here is the money you lent me last night for my cab."

He worked till seven o'clock. Then he went and dined taking another three francs. The two evening bocks brought the expenditure of the day up to nine francs thirty centimes. But as he could not re-establish a credit or create fresh resources in twenty-four hours, he borrowed another six francs fifty centimes the next day from the twenty he was going to return that very evening, so that he came to keep his appointment with just four francs twenty centimes in his pocket.

He was in a deuce of a temper, and promised himself that he would pretty soon explain things. He would say to his mistress: "You know, I found the twenty francs you slipped into my pocket the other day. I cannot give them back to you now, because my situation is unaltered, and I have not had time to occupy myself with money matters. But I will give them to you the next time we meet."

She arrived, loving, eager, full of alarm. How would he receive her? She kissed him persistently to avoid an explanation at the outset.

He said to himself: "It will be time enough to enter on the matter by-and-by. I will find an opportunity of doing so."

He did not find the opportunity, and said nothing, shirking before the difficulty of opening this delicate subject. She did not speak of going out, and was in every way charming. They separated about midnight, after making an appointment for the Wednesday of the following week, for Madame de Marelle was engaged to dine out several days in succession.

The next day, as Duroy, on paying for his breakfast, felt for the four coins that ought to be remaining to him, he perceived that they were five, and one of them a gold one. At the outset he thought that he had received it by mistake in his change the day before, then he understood it, and his heart throbbed with humiliation at this persistent charity. How he now regretted not having said anything! If he had spoken energetically this would not have happened.

For four days he made efforts, as numerous as they were fruitless, to raise five louis, and spent Clotilde's second one. She managed, although he had said to her savagely, "Don't play that joke of the other evening's again, or I shall get angry," to slip another twenty francs into his trouser pockets the first time they met. When he found them he swore bitterly, and transferred them to his waistcoat to have them under his hand, for he had not a rap. He appeased his conscience by this argument: "I will give it all back to her in a lump. After all, it is only borrowed money."

At length the cashier of the paper agreed, on his desperate appeals, to let him have five francs daily. It was just enough to live upon, but not enough to repay sixty francs with. But as Clotilde was again seized by her passion for nocturnal excursions in all the suspicious localities in Paris, he ended by not being unbearably annoyed to find a yellow boy in one of his pockets, once even in his boot, and another time in his watch-case, after their adventurous excursions. Since she had wishes which he could not for the moment gratify himself, was it not natural that she should pay for them rather than go without them? He kept an account, too, of all he received in this way, in order to return it to her some day.

One evening she said to him: "Would you believe that I have never been to the Folies-Bergère? Will you take me there?"

He hesitated a moment, afraid of meeting Rachel. Then he thought: "Bah! I am not married, after all. If that girl sees me she will understand the state of things, and will not speak to me. Besides, we will have a box."

Another reason helped his decision. He was well pleased of this opportunity of offering Madame de Marelle a box at the theater without its costing anything. It was a kind of compensation.

He left her in the cab while he got the order for the box, in order that she might not see it offered him, and then came to fetch her. They went in, and were received with bows by the acting manager. An immense crowd filled the lounge, and they had great difficulty in making their way through the swarm of men and women. At length they reached the box and settled themselves in it, shut in between the motionless orchestra and the eddy of the gallery. But Madame de Marelle rarely glanced at the stage. Wholly taken up with the women promenading behind her back, she constantly turned round to look at them, with a longing to touch them, to feel their bodices, their skirts, their hair, to know what these creatures were made of.

Suddenly she said: "There is a stout, dark girl who keeps watching us all the time. I thought just now that she was going to speak to us. Did you notice her?"

He answered: "No, you must be mistaken." But he had already noticed her for some time back. It was Rachel who was prowling about in their neighborhood, with anger in her eyes and hard words upon her lips.

Duroy had brushed against her in making his way through the crowd, and she had whispered, "Good evening," with a wink which signified, "I understand." But he had not replied to this mark of attention for fear of being seen by his mistress, and he had passed on coldly, with haughty look and disdainful lip. The woman, whom unconscious jealousy already assailed, turned back, brushed against him again, and said in louder tones: "Good evening, George." He had not answered even then. Then she made up her mind to be recognized and bowed to, and she kept continually passing in the rear of the box, awaiting a favorable moment.

As soon as she saw that Madame de Marelle was looking at her she touched Duroy's shoulder, saying: "Good evening, are you quite well?"

He did not turn round, and she went on: "What, have you grown deaf since Thursday?" He did not reply, affecting a contempt which would not allow him to compromise himself even by a word with this slut.

She began to laugh an angry laugh, and said: "So you are dumb, then? Perhaps the lady has bitten your tongue off?"

He made an angry movement, and exclaimed, in an exasperated tone: "What do you mean by speaking to me? Be off, or I will have you locked up."

Then, with fiery eye and swelling bosom, she screeched out: "So that's it, is it? Ah! you lout. When a man sleeps with a woman the least he can do is to nod to her. It is no reason because you are with someone else that you should cut me to-day. If you had only nodded to me when I passed you just now, I should have left you alone. But you wanted to do the grand. I'll pay you out! Ah, so you won't say good evening when you meet me!"

She would have gone on for a long time, but Madame de Marelle had opened the door of the box and fled through the crowd, blindly seeking the way out. Duroy started off in her rear and strove to catch her up, while Rachel, seeing them flee, yelled triumphantly: "Stop her, she has stolen my sweetheart."

People began to laugh. Two gentlemen for fun seized the fugitive by the shoulders and sought to bring her back, trying, too, to kiss her. But Duroy, having caught her up, freed her forcibly and led her away into the street. She jumped into an empty cab standing at the door. He jumped in after her, and when the driver asked, "Where to, sir?" replied, "Wherever you like."

The cab slowly moved off, jolting over the paving stones. Clotilde, seized by a kind of hysterical attack, sat choking and gasping with her hands covering her face, and Duroy neither knew what to do nor what to say. At last, as he heard her sobbing, he stammered out: "Clo, my dear little Clo, just listen, let me explain. It is not my fault. I used to know that woman, some time ago, you know—"

She suddenly took her hands from her face, and overcome by the wrath of a loving and deceitful woman, a furious wrath that enabled her to recover her speech, she pantingly jerked out, in rapid and broken sentences: "Oh!—you wretch—you wretch—what a scoundrel you are—can it be possible? How shameful—O Lord—how shameful!" Then, getting angrier and angrier as her ideas grew clearer and arguments suggested themselves to her, she went on: "It was with my money you paid her, wasn't it? And I was giving him money—for that creature. Oh, the scoundrel!" She seemed for a few minutes to be seeking some stronger expression that would not come, and then all at once she spat out, as it were, the words: "Oh! you swine—you swine—you swine—you paid her with my money—you swine—you swine!" She could not think of anything else, and kept repeating, "You swine, you swine!"

Suddenly she leant out of the window, and catching the driver by the sleeve, cried, "Stop," and opening the door, sprang out.

George wanted to follow, but she cried, "I won't have you get out," in such loud tones that the passers-by began to gather about her, and Duroy did not move for fear of a scandal. She took her purse from her pocket and looked for some change by the light of the cab lantern, then taking two francs fifty centimes she put them in the driver's hand, saying, in ringing tones: "There is your fare—I pay you, now take this blackguard to the Rue Boursault, Batignolles."

Mirth was aroused in the group surrounding her. A gentleman said: "Well done, little woman," and a young rapscallion standing close to the cab thrust his head into the open door and sang out, in shrill tones, "Goodnight, lovey!" Then the cab started off again, followed by a burst of laughter.

VI

George Duroy woke up chapfallen the next morning.

He dressed himself slowly, and then sat down at his window and began to reflect. He felt a kind of aching sensation all over, just as though he had received a drubbing over night. At last the necessity of finding some money spurred him up, and he went first to Forestier.

His friend received him in his study with his feet on the fender.

"What has brought you out so early?" said he.

"A very serious matter, a debt of honor."

"At play?"

He hesitated a moment, and then said: "At play."

"Heavy?"

"Five hundred francs."

He only owed two hundred and eighty.

Forestier, skeptical on the point, inquired: "Whom do you owe it to?"

Duroy could not answer right off. "To—to—a Monsieur de Carleville."

"Ah! and where does he live?"

"At—at—"

Forestier began to laugh. "Number ought, Nowhere Street, eh? I know that gentleman, my dear fellow. If you want twenty francs, I have still that much at your service, but no more."

Duroy took the offered louis. Then he went from door to door among the people he knew, and wound up by having collected at about five o'clock the sum of eighty francs. And he still needed two hundred more; he made up his mind, and keeping for himself what he had thus gleaned, murmured: "Bah! I am not going to put myself out for that cat. I will pay her when I can."

For a fortnight he lived regularly, economically, and chastely, his mind filled with energetic resolves. Then he was seized with a strong longing for love. It seemed to him that several years had passed since he last clasped a woman in his arms, and like the sailor who goes wild on seeing land, every passing petticoat made him quiver. So he went one evening to the Folies

Bergère in the hope of finding Rachel. He caught sight of her indeed, directly he entered, for she scarcely went elsewhere, and went up to her smiling with outstretched hand. But she merely looked him down from head to foot, saying: "What do you want with me?"

He tried to laugh it off with, "Come, don't be stuck-up."

She turned on her heels, saying: "I don't associate with ponces."

She had picked out the bitterest insult. He felt the blood rush to his face, and went home alone.

Forestier, ill, weak, always coughing, led him a hard life at the paper, and seemed to rack his brain to find him tiresome jobs. One day, even, in a moment of nervous irritation, and after a long fit of coughing, as Duroy had not brought him a piece of information he wanted, he growled out: "Confound it! you are a bigger fool than I thought."

The other almost struck him, but restrained himself, and went away muttering: "I'll manage to pay you out some day." An idea shot through his mind, and he added: "I will make a cuckold of you, old fellow!" And he took himself off, rubbing his hands, delighted at this project.

He resolved to set about it the very next day. He paid Madame Forestier a visit as a reconnaissance. He found her lying at full length on a couch, reading a book. She held out her hand without rising, merely turning her head, and said: "Good-day, Pretty-boy!"

He felt as though he had received a blow. "Why do you call me that?" he said.

She replied, with a smile: "I saw Madame de Marelle the other day, and learned how you had been baptized at her place."

He felt reassured by her amiable air. Besides, what was there for him to be afraid of?

She resumed: "You spoil her. As to me, people come to see me when they think of it—the thirty-second of the month, or something like it."

He sat down near her, and regarded her with a new species of curiosity, the curiosity of the amateur who is bargain-hunting. She was charming, a soft and tender blonde, made for caresses, and he thought: "She is better than the other, certainly." He did not doubt his success, it seemed to him that he had only to stretch out his hand and take her, as one gathers a fruit.

He said, resolutely: "I did not come to see you, because it was better so."

She asked, without understanding: "What? Why?"

"No, not at all."

"Because I am in love with you; oh! only a little, and I do not want to be head over ears."

She seemed neither astonished, nor shocked, nor flattered; she went on smiling the same indifferent smile, and replied with the same tranquillity: "Oh! you can come all the same. No one is in love with me long."

He was surprised, more by the tone than by the words, and asked: "Why not?"

"Because it is useless. I let this be understood at once. If you had told me of your fear before, I should have reassured you, and invited you, on the contrary, to come as often as possible."

He exclaimed, in a pathetic tone: "Can we command our feelings?"

She turned towards him: "My dear friend, for me a man in love is struck off the list of the living. He becomes idiotic, and not only idiotic, but dangerous. I cease all intimate relations with people who are in love with me, or who pretend to be so—because they bore me, in the first place; and, secondly, because they are as much objects of suspicion to me as a mad dog, which may have a fit of biting. I therefore put them into a kind of moral quarantine until their illness is over. Do not forget this. I know very well that in your case love is only a species of appetite, while with me it would be, on the contrary, a kind of—of—of communion of souls, which does not enter into a man's religion. You understand its letter, and its spirit. But look me well in the face." She no longer smiled. Her face was calm and cold, and she continued, emphatically: "I will never, never be your mistress; you understand. It is therefore absolutely useless, it would even be hurtful, for you to persist in this desire. And now that the operation is over, will you agree to be friends—good friends—real friends, I mean, without any mental reservation."

He had understood that any attempt would be useless in face of this irrevocable sentence. He made up his mind at once, frankly, and, delighted at being able to secure this ally in the battle of life, held out both hands, saying: "I am yours, madame, as you will."

She read the sincerity of his intention in his voice, and gave him her hands. He kissed them both, one after the other, and then said simply, as he raised his head: "Ah, if I had found a woman like you, how gladly I would have married her."

She was touched this time—soothed by this phrase, as women are by the compliments which reach their hearts, and she gave him one of those rapid and grateful looks which make us their slaves. Then, as he could find no change of subject to renew the conversation, she said softly, laying her finger on his arm: "And I am going to play my part of a friend at once. You are clumsy." She hesitated a moment, and then asked: "May I speak plainly?"

"Yes."

"Quite plainly?"

"Quite."

"Well, go and see Madame Walter, who greatly appreciates you, and do your best to please her. You will find a place there for your compliments, although she is virtuous, you understand me, perfectly virtuous. Oh! there is no hope of—of poaching there, either. You may find something better, though, by showing yourself. I know that you still hold an inferior position on the paper. But do not be afraid, they receive all their staff with the same kindness. Go there—believe me."

He said, with a smile: "Thanks, you are an angel, a guardian angel."

They spoke of one thing and another. He stayed for some time, wishing to prove that he took pleasure in being with her, and on leaving, remarked: "It is understood, then, that we are friends?"

"It is."

As he had noted the effect of the compliment he had paid her shortly before, he seconded it by adding: "And if ever you become a widow, I enter the lists."

Then he hurried away, so as not to give her time to get angry.

A visit to Madame Walter was rather awkward for Duroy, for he had not been authorized to call, and he did not want to commit a blunder. The governor displayed some good will towards him, appreciated his services, and employed him by preference on difficult jobs, so why should he not profit by this favor to enter the house? One day, then, having risen early, he went to the market while the morning sales were in progress, and for ten francs obtained a score of splendid pears. Having carefully packed them in a hamper to make it appear that they had come from a distance, he left them with the doorkeeper at Madame Walter's with his card, on which he had written: "George Duroy begs Madame Walter to accept a little fruit which he received this morning from Normandy."

He found the next morning, among his letters at the office, an envelope in reply, containing the card of Madame Walter, who "thanked Monsieur George Duroy, and was at home every Saturday."

On the following Saturday he called. Monsieur Walter occupied, on the Boulevard Malesherbes, a double house, which belonged to him, and of which a part was let off, in the economical way of practical people. A single doorkeeper, quartered between the two carriage entrances, opened the door for both landlord and tenant, and imparted to each of the entrances an air of wealth by his get-up like a beadle, his big calves in white stockings, and his coat with gilt buttons and scarlet facings. The reception-rooms were on the first floor, preceded by an ante-room hung with tapestry, and shut in by curtains over the doorways. Two footmen were dozing on benches. One of them took Duroy's overcoat and the other relieved him of his cane, opened the door, advanced a few steps in front of the visitor, and then drawing aside, let him pass, calling out his name, into an empty room.

The young fellow, somewhat embarrassed, looked round on all sides when he perceived in a glass some people sitting down who seemed very far off. He was at sea at first as to the direction in which they were, the mirror having deceived his eyes. Then he passed through two empty drawing-rooms and reached a small boudoir hung with blue silk, where four ladies were chatting round a table bearing cups of tea. Despite the assurance he had acquired in course of his Parisian life, and above all in his career as a reporter, which constantly brought him into contact with important personages, Duroy felt somewhat intimidated by the get-up of the entrance and the passage through the deserted drawing-room. He stammered: "Madame, I have ventured," as his eyes sought the mistress of the house.

She held out her hand, which he took with a bow, and having remarked: "You are very kind sir, to call and see me," she pointed to a chair, in seeking to sit down in which he almost fell, having thought it much higher.

They had become silent. One of the ladies began to talk again. It was a question of the frost, which was becoming sharper, though not enough, however, to check the epidemic of typhoid fever, nor to allow skating. Every one gave her opinion on this advent of frost in Paris, then they expressed their preference for the different seasons with all the trivial reasons that lie about in people's minds like dust in rooms. The faint noise made by a door caused Duroy to turn his head, and he saw in a glass a stout lady approaching. As soon as she made her appearance in the boudoir one of the other visitors rose, shook hands and left, and the young fellow followed her black back glittering with jet through the drawing-rooms with his eyes. When the agitation due to this change had subsided they spoke without transition of the Morocco question and the war in the East and also of the difficulties of England in South Africa. These ladies discussed these matters from memory, as if they had been reciting passages from a fashionable play, frequently rehearsed.

A fresh arrival took place, that of a little curly-headed blonde, which brought about the departure of a tall, thin lady of middle age. They now spoke of the chance Monsieur Linet had of getting into the Academie-Francaise. The new-comer formerly believed that he would be beaten by Monsieur Cabanon-Lebas, the author of the fine dramatic adaption of Don Quixote in verse.

"You know it is to be played at the Odeon next winter?"

"Really, I shall certainly go and see such a very excellent literary effort."

Madame Walter answered gracefully with calm indifference, without ever hesitating as to what she should say, her mind being always made up beforehand. But she saw that night was coming on, and rang for the lamps, while listening to the conversation that trickled on like a stream of honey, and thinking that she had forgotten to call on the stationer about the invitation cards for her next dinner. She was a little too stout, though still beautiful, at the dangerous age when the general break-up is at hand. She preserved herself by dint of care, hygienic precautions, and salves for the skin. She seemed discreet in all matters; moderate and reasonable; one of those women whose mind is correctly laid out like a French garden. One walks through it with surprise, but experiencing a certain charm. She had keen, discreet, and sound sense, that stood her instead of fancy, generosity, and affection, together with a calm kindness for everybody and everything.

She noted that Duroy had not said anything, that he had not been spoken to, and that he seemed slightly ill at ease; and as the ladies had not yet quitted the Academy, that favorite subject always occupying them some time, she said: "And you who should be better informed than any one, Monsieur Duroy, who is your favorite?"

He replied unhesitatingly: "In this matter, madame, I should never consider the merit, always disputable, of the candidates, but their age and their state of health. I should not ask about their credentials, but their disease. I should not seek to learn whether they have made a metrical translation of Lope de Vega, but I should take care to obtain information as to the state of their liver, their heart, their lungs, and their spinal marrow. For me a good hypertrophy, a good aneurism, and above all, a good beginning of locomotor ataxy, would be a hundred times more valuable than forty volumes of disgressions on the idea of patriotism as embodied in barbaric poetry."

An astonished silence followed this opinion, and Madame Walter asked with a smile: "But why?"

He replied: "Because I never seek aught else than the pleasure that any one can give the ladies. But, Madame, the Academy only has any real interest for you when an Academician dies. The more of them die the happier you must be. But in order that they may die quickly they must be elected sick and old." As they still remained somewhat surprised, he continued. "Besides, I am like you, and I like to read of the death of an Academician. I at once ask myself: 'Who will replace him?' And I draw up my list. It is a game, a very pretty little game that is played in all Parisian salons at each decease of one of the Immortals, the game of 'Death and the Forty Fogies.'"

The ladies, still slightly disconcerted, began however, to smile, so true were his remarks. He concluded, as he rose: "It is you who really elect them, ladies, and you only elect them to see them die. Choose them old, therefore, very old; as old as possible, and do not trouble yourselves about anything else."

He then retired very gracefully. As soon as he was gone, one of the ladies said: "He is very funny, that young fellow. Who is he?"

Madame Walter replied: "One of the staff of our paper, who does not do much yet; but I feel sure that he will get on."

Duroy strode gayly down the Boulevard Malesherbes, content with his exit, and murmuring: "A capital start."

He made it up with Rachel that evening.

The following week two things happened to him. He was appointed chief reporter and invited to dinner at Madame Walter's. He saw at once a connection between these things. The *Vie Francaise* was before everything a financial paper, the head of it being a financier, to whom the press and the position of a deputy served as levers. Making use of every cordiality as a weapon, he had always worked under the smiling mask of a good fellow; but he only employed men whom he had sounded, tried, and proved; whom he knew to be crafty, bold, and supple. Duroy, appointed chief of the reporting staff, seemed to him a valuable fellow.

This duty had been filled up till then by the chief sub-editor, Monsieur Boisrenard, an old journalist, as correct, punctual, and scrupulous as a clerk. In course of thirty years he had been sub-editor of eleven different papers, without in any way modifying his way of thinking or acting. He passed from one office to another as one changes one's restaurant, scarcely noticing that the cookery was not quite the same. Political and religious opinions were foreign to him. He was devoted to his paper, whatever it might be, well up in his work, and valuable from his experience. He worked like a blind man who sees nothing, like a deaf man who hears nothing, and like a dumb man who never speaks of anything. He had, however, a strong instinct of professional loyalty, and would not stoop to aught he did not think honest and right from the special point of view of his business.

Monsieur Walter, who thoroughly appreciated him, had however, often wished for another man to whom to entrust the "Echoes," which he held to be the very marrow of the paper. It is through them that rumors are set afloat and the public and the funds influenced. It is necessary to know how to slip the all-important matter, rather hinted at than said right out, in between the description of two fashionable entertainments, without appearing to intend it. It is necessary to imply a thing by judicious reservations; let what is desired be guessed at; contradict in such a fashion as to confirm, or affirm in such a way that no one shall believe the statement. It is necessary that in the "Echoes" everyone shall find every day at least one line of interest, in order that every one may read them. Every one must be thought of, all classes, all professions, Paris and the provinces, the army and the art world, the clergy and the university, the bar and the world of gallantry. The man who has the conduct of them, and who commands an army of reporters, must be always on the alert and always on his guard; mistrustful, far-seeing, cunning, alert, and supple; armed with every kind of cunning, and gifted with an infallible knack of spotting false news at the first glance, of judging which is good to announce and good to hide, of divining what will catch the public, and of putting it forward in such a way as to double its effect.

Monsieur Boisrenard, who had in his favor the skill acquired by long habit, nevertheless lacked mastery and dash; he lacked, above all, the native cunning needed to put forth day by day the secret ideas of the manager. Duroy could do it to perfection, and was an admirable addition to the staff. The wire-pullers and real editors of the *Vie Francaise* were half a dozen deputies, interested in all the speculations brought out or backed up by the manager. They were known in the Chamber as "Walter's gang," and envied because they gained money with him and through him. Forestier, the political editor, was only the man of straw of these men of business, the worker-out of ideas suggested by them. They prompted his leaders, which he always wrote at home, so as to do so in quiet, he said. But in order to give the paper a literary and truly Parisian smack, the services of two celebrated writers in different styles had been secured—Jacques Rival, a descriptive writer, and Norbert de Varenne, a poet and story-writer. To these had been added, at a cheap rate, theatrical, musical and art critics, a law reporter, and a sporting reporter, from the mercenary tribe of all-round pressmen. Two ladies, "Pink Domino" and "Lily Fingers," sent in fashion articles, and dealt with questions of dress, etiquette, and society.

Duroy was in all the joy of his appointment as chief of the "Echoes" when he received a printed card on which he read: "Monsieur and Madame

Walter request the pleasure of Monsieur Geo. Duroy's company at dinner, on Thursday, January 20." This new mark of favor following on the other filled him with such joy that he kissed the invitation as he would have done a love letter. Then he went in search of the cashier to deal with the important question of money. A chief of the reporting staff on a Paris paper generally has his budget out of which he pays his reporters for the intelligence, important or trifling, brought in by them, as gardeners bring in their fruits to a dealer. Twelve hundred francs a month were allotted at the outset to Duroy, who proposed to himself to retain a considerable share of it. The cashier, on his pressing instances, ended by advancing him four hundred francs. He had at first the intention of sending Madame de Marelle the two hundred and eighty francs he owed her, but he almost immediately reflected that he would only have a hundred and twenty left, a sum utterly insufficient to carry on his new duties in suitable fashion, and so put off this resolution to a future day.

During a couple of days he was engaged in settling down, for he had inherited a special table and a set of pigeon holes in the large room serving for the whole of the staff. He occupied one end of the room, while Boisrenard, whose head, black as a crow's, despite his age, was always bent over a sheet of paper, had the other. The long table in the middle belonged to the staff. Generally it served them to sit on, either with their legs dangling over the edges, or squatted like tailors in the center. Sometimes five or six would be sitting on it in that fashion, perseveringly playing cup and ball. Duroy had ended by having a taste for this amusement, and was beginning to get expert at it, under the guidance, and thanks to the advice of Saint-Potin. Forestier, grown worse, had lent him his fine cup and ball in West Indian wood, the last he had bought, and which he found rather too heavy for him, and Duroy swung with vigorous arm the big black ball at the end of its string, counting quickly to himself: "One—two—three—four—five—six." It happened precisely that for the first time he spiked the ball twenty times running, the very day that he was to dine at Madame Walter's. "A good day," he thought, "I am successful in everything." For skill at cup and ball really conferred a kind of superiority in the office of the *Vie Francaise*.

He left the office early to have time to dress, and was going up the Rue de Londres when he saw, trotting along in front of him, a little woman whose figure recalled that of Madame de Marelle. He felt his cheeks flush, and his heart began to beat. He crossed the road to get a view of her. She stopped, in order to cross over, too. He had made a mistake, and breathed again. He had often asked how he ought to behave if he met her face to face. Should he bow, or should he seem not to have seen her. "I should not see her," he thought.

It was cold; the gutters were frozen, and the pavement dry and gray in the gas-light. When he got home he thought: "I must change my lodgings; this is no longer good enough for me." He felt nervous and lively, capable of anything; and he said aloud, as he walked from his bed to the window: "It is fortune at last—it is fortune! I must write to father." From time to time he wrote to his father, and the letter always brought happiness to the little Norman inn by the roadside, at the summit of the slope overlooking Rouen and the broad valley of the Seine. From time to time, too, he received a blue envelope, addressed in a large, shaky hand, and read the same unvarying lines at the beginning of the paternal epistle. "My Dear Son: This leaves your mother and myself in good health. There is not much news here. I must tell you, however," etc. In his heart he retained a feeling of interest for the village matters, for the news of the neighbours, and the condition of the crops.

He repeated to himself, as he tied his white tie before his little looking-glass: "I must write to father to-morrow. Wouldn't the old fellow be staggered if he could see me this evening in the house I am going to? By Jove! I am going to have such a dinner as he never tasted." And he suddenly saw the dark kitchen behind the empty *café*; the copper stewpans casting their yellow reflections on the wall; the cat on the hearth, with her nose to the fire, in sphinx-like attitude; the wooden table, greasy with time and spilt liquids, a soup tureen smoking upon it, and a lighted candle between two plates. He saw them, too—his father and mother, two slow-moving peasants, eating their soup. He knew the smallest wrinkles on their old faces, the slightest movements of their arms and heads. He knew even what they talked about every evening as they sat at supper. He thought, too: "I must really go and see them;" but his toilet being ended, he blew out his light and went downstairs.

As he passed along the outer boulevard girls accosted him from time to time. He replied, as he pulled away his arm: "Go to the devil!" with a violent disdain, as though they had insulted him. What did they take him for? Could not these hussies tell what a man was? The sensation of his dress coat, put on in order to go to dinner with such well-known and important people, inspired him with the sentiment of a new impersonality—the sense of having become another man, a man in society, genuine society.

He entered the ante-room, lit by tall bronze candelabra, with confidence, and handed in easy fashion his cane and overcoat to two valets who approached. All the drawing-rooms were lit up. Madame Walter received her guests in the second, the largest. She welcomed him with a charming smile, and he shook hands with two gentlemen who had arrived before him—Monsieur Firmin and Monsieur Laroche-Mathieu, deputies, and anonymous editors of the *Vie Francaise*. Monsieur Laroche-Mathieu had a special authority at the paper, due to a great influence he enjoyed in the Chamber. No one doubted his being a minister some day. Then came the Forestiers; the wife in pink, and looking charming. Duroy was stupefied to see her on terms of intimacy with the two deputies. She chatted in low tones beside the fireplace, for more than five minutes, with Monsieur Laroche-Mathieu. Charles seemed worn out. He had grown much thinner during the past month, and coughed incessantly as he repeated: "I must make up my mind to finish the winter in the south." Norbert de Varenne and Jacques Rival made their appearance together. Then a door having opened at the further end of the room, Monsieur Walter came in with two tall young girls, of from sixteen to eighteen, one ugly and the other pretty.

Duroy knew that the governor was the father of a family; but he was struck with astonishment. He had never thought of his daughters, save as one thinks of distant countries which one will never see. And then he had fancied them quite young, and here they were grown-up women. They held out their hands to him after being introduced, and then went and sat down at a little table, without doubt reserved to them, at which they began to turn over a number of reels of silk in a work-basket. They were still awaiting someone, and all were silent with that sense of oppression, preceding dinners, between people who do not find themselves in the same mental atmosphere after the different occupations of the day.

Duroy having, for want of occupation, raised his eyes towards the wall, Monsieur Walter called to him from a distance, with an evident wish to show off his property: "Are you looking at my pictures? I will show them to you," and he took a lamp, so that the details might be distinguished.

"Here we have landscapes," said he.

In the center of the wall was a large canvas by Guillemet, a bit of the Normandy coast under a lowering sky. Below it a wood, by Harpignies, and a plain in Algeria, by Guillemet, with a camel on the horizon, a tall camel with long legs, like some strange monument. Monsieur Walter passed on to the next wall, and announced in a grave tone, like a master of the ceremonies: "High Art." There were four: "A Hospital Visit," by Gervex; "A Harvester," by Bastien-Lepage; "A Widow," by Bouguereau; and "An Execution," by Jean Paul Laurens. The last work represented a Vendean priest shot against the wall of his church by a detachment of Blues. A smile flitted across the governor's grave countenance as he indicated the next wall. "Here the fanciful school." First came a little canvas by Jean Beraud, entitled, "Above and Below." It was a pretty Parisian mounting to the roof of a tramcar in motion. Her head appeared on a level with the top, and the gentlemen on the seats viewed with satisfaction the pretty face approaching them, while those standing on the platform below considered the young woman's legs with a different expression of envy and desire. Monsieur Walter held the lamp at arm's length, and repeated, with a sly laugh: "It is funny, isn't it?" Then he lit up "A Rescue," by Lambert. In the middle of a table a kitten, squatted on its haunches, was watching with astonishment and perplexity a fly drowning in a glass of water. It had its paw raised ready to fish out the insect with a rapid sweep of it. But it had not quite made up its mind. It hesitated. What would it do? Then the governor showed a Detaille, "The Lesson," which represented a soldier in a barrack-room teaching a poodle to play the drum, and said: "That is very witty."

Duroy laughed a laugh of approbation, and exclaimed: "It is charming, charm—" He stopped short on hearing behind him the voice of Madame de Marelle, who had just come in.

The governor continued to light up the pictures as he explained them. He now showed a water-color by Maurice Leloir, "The Obstacle." It was a sedan chair checked on its way, the street being blocked by a fight between two laborers, two fellows struggling like Hercules. From out of the window of the chair peered the head of a charming woman, who watched without impatience, without alarm, and with a certain admiration, the combat of these two brutes. Monsieur Walter continued: "I have others in the adjoining rooms, but they are by less known men. I buy of the young artists now, the very young ones, and hang their works in the more private rooms until they become known." He then went on in a low tone: "Now is the time to buy! The painters are all dying of hunger! They have not a sou, not a sou!"

But Duroy saw nothing, and heard without understanding. Madame de Marelle was there behind him. What ought he to do? If he spoke to her, might she not turn her back on him, or treat him with insolence? If he did not approach her, what would people think? He said to himself: "I will gain time, at any rate." He was so moved that for a moment he thought of feigning a sudden illness, which would allow him to withdraw. The examination of the walls was over. The governor went to put down his lamp and welcome the last comer, while Duroy began to re-examine the pictures as if he could not tire of admiring them. He was quite upset. What should he do? Madame Forestier called to him: "Monsieur Duroy." He went to her. It was to speak to him of a friend of hers who was about to give a fête, and who would like to have a line to that effect in the *Vie Francaise*. He gasped out: "Certainly, Madame, certainly."

Madame de Marelle was now quite close to him. He dared not turn round to go away. All at once he thought he was going mad; she had said aloud: "Good evening, Pretty-boy. So you no longer recognize me."

He rapidly turned on his heels. She stood before him smiling, her eyes beaming with sprightliness and affection, and held out her hand. He took it tremblingly, still fearing some trick, some perfidy. She added, calmly: "What has become of you? One no longer sees anything of you."

He stammered, without being able to recover his coolness: "I have a great deal to do, Madame, a great deal to do. Monsieur Walter has entrusted me with new duties which give me a great deal of occupation."

She replied, still looking him in the face, but without his being able to discover anything save good will in her glance: "I know it. But that is no reason for forgetting your friends."

They were separated by a lady who came in, with red arms and red face, a stout lady in a very low dress, got up with pretentiousness, and walking so heavily that one guessed by her motions the size and weight of her legs. As she seemed to be treated with great attention, Duroy asked Madame Forestier: "Who is that lady?"

"The Viscomtesse de Percemur, who signs her articles 'Lily Fingers.'"

He was astounded, and seized on by an inclination to laugh.

"'Lily Fingers!' 'Lily Fingers!' and I imagined her young like yourself. So that is 'Lily Fingers.' That is very funny, very funny."

A servant appeared in the doorway and announced dinner. The dinner was commonplace and lively, one of those dinners at which people talk about everything, without saying anything. Duroy found himself between the elder daughter of the master of the house, the ugly one, Mademoiselle Rose and Madame de Marelle. The neighborhood of the latter made him feel very ill at ease, although she seemed very much at her ease, and chatted with her usual vivacity. He was troubled at first, constrained, hesitating, like a musician who has lost the keynote. By degrees, however, he recovered his assurance, and their eyes continually meeting questioned one another, exchanging looks in an intimate, almost sensual, fashion as of old. All at once he thought he felt something brush against his foot under the table. He softly pushed forward his leg and encountered that of his neighbor, which did not shrink from the contact. They did not speak, each being at that moment turned towards their neighbor. Duroy, his heart beating, pushed a little harder with his knee. A slight pressure replied to him. Then he understood that their loves were beginning anew. What did they say then? Not much, but their lips quivered every time that they looked at one another.

The young fellow, however, wishing to do the amiable to his employer's daughter, spoke to her from time to time. She replied as the mother would have done, never hesitating as to what she should say. On the right of Monsieur Walter the Viscomtesse de Percemur gave herself the airs of a princess, and Duroy, amused at watching her, said in a low voice to Madame de Marelle. "Do you know the other, the one who signs herself 'Pink Domino'?"

"Yes, very well, the Baroness de Livar."

"Is she of the same breed?"

"No, but quite as funny. A tall, dried-up woman of sixty, false curls, projecting teeth, ideas dating from the Restoration, and toilets of the same epoch."

"Where did they unearth these literary phenomena?"

"The scattered waifs of the nobility are always sheltered by enriched cits."

"No other reason?"

"None."

Then a political discussion began between the master of the house, the two deputies, Norbert de Varenne, and Jacques Rival, and lasted till dessert.

When they returned to the drawing-room, Duroy again approached Madame de Marelle, and looking her in the eyes, said: "Shall I see you home to-night?"

"No."

"Why not?"

"Because Monsieur Laroche Mathieu, who is my neighbor, drops me at my door every time I dine here."

"When shall I see you?"

"Come and lunch with me to-morrow."

And they separated without saying anything more.

Duroy did not remain late, finding the evening dull. As he went downstairs he overtook Norbert de Varenne, who was also leaving. The old poet took him by the arm. No longer having to fear any rivalry as regards the paper, their work being essentially different, he now manifested a fatherly kindness towards the young fellow.

"Well, will you walk home a bit of my way with me?" said he.

"With pleasure, my dear master," replied Duroy.

And they went out, walking slowly along the Boulevard Malesherbes. Paris was almost deserted that night—a cold night—one of those nights that seem vaster, as it were, than others, when the stars seem higher above, and the air seems to bear on its icy breath something coming from further than even the stars. The two men did not speak at first. Then Duroy, in order to say something, remarked: "Monsieur Laroche Mathieu seems very intelligent and well informed."

The old poet murmured: "Do you think so?"

The young fellow, surprised at this remark, hesitated in replying: "Yes; besides, he passes for one of the most capable men in the Chamber."

"It is possible. In the kingdom of the blind the one-eyed man is king. All these people are commonplace because their mind is shut in between two walls, money and politics. They are dullards, my dear fellow, with whom it is impossible to talk about anything we care for. Their minds are at the bottom mud, or rather sewage; like the Seine Asnières. Ah! how difficult it is to find a man with breadth of thought, one who causes you the same sensation as the breeze from across the broad ocean one breathes on the seashore. I have known some such; they are dead."

Norbert de Varenne spoke with a clear but restrained voice, which would have rung out in the silence of the night had he given it rein. He seemed excited and sad, and went on: "What matter, besides, a little more or less talent, since all must come to an end."

He was silent, and Duroy, who felt light hearted that evening, said with a smile: "You are gloomy to-day, dear master."

The poet replied: "I am always so, my lad, so will you be in a few years. Life is a hill. As long as one is climbing up one looks towards the summit and is happy, but when one reaches the top one suddenly perceives the descent before one, and its bottom, which is death. One climbs up slowly, but one goes down quickly. At your age a man is happy. He hopes for many things, which, by the way, never come to pass. At mine, one no longer expects anything—but death."

Duroy began to laugh: "You make me shudder all over."

Norbert de Varenne went on: "No, you do not understand me now, but later on you will remember what I am saying to you at this moment. A day comes, and it comes early for many, when there is an end to mirth, for behind everything one looks at one sees death. You do not even understand the word. At your age it means nothing; at mine it is terrible. Yes, one understands it all at once, one does not know how or why, and then everything in life changes its aspect. For fifteen years I have felt death assail me as if I bore within me some gnawing beast. I have felt myself decaying little by little, month by month, hour by hour, like a house crumbling to ruin. Death has disfigured me so completely that I do not recognize myself. I have no longer anything about me of myself—of the fresh, strong man I was at thirty. I have seen death whiten my black hairs, and with what skillful and spiteful slowness. Death has taken my firm skin, my muscles, my teeth, my whole body of old, only leaving me a despairing soul, soon to be taken too. Every step brings me nearer to death, every moment, every breath hastens his odious work. To breathe, sleep, drink, eat, work, dream, everything we do is to die. To live, in short, is to die. I now see death so near that I often want to stretch my arms to push it back. I see it everywhere. The insects crushed on the path, the falling leaves, the white hair in a friend's head, rend my heart and cry to me, "Behold it!" It spoils for me all I do, all I see, all that I eat and drink, all that I love; the bright moonlight, the sunrise, the broad ocean, the noble rivers, and the soft summer evening air so sweet to breathe."

He walked on slowly, dreaming aloud, almost forgetting that he had a listener: "And no one ever returns—never. The model of a statue may be preserved, but my body, my face, my thoughts, my desires will never reappear again. And yet millions of beings will be born with a nose, eyes, forehead, cheeks, and mouth like me, and also a soul like me, without my ever returning, without even anything recognizable of me appearing in these countless different beings. What can we cling to? What can we believe in? All religions are stupid, with their puerile morality and their egoistical promises, monstrously absurd. Death alone is certain."

He stopped, reflected for a few moments, and then, with a look of resignation, said: "I am a lost creature. I have neither father nor mother, nor sister nor brother; no wife, no children, no God."

He added, after a pause: "I have only verse."

They reached the Pont de la Concorde, crossed it in silence, and walked past the Palais Bourbon. Norbert de Varenne began to speak again, saying: "Marry, my friend; you do not know what it is to live alone at my age. Solitude now fills me with horrible agony—solitude at home by the fireside of a night. It is so profound, so sad; the silence of the room in which one dwells alone. It is not alone silence about the body, but silence about the soul; and when the furniture creaks I shudder to the heart, for no sound but is unexpected in my gloomy dwelling." He was silent again for a moment, and then added: "When one is old it is well, all the same, to have children."

They had got half way down the Rue de Bourgoyne. The poet halted in front of a tall house, rang the bell, shook Duroy by the hand, and said:

"Forget all this old man's doddering, youngster, and live as befits your age. Good-night."

And he disappeared in the dark passage.

Duroy resumed his route with a pain at his heart. It seemed to him as though he had been shown a hole filled with bones, an unavoidable gulf into which all must fall one day. He muttered: "By Jove, it can't be very lively in his place. I should not care for a front seat to see the procession of his thoughts go by. The deuce, no."

But having paused to allow a perfumed lady, alighting from her carriage and entering her house, to pass before him, he drew in with eager breath the scent of vervain and orris root floating in the air. His lungs and heart throbbed suddenly with hope and joy, and the recollection of Madame de Marelle, whom he was to see the next day, assailed him from head to foot. All smiled on him, life welcomed him with kindness. How sweet was the realization of hopes!

He fell asleep, intoxicated with this idea, and rose early to take a stroll down the Avenue du Bois de Boulogne before keeping his appointment. The wind having changed, the weather had grown milder during the night, and it was as warm and as sunny as in April. All the frequenters of the Bois had sallied out that morning, yielding to the summons of a bright, clear day. Duroy walked along slowly. He passed the Arc de Triomphe, and went along the main avenue. He watched the people on horseback, ladies and gentlemen, trotting and galloping, the rich folk of the world, and scarcely envied them now. He knew them almost all by name—knew the amount of their fortune, and the secret history of their life, his duties having made him a kind of directory of the celebrities and the scandals of Paris.

Ladies rode past, slender, and sharply outlined in the dark cloth of their habits, with that proud and unassailable air many women have on horseback, and Duroy amused himself by murmuring the names, titles, and qualities of the lovers whom they had had, or who were attributed to them. Sometimes, instead of saying "Baron de Tanquelot," "Prince de la Tour-Enguerrand," he murmured "Lesbian fashion, Louise Michot of the Vaudeville, Rose Marquetin of the Opera."

The game greatly amused him, as if he had verified, beneath grave outward appearances, the deep, eternal infamy of mankind, and as if this had excited, rejoiced, and consoled him. Then he said aloud: "Set of hypocrites!" and sought out with his eye the horsemen concerning whom the worst tales were current. He saw many, suspected of cheating at play, for whom their clubs were, at all events, their chief, their sole source of livelihood, a suspicious one, at any rate. Others, very celebrated, lived only, it was well known, on the income of their wives; others, again, it was affirmed, on that of their mistresses. Many had paid their debts, an honorable action, without it ever being guessed whence the money had come—a very equivocal mystery. He saw financiers whose immense fortune had had its origin in a theft, and who were received everywhere, even in the most noble houses; then men so respected that the lower middle-class took off their hats on their passage, but whose shameless speculations in connection with great national enterprises were a mystery for none of those really acquainted with the inner side of things. All had a haughty look, a proud lip, an insolent eye. Duroy still laughed, repeating: "A fine lot; a lot of blackguards, of sharpers."

But a pretty little open carriage passed, drawn by two white ponies with flowing manes and tails, and driven by a pretty fair girl, a well-known courtesan, who had two grooms seated behind her. Duroy halted with a desire to applaud this mushroom of love, who displayed so boldly at this place and time set apart for aristocratic hypocrites the dashing luxury earned between her sheets. He felt, perhaps vaguely, that there was something in common between them—a tie of nature, that they were of the same race, the same spirit, and that his success would be achieved by daring steps of the same kind. He walked back more slowly, his heart aglow with satisfaction, and arrived a little in advance of the time at the door of his former mistress.

She received him with proffered lips, as though no rupture had taken place, and she even forgot for a few moments the prudence that made her opposed to all caresses at her home. Then she said, as she kissed the ends of his moustache: "You don't know what a vexation has happened to me, darling? I was hoping for a nice honeymoon, and here is my husband home for six weeks. He has obtained leave. But I won't remain six weeks without seeing you, especially after our little tiff, and this is how I have arranged matters. You are to come and dine with us on Monday. I have already spoken to him about you, and I will introduce you."

Duroy hesitated, somewhat perplexed, never yet having found himself face to face with a man whose wife he had enjoyed. He was afraid lest something might betray him—a slight embarrassment, a look, no matter what. He stammered out: "No, I would rather not make your husband's acquaintance."

She insisted, very much astonished, standing before him with wide open, wondering eyes. "But why? What a funny thing. It happens every day. I should not have thought you such a goose."

He was hurt, and said: "Very well, I will come to dinner on Monday."

She went on: "In order that it may seem more natural I will ask the Forestiers, though I really do not like entertaining people at home."

Until Monday Duroy scarcely thought any more about the interview, but on mounting the stairs at Madame de Marelle's he felt strangely uneasy, not that it was so repugnant to him to take her husband's hand, to drink his wine, and eat his bread, but because he felt afraid of something without knowing what. He was shown into the drawing-room and waited as usual. Soon the door of the inner room opened, and he saw a tall, white-bearded man, wearing the ribbon of the Legion of Honor, grave and correct, who advanced towards him with punctilious politeness, saying: "My wife has often spoken to me of you, sir, and I am delighted to make your acquaintance."

Duroy stepped forward, seeking to impart to his face a look of expressive cordiality, and grasped his host's hand with exaggerated energy. Then, having sat down, he could find nothing to say.

Monsieur de Marelle placed a log upon the fire, and inquired: "Have you been long engaged in journalism?"

"Only a few months."

"Ah! you have got on quickly?"

"Yes, fairly so," and he began to chat at random, without thinking very much about what he was saying, talking of all the trifles customary among men who do not know one another. He was growing seasoned now, and thought the situation a very amusing one. He looked at Monsieur de Marelle's serious and respectable face, with a temptation to laugh, as he thought: "I have cuckolded you, old fellow, I have cuckolded you." A vicious, inward satisfaction stole over him—the satisfaction of a thief who has been successful, and is not even suspected—a delicious, roguish joy. He suddenly longed to be the friend of this man, to win his confidence, to get him to relate the secrets of his life.

Madame de Marelle came in suddenly, and having taken them in with a smiling and impenetrable glance, went toward Duroy, who dared not, in the presence of her husband, kiss her hand as he always did. She was calm, and light-hearted as a person accustomed to everything, finding this meeting simple and natural in her frank and native trickery. Laurine appeared, and went and held up her forehead to George more quietly than usual, her father's presence intimidating her. Her mother said to her: "Well, you don't call him Pretty-boy to-day." And the child blushed as if a serious indiscretion had been committed, a thing that ought not to have been mentioned, revealed, an intimate and, so to say, guilty secret of her heart laid bare.

When the Forestiers arrived, all were alarmed at the condition of Charles. He had grown frightfully thin and pale within a week, and coughed incessantly. He stated, besides, that he was leaving for Cannes on the following Thursday, by the doctor's imperative orders. They left early, and Duroy said, shaking his head: "I think he is very bad. He will never make old bones."

Madame de Marelle said, calmly: "Oh! he is done for. There is a man who was lucky in finding the wife he did."

Duroy asked: "Does she help him much?"

"She does everything. She is acquainted with everything that is going on; she knows everyone without seeming to go and see anybody; she obtains what she wants as she likes. Oh! she is keen, clever, and intriguing as no one else is. She is a treasure for anyone wanting to get on."

George said: "She will marry again very quickly, no doubt?"

Madame de Marelle replied: "Yes. I should not be surprised if she had some one already in her eye—a deputy, unless, indeed, he objects—for—for—there may be serious—moral—obstacles. But then—I don't really know."

Monsieur de Marelle grumbled with slow impatience: "You are always suspecting a number of things that I do not like. Do not let us meddle with the affairs of others. Our conscience is enough to guide us. That should be a rule with everyone."

Duroy withdrew, uneasy at heart, and with his mind full of vague plans. The next day he paid a visit to the Forestiers, and found them finishing their packing up. Charles, stretched on a sofa, exaggerated his difficulty of breathing, and repeated: "I ought to have been off a month ago."

Then he gave George a series of recommendations concerning the paper, although everything had been agreed upon and settled with Monsieur Walter. As George left, he energetically squeezed his old comrade's hand, saying: "Well, old fellow, we shall have you back soon." But as Madame Forestier was showing him out, he said to her, quickly: "You have not forgotten our agreement? We are friends and allies, are we not? So if you have need of me, for no matter what, do not hesitate. Send a letter or a telegram, and I will obey."

She murmured: "Thanks, I will not forget." And her eye, too, said "Thanks," in a deeper and tenderer fashion.

As Duroy went downstairs, he met slowly coming up Monsieur de Vaudrec, whom he had met there once before. The Count appeared sad, at this departure, perhaps. Wishing to show his good breeding, the journalist eagerly bowed. The other returned the salutation courteously, but in a somewhat dignified manner.

The Forestiers left on Thursday evening.

VII

Charles's absence gave Duroy increased importance in the editorial department of the *Vie Francaise*. He signed several leaders besides his "Echoes," for the governor insisted on everyone assuming the responsibility of his "copy." He became engaged in several newspaper controversies, in which he acquitted himself creditably, and his constant relations with different statesmen were gradually preparing him to become in his turn a clever and perspicuous political editor. There was only one cloud on his horizon. It came from a little free-lance newspaper, which continually assailed him, or rather in him assailed the chief writer of "Echoes" in the *Vie Francaise*, the chief of "Monsieur Walter's startlers," as it was put by the anonymous writer of the *Plume*. Day by day cutting paragraphs, insinuations of every kind, appeared in it.

One day Jacques Rival said to Duroy: "You are very patient."

Duroy replied: "What can I do, there is no direct attack?"

But one afternoon, as he entered the editor's room, Boisrenard held out the current number of the *Plume*, saying: "Here's another spiteful dig at you."

"Ah! what about?"

"Oh! a mere nothing—the arrest of a Madame Aubert by the police."

George took the paper, and read, under the heading, "Duroy's Latest":

"The illustrious reporter of the *Vie Francaise* to-day informs us that Madame Aubert, whose arrest by a police agent belonging to the odious *brigade des mœurs* we announced, exists only in our imagination. Now the person in question lives at 18 Rue de l'Ecureuil, Montmartre. We understand only too well, however, the interest the agents of Walter's bank have in supporting those of the Prefect of Police, who tolerates their commerce. As to the reporter of whom it is a question, he would do better to give us one of those good sensational bits of news of which he has the secret—news of deaths contradicted the following day, news of battles which have never taken place, announcements of important utterances by sovereigns who have not said anything—all the news, in short, which constitutes Walter's profits, or even one of those little indiscretions concerning entertainments given by would-be fashionable ladies, or the excellence of certain articles of consumption which are of such resource to some of our compeers."

The young fellow was more astonished than annoyed, only understanding that there was something very disagreeable for him in all this.

Boisrenard went on: "Who gave you this 'Echo'?"

Duroy thought for a moment, having forgotten. Then all at once the recollection occurred to him, "Saint-Potin." He re-read the paragraph in the *Plume* and reddened, roused by the accusation of venality. He exclaimed: "What! do they mean to assert that I am paid—"

Boisrenard interrupted him: "They do, though. It is very annoying for you. The governor is very strict about that sort of thing. It might happen so often in the 'Echoes.'"

Saint-Potin came in at that moment. Duroy hastened to him. "Have you seen the paragraph in the *Plume*?"

"Yes, and I have just come from Madame Aubert. She does exist, but she was not arrested. That much of the report has no foundation."

Duroy hastened to the room of the governor, whom he found somewhat cool, and with a look of suspicion in his eye. After having listened to the statement of the case, Monsieur Walter said: "Go and see the woman yourself, and contradict the paragraph in such terms as will put a stop to such things being written about you any more. I mean the latter part of the paragraph. It is very annoying for the paper, for yourself, and for me. A journalist should no more be suspected than Cæsar's wife."

Duroy got into a cab, with Saint-Potin as his guide, and called out to the driver: "Number 18 Rue de l'Ecureuil, Montmartre."

It was a huge house, in which they had to go up six flights of stairs. An old woman in a woolen jacket opened the door to them. "What is it you want with me now?" said she, on catching sight of Saint-Potin.

He replied: "I have brought this gentleman, who is an inspector of police, and who would like to hear your story."

Then she let him in, saying: "Two more have been here since you, for some paper or other, I don't know which," and turning towards Duroy, added: "So this gentleman wants to know about it?"

"Yes. Were you arrested by an *agent des mœurs*?"

She lifted her arms into the air. "Never in my life, sir, never in my life. This is what it is all about. I have a butcher who sells good meat, but who gives bad weight. I have often noticed it without saying anything; but the other day, when I asked him for two pounds of chops, as I had my daughter and my son-in-law to dinner, I caught him weighing in bits of trimmings— trimmings of chops, it is true, but not of mine. I could have made a stew of them, it is true, as well, but when I ask for chops it is not to get other people's trimmings. I refused to take them, and he calls me an old shark. I called him an old rogue, and from one thing to another we picked up such a row that there were over a hundred people round the shop, some of them laughing fit to split. So that at last a police agent came up and asked us to settle it before the commissary. We went, and he dismissed the case. Since then I get my meat elsewhere, and don't even pass his door, in order to avoid his slanders."

She ceased talking, and Duroy asked: "Is that all?"

"It is the whole truth, sir," and having offered him a glass of cordial, which he declined, the old woman insisted on the short weight of the butcher being spoken of in the report.

On his return to the office, Duroy wrote his reply:

> "An anonymous scribbler in the *Plume* seeks to pick a quarrel with me on the subject of an old woman whom he states was arrested by an *agent des mœurs*, which fact I deny. I have myself seen Madame Aubert—who is at least sixty years of age—and she told me in detail her quarrel with the butcher over the weighing of some chops, which led to an explanation before the commissary of police. This is the whole truth. As to the other insinuations of the writer in the *Plume*, I despise them. Besides, a man does not reply to such things when they are written under a mask.
>
> "GEORGE DUROY."

Monsieur Walter and Jacques Rival, who had come in, thought this note satisfactory, and it was settled that it should go in at once.

Duroy went home early, somewhat agitated and slightly uneasy. What reply would the other man make? Who was he? Why this brutal attack? With the brusque manners of journalists this affair might go very far. He slept badly. When he read his reply in the paper next morning, it seemed to him more aggressive in print than in manuscript. He might, it seemed to him, have softened certain phrases. He felt feverish all day, and slept badly again at night. He rose at dawn to get the number of the *Plume* that must contain a reply to him.

The weather had turned cold again, it was freezing hard. The gutters, frozen while still flowing, showed like two ribbons of ice alongside the pavement. The morning papers had not yet come in, and Duroy recalled the day of his first article, "The Recollections of a Chasseur d'Afrique." His hands and feet getting numbed, grew painful, especially the tips of his fingers, and he began to trot round the glazed kiosque in which the newspaper seller, squatting over her foot warmer, only showed through the little window a red nose and a pair of cheeks to match in a woolen hood. At length the newspaper porter passed the expected parcel through the opening, and the woman held out to Duroy an unfolded copy of the *Plume*.

He glanced through it in search of his name, and at first saw nothing. He was breathing again, when he saw between two dashes:

> "Monsieur Duroy, of the *Vie Francaise*, contradicts us, and in contradicting us, lies. He admits, however, that there is a Madame Aubert, and that an agent took her before the commissary of police. It only remains, therefore, to add two words, '*des mœurs*,' after the word 'agent,' and he is right. But the conscience of certain journalists is on a level with their talent. And I sign,
>
> "LOUIS LANGREMONT."

George's heart began to beat violently, and he went home to dress without being too well aware of what he was doing. So he had been insulted, and in such a way that no hesitation was possible. And why? For nothing at all. On account of an old woman who had quarreled with her butcher.

He dressed quickly and went to see Monsieur Walter, although it was barely eight o'clock. Monsieur Walter, already up, was reading the *Plume*. "Well," said he, with a grave face, on seeing Duroy, "you cannot draw back now." The young fellow did not answer, and the other went on: "Go at once and see Rival, who will act for you."

Duroy stammered a few vague words, and went out in quest of the descriptive writer, who was still asleep. He jumped out of bed, and, having read the paragraph, said: "By Jove, you must go out. Whom do you think of for the other second?"

"I really don't know."

"Boisrenard? What do you think?"

"Yes. Boisrenard."

"Are you a good swordsman?"

"Not at all."

"The devil! And with the pistol?"

"I can shoot a little."

"Good. You shall practice while I look after everything else. Wait for me a moment."

He went into his dressing-room, and soon reappeared washed, shaved, correct-looking.

"Come with me," said he.

He lived on the ground floor of a small house, and he led Duroy to the cellar, an enormous cellar, converted into a fencing-room and shooting gallery, all the openings on the street being closed. After having lit a row of gas jets running the whole length of a second cellar, at the end of which was an iron man painted red and blue; he placed on a table two pairs of breech-loading pistols, and began to give the word of command in a sharp tone, as though on the ground: "Ready? Fire—one—two—three."

Duroy, dumbfounded, obeyed, raising his arm, aiming and firing, and as he often hit the mark fair on the body, having frequently made use of an old horse pistol of his father's when a boy, against the birds, Jacques Rival, well satisfied, exclaimed: "Good—very good—very good—you will do—you will do."

Then he left George, saying: "Go on shooting till noon; here is plenty of ammunition, don't be afraid to use it. I will come back to take you to lunch and tell you how things are going."

Left to himself, Duroy fired a few more shots, and then sat down and began to reflect. How absurd these things were, all the same! What did a duel prove? Was a rascal less of a rascal after going out? What did an honest man, who had been insulted, gain by risking his life against a scoundrel? And his mind, gloomily inclined, recalled the words of Norbert de Varenne.

Then he felt thirsty, and having heard the sound of water dropping behind him, found that there was a hydrant serving as a douche bath, and drank from the nozzle of the hose. Then he began to think again. It was gloomy in this cellar, as gloomy as a tomb. The dull and distant rolling of vehicles sounded like the rumblings of a far-off storm. What o'clock could it be? The hours passed by there as they must pass in prisons, without anything to indicate or mark them save the visits of the warder. He waited a long time. Then all at once he heard footsteps and voices, and Jacques Rival reappeared, accompanied by Boisrenard. He called out as soon as he saw Duroy: "It's all settled."

The latter thought the matter terminated by a letter of apology, his heart beat, and he stammered: "Ah! thanks."

The descriptive writer continued: "That fellow Langremont is very square; he accepted all our conditions. Twenty-five paces, one shot, at the word of command raising the pistol. The hand is much steadier that way than bringing it down. See here, Boisrenard, what I told you."

And taking a pistol he began to fire, pointed out how much better one kept the line by raising the arm. Then he said: "Now let's go and lunch; it is past twelve o'clock."

They went to a neighboring restaurant. Duroy scarcely spoke. He ate in order not to appear afraid, and then, in course of the afternoon, accompanied Boisrenard to the office, where he got through his work in an abstracted and mechanical fashion. They thought him plucky. Jacques Rival dropped in in the course of the afternoon, and it was settled that his seconds should call for him in a landau at seven o'clock the next morning, and drive to the Bois de Vesinet, where the meeting was to take place. All this had been done so unexpectedly, without his taking part in it, without his saying a word, without his giving his opinion, without accepting or refusing, and with such rapidity, too, that he was bewildered, scared, and scarcely able to understand what was going on.

He found himself at home at nine o'clock, after having dined with Boisrenard, who, out of self-devotion, had not left him all day. As soon as he was alone he strode quickly up and down his room for several minutes. He was too uneasy to think about anything. One solitary idea filled his mind, that of a duel on the morrow, without this idea awakening in him anything else save a powerful emotion. He had been a soldier, he had been engaged with the Arabs, without much danger to himself though, any more than when one hunts a wild boar.

To reckon things up, he had done his duty. He had shown himself what he should be. He would be talked of, approved of, and congratulated. Then he said aloud, as one does under powerful impressions: "What a brute of a fellow."

He sat down and began to reflect. He had thrown upon his little table one of his adversary's cards, given him by Rival in order to retain his address. He read, as he had already done a score of times during the day: "Louis Langremont, 176 Rue Montmartre." Nothing more. He examined these assembled letters, which seemed to him mysterious and full of some disturbing import. Louis Langremont. Who was this man? What was his age, his height, his appearance? Was it not disgusting that a stranger, an unknown, should thus come and suddenly disturb one's existence without cause and from sheer caprice, on account of an old woman who had had a quarrel with her butcher. He again repeated aloud: "What a brute."

And he stood lost in thought, his eyes fixed on the card. Anger was aroused in him against this bit of paper, an anger with which was blended a strange sense of uneasiness. What a stupid business it was. He took a pair of nail scissors which were lying about, and stuck their points into the printed name, as though he was stabbing someone. So he was to fight, and with pistols. Why had he not chosen swords? He would have got off with a prick in the hand or arm, while with the pistols one never knew the possible result. He said: "Come, I must keep my pluck up."

The sound of his own voice made him shudder, and he glanced about him. He began to feel very nervous. He drank a glass of water and went to bed.

As soon as he was in bed he blew out his candle and closed his eyes. He was warm between the sheets, though it was very cold in his room, but he could not manage to doze off. He turned over and over, remained five minutes on his back, then lay on his left side, then rolled on the right. He was still thirsty, and got up to drink. Then a sense of uneasiness assailed him. Was he going to be afraid? Why did his heart beat wildly at each well-known sound in the room? When his clock was going to strike, the faint squeak of the lever made him jump, and he had to open his mouth for some moments in order to breathe, so oppressed did he feel. He began to reason philosophically on the possibility of his being afraid.

No, certainly he would not be afraid, now he had made up his mind to go through with it to the end, since he was firmly decided to fight and not to tremble. But he felt so deeply moved that he asked himself: "Can one be afraid in spite of one's self?" This doubt assailed him. If some power stronger than his will overcame it, what would happen? Yes, what would happen? Certainly he would go on the ground, since he meant to. But suppose he shook? suppose he fainted? And he thought of his position, his reputation, his future.

A strange need of getting up to look at himself in the glass suddenly seized him. He relit the candle. When he saw his face so reflected, he scarcely recognized himself, and it seemed to him that he had never seen himself before. His eyes appeared enormous, and he was pale; yes, he was certainly pale, very pale. Suddenly the thought shot through his mind: "By this time to-morrow I may be dead." And his heart began to beat again furiously. He turned towards his bed, and distinctly saw himself stretched on his back between the same sheets as he had just left. He had the hollow cheeks of the dead, and the whiteness of those hands that no longer move. Then he grew afraid of his bed, and in order to see it no longer he opened the window to look out. An icy coldness assailed him from head to foot, and he drew back breathless.

The thought occurred to him to make a fire. He built it up slowly, without looking around. His hands shook slightly with a kind of nervous tremor when he touched anything. His head wandered, his disjointed, drifting thoughts became fleeting and painful, an intoxication invaded his mind as though he had been drinking. And he kept asking himself: "What shall I do? What will become of me?"

He began to walk up and down, repeating mechanically: "I must pull myself together. I must pull myself together." Then he added: "I will write to my parents, in case of accident." He sat down again, took some notepaper, and wrote: "Dear papa, dear mamma." Then, thinking these words rather too familiar under such tragic circumstances, he tore up the first sheet, and began anew, "My dear father, my dear mother, I am to fight a duel at daybreak, and as it might happen that—" He did not dare write the rest, and sprang up with a jump. He was now crushed by one besetting idea. He was going to fight a duel. He could no longer avoid it. What was the matter with him, then? He meant to fight, his mind was firmly made up to do so, and yet it seemed to him that, despite every effort of will, he could not retain strength enough to go to the place appointed for the meeting. From time to time his teeth absolutely chattered, and he asked himself: "Has my adversary been out before? Is he a frequenter of the shooting galleries? Is he known and classed as a shot?" He had never heard his name mentioned. And yet, if this man was not a remarkably good pistol shot, he would scarcely have accepted that dangerous weapon without discussion or hesitation.

Then Duroy pictured to himself their meeting, his own attitude, and the bearing of his opponent. He wearied himself in imagining the slightest details of the duel, and all at once saw in front of him the little round black hole in the barrel from which the ball was about to issue. He was suddenly seized with a fit of terrible despair. His whole body quivered, shaken by short, sharp shudderings. He clenched his teeth to avoid crying out, and was assailed by a wild desire to roll on the ground, to tear something to pieces, to bite. But he caught sight of a glass on the mantelpiece, and remembered that there was in the cupboard a bottle of brandy almost full, for he had kept up a military habit of a morning dram. He seized the bottle and greedily drank from its mouth in long gulps. He only put it down when his breath failed him. It was a third empty. A warmth like that of flame soon kindled within his body, and spreading through his limbs, buoyed up his mind by deadening his thoughts. He said to himself: "I have hit upon the right plan." And as his skin now seemed burning he reopened the window.

Day was breaking, calm and icy cold. On high the stars seemed dying away in the brightening sky, and in the deep cutting of the railway, the red, green, and white signal lamps were paling. The first locomotives were leaving the engine shed, and went off whistling, to be coupled to the first trains. Others, in the distance, gave vent to shrill and repeated screeches, their awakening cries, like cocks of the country. Duroy thought: "Perhaps I shall never see all this again." But as he felt that he was going again to be moved by the prospect of his own fate, he fought against it strongly, saying: "Come, I must not think of anything till the moment of the meeting; it is the only way to keep up my pluck."

And he set about his toilet. He had another moment of weakness while shaving, in thinking that it was perhaps the last time he should see his face. But he swallowed another mouthful of brandy, and finished dressing. The hour which followed was difficult to get through. He walked up and down, trying to keep from thinking. When he heard a knock at the door he almost dropped, so violent was the shock to him. It was his seconds. Already!

They were wrapped up in furs, and Rival, after shaking his principal's hand, said: "It is as cold as Siberia." Then he added: "Well, how goes it?"

"Very well."

"You are quite steady?"

"Quite."

"That's it; we shall get on all right. Have you had something to eat and drink?"

"Yes; I don't need anything."

Boisrenard, in honor of the occasion, sported a foreign order, yellow and green, that Duroy had never seen him display before.

They went downstairs. A gentleman was awaiting them in the carriage. Rival introduced him as "Doctor Le Brument." Duroy shook hands, saying, "I am very much obliged to you," and sought to take his place on the front seat. He sat down on something hard that made him spring up again, as though impelled by a spring. It was the pistol case.

Rival observed: "No, the back seat for the doctor and the principal, the back seat."

Duroy ended by understanding him, and sank down beside the doctor. The two seconds got in in their turn, and the driver started. He knew where to go. But the pistol case was in the way of everyone, above all of Duroy, who would have preferred it out of sight. They tried to put it at the back of the seat and it hurt their own; they stuck it upright between Rival and Boisrenard, and it kept falling all the time. They finished by stowing it away under their feet. Conversation languished, although the doctor related some anecdotes. Rival alone replied to him. Duroy would have liked to have given a proof of presence of mind, but he was afraid of losing the thread of his ideas, of showing the troubled state of his mind, and was haunted, too, by the disturbing fear of beginning to tremble.

The carriage was soon right out in the country. It was about nine o'clock. It was one of those sharp winter mornings when everything is as bright and brittle as glass. The trees, coated with hoar frost, seemed to have been sweating ice; the earth rang under a footstep, the dry air carried the slightest sound to a distance, the blue sky seemed to shine like a mirror, and the sun, dazzling and cold itself, shed upon the frozen universe rays which did not warm anything.

Rival observed to Duroy: "I got the pistols at Gastine Renette's. He loaded them himself. The box is sealed. We shall toss up, besides, whether we use them or those of our adversary."

Duroy mechanically replied: "I am very much obliged to you."

Then Rival gave him a series of circumstantial recommendations, for he was anxious that his principal should not make any mistake. He emphasized each point several times, saying: "When they say, 'Are you ready, gentlemen?' you must answer 'Yes' in a loud tone. When they give the word 'Fire!' you must raise your arm quickly, and you must fire before they have finished counting 'One, two, three.'"

And Duroy kept on repeating to himself: "When they give the word to fire, I must raise my arm. When they give the word to fire, I must raise my arm." He learnt it as children learn their lessons, by murmuring them to satiety in order to fix them on their minds. "When they give the word to fire, I must raise my arm."

The carriage entered a wood, turned down an avenue on the right, and then to the right again. Rival suddenly opened the door to cry to the driver: "That way, down the narrow road." The carriage turned into a rutty road between two copses, in which dead leaves fringed with ice were quivering. Duroy was still murmuring: "When they give the word to fire, I must raise my arm." And he thought how a carriage accident would settle the whole affair. "Oh! if they could only upset, what luck; if he could only break a leg."

But he caught sight, at the further side of a clearing, of another carriage drawn up, and four gentlemen stamping to keep their feet warm, and he was obliged to open his mouth, so difficult did his breathing become.

The seconds got out first, and then the doctor and the principal. Rival had taken the pistol-case and walked away with Boisrenard to meet two of the strangers who came towards them. Duroy watched them salute one another ceremoniously, and then walk up and down the clearing, looking now on the ground and now at the trees, as though they were looking for something that had fallen down or might fly away. Then they measured off a certain number of paces, and with great difficulty stuck two walking sticks into the frozen ground. They then reassembled in a group and went through the action of tossing, like children playing heads or tails.

Doctor Le Brument said to Duroy: "Do you feel all right? Do you want anything?"

"No, nothing, thanks."

It seemed to him that he was mad, that he was asleep, that he was dreaming, that supernatural influences enveloped him. Was he afraid? Perhaps. But he did not know. Everything about him had altered.

Jacques Rival returned, and announced in low tones of satisfaction: "It is all ready. Luck has favored us as regards the pistols."

That, so far as Duroy was concerned, was a matter of profound indifference.

They took off his overcoat, which he let them do mechanically. They felt the breast-pocket of his frock-coat to make certain that he had no pocketbook or papers likely to deaden a ball. He kept repeating to himself like a prayer: "When the word is given to fire, I must raise my arm."

They led him up to one of the sticks stuck in the ground and handed him his pistol. Then he saw a man standing just in front of him—a short, stout, bald-headed man, wearing spectacles. It was his adversary. He saw him very plainly, but he could only think: "When the word to fire is given, I must raise my arm and fire at once."

A voice rang out in the deep silence, a voice that seemed to come from a great distance, saying: "Are you ready, gentlemen?"

George exclaimed "Yes."

The same voice gave the word "Fire!"

He heard nothing more, he saw nothing more, he took note of nothing more, he only knew that he raised his arm, pressing strongly on the trigger. And he heard nothing. But he saw all at once a little smoke at the end of his pistol barrel, and as the man in front of him still stood in the same position, he perceived, too, a little cloud of smoke drifting off over his head.

They had both fired. It was over.

His seconds and the doctor touched him, felt him and unbuttoned his clothes, asking, anxiously: "Are you hit?"

He replied at haphazard: "No, I do not think so."

Langremont, too, was as unhurt as his enemy, and Jacques Rival murmured in a discontented tone: "It is always so with those damned pistols; you either miss or kill. What a filthy weapon."

Duroy did not move, paralyzed by surprise and joy. It was over. They had to take away his weapon, which he still had clenched in his hand. It seemed to him now that he could have done battle with the whole world. It was over. What happiness! He felt suddenly brave enough to defy no matter whom.

The whole of the seconds conversed together for a few moments, making an appointment to draw up their report of the proceedings in the course of the day. Then they got into the carriage again, and the driver, who was laughing on the box, started off, cracking his whip. They breakfasted together on the boulevards, and in chatting over the event, Duroy narrated his impressions. "I felt quite unconcerned, quite. You must, besides, have seen it yourself."

Rival replied: "Yes, you bore yourself very well."

When the report was drawn up it was handed to Duroy, who was to insert it in the paper. He was astonished to read that he had exchanged a couple of shots with Monsieur Louis Langremont, and rather uneasily interrogated Rival, saying: "But we only fired once."

The other smiled. "Yes, one shot apiece, that makes a couple of shots."

Duroy, deeming the explanation satisfactory, did not persist. Daddy Walter embraced him, saying: "Bravo, bravo, you have defended the colors of *Vie Francaise*; bravo!"

George showed himself in the course of the evening at the principal newspaper offices, and at the chief *cafés* on the boulevards. He twice encountered his adversary, who was also showing himself. They did not bow to one another. If one of them had been wounded they would have shaken hands. Each of them, moreover, swore with conviction that he had heard the whistling of the other's bullet.

The next day, at about eleven, Duroy received a telegram. "Awfully alarmed. Come at once. Rue de Constantinople.—Clo."

He hastened to their meeting-place, and she threw herself into his arms, smothering him with kisses.

"Oh, my darling! if you only knew what I felt when I saw the papers this morning. Oh, tell me all about it! I want to know everything."

He had to give minute details. She said: "What a dreadful night you must have passed before the duel."

"No, I slept very well."

"I should not have closed an eye. And on the ground—tell me all that happened."

He gave a dramatic account. "When we were face to face with one another at twenty paces, only four times the length of this room, Jacques, after asking if we were ready, gave the word 'Fire.' I raised my arm at once, keeping a good line, but I made the mistake of trying to aim at the head. I had a pistol with an unusually stiff pull, and I am accustomed to very easy ones, so that the resistance of the trigger caused me to fire too high. No matter, it could not have gone very far off him. He shoots well, too, the rascal. His bullet skimmed by my temple. I felt the wind of it."

She was sitting on his knees, and holding him in her arms as though to share his dangers. She murmured: "Oh, my poor darling! my poor darling!"

When he had finished his narration, she said: "Do you know, I cannot live without you. I must see you, and with my husband in Paris it is not easy. Often I could find an hour in the morning before you were up to run in and kiss you, but I won't enter that awful house of yours. What is to be done?"

He suddenly had an inspiration, and asked: "What is the rent here?"

"A hundred francs a month."

"Well, I will take the rooms over on my own account, and live here altogether. Mine are no longer good enough for my new position."

She reflected a few moments, and then said: "No, I won't have that."

He was astonished, and asked: "Why not?"

"Because I won't."

"That is not a reason. These rooms suit me very well. I am here, and shall remain here. Besides," he added, with a laugh, "they are taken in my name."

But she kept on refusing, "No, no, I won't have it."

"Why not, then?"

Then she whispered tenderly: "Because you would bring women here, and I won't have it."

He grew indignant. "Never. I can promise you that."

"No, you will bring them all the same."

"I swear I won't."

"Truly?"

"Truly, on my word of honor. This is our place, our very own."

She clasped him to her in an outburst of love, exclaiming: "Very well, then, darling. But you know if you once deceive me, only once, it will be all over between us, all over for ever."

He swore again with many protestations, and it was agreed that he should install himself there that very day, so that she could look in on him as she passed the door. Then she said: "In any case, come and dine with us on Sunday. My husband thinks you are charming."

He was flattered "Really!"

"Yes, you have captivated him. And then, listen, you have told me that you were brought up in a country-house."

"Yes; why?"

"Then you must know something about agriculture?"

"Yes."

"Well, talk to him about gardening and the crops. He is very fond of that sort of thing."

"Good; I will not forget."

She left him, after kissing him to an indefinite extent, the duel having stimulated her affection.

Duroy thought, as he made his way to the office, "What a strange being. What a feather brain. Can one tell what she wants and what she cares for? And what a strange household. What fanciful being arranged the union of that old man and this madcap? What made the inspector marry this giddy girl? A mystery. Who knows? Love, perhaps." And he concluded: "After all, she is a very nice little mistress, and I should be a very big fool to let her slip away from me."

VIII

His duel had given Duroy a position among the leader-writers of the *Vie Francaise*, but as he had great difficulty in finding ideas, he made a specialty of declamatory articles on the decadence of morality, the lowering of the standard of character, the weakening of the patriotic fiber and the anemia of French honor. He had discovered the word anemia, and was very proud of it. And when Madame de Marelle, filled with that skeptical, mocking, and incredulous spirit characteristic of the Parisian, laughed at his tirades, which she demolished with an epigram, he replied with a smile: "Bah! this sort of thing will give me a good reputation later on."

He now resided in the Rue de Constantinople, whither he had shifted his portmanteau, his hair-brush, his razor, and his soap, which was what his moving amounted to. Twice or thrice a week she would call before he was up, undress in a twinkling, and slip into bed, shivering from the cold prevailing out of doors. As a set off, Duroy dined every Thursday at her residence, and paid court to her husband by talking agriculture with him. As he was himself fond of everything relating to the cultivation of the soil, they sometimes both grew so interested in the subject of their conversation that they quite forgot the wife dozing on the sofa. Laurine would also go to sleep, now on the knee of her father and now on that of Pretty-boy. And when the journalist had left, Monsieur de Marelle never failed to assert, in that doctrinal tone in which he said the least thing: "That young fellow is really very pleasant company, he has a well-informed mind."

February was drawing to a close. One began to smell the violets in the street, as one passed the barrows of the flower-sellers of a morning. Duroy was living beneath a sky without a cloud.

One night, on returning home, he found a letter that had been slipped under his door. He glanced at the post-mark, and read "Cannes." Having opened it, he read:

> "Villa Jolie, Cannes.
>
> "DEAR SIR AND FRIEND,—You told me, did you not, that I could reckon upon you for anything? Well, I have a very painful service to ask of you; it is to come and help me, so that I may not be left alone during the last moments of Charles, who is dying. He may not last out the week, as the doctor has forewarned me, although he has not yet taken to his bed. I have no longer strength nor courage to

witness this hourly death, and I think with terror of those last moments which are drawing near. I can only ask such a service of you, as my husband has no relatives. You were his comrade; he opened the door of the paper to you. Come, I beg of you; I have no one else to ask.

"Believe me, your very sincere friend,

"MADELEINE FORESTIER."

A strange feeling filled George's heart, a sense of freedom and of a space opening before him, and he murmured: "To be sure, I'll go. Poor Charles! What are we, after all?"

The governor, to whom he read the letter, grumblingly granted permission, repeating: "But be back soon, you are indispensable to us."

George left for Cannes next day by the seven o'clock express, after letting the Marelles know of his departure by a telegram. He arrived the following evening about four o'clock. A commissionaire guided him to the Villa Jolie, built half-way up the slope of the pine forest clothed with white houses, which extends from Cannes to the Golfe Juan. The house—small, low, and in the Italian style—was built beside the road which winds zig-zag fashion up through the trees, revealing a succession of charming views at every turning it makes.

The man servant opened the door, and exclaimed: "Oh! Sir, madame is expecting you most impatiently."

"How is your master?" inquired Duroy.

"Not at all well, sir. He cannot last much longer."

The drawing-room, into which George was shown, was hung with pink and blue chintz. The tall and wide windows overlooked the town and the sea. Duroy muttered: "By Jove, this is nice and swell for a country house. Where the deuce do they get the money from?"

The rustle of a dress made him turn round. Madame Forestier held out both hands to him. "How good of you to come, how good of you to come," said she.

And suddenly she kissed him on the cheek. Then they looked at one another. She was somewhat paler and thinner, but still fresh-complexioned, and perhaps still prettier for her additional delicacy. She murmured: "He is dreadful, do you know; he knows that he is doomed, and he leads me a fearful life. But where is your portmanteau?"

"I have left it at the station, not knowing what hotel you would like me to stop at in order to be near you."

She hesitated a moment, and then said: "You must stay here. Besides, your room is all ready. He might die at any moment, and if it were to happen during the night I should be alone. I will send for your luggage."

He bowed, saying: "As you please."

"Now let us go upstairs," she said.

He followed her. She opened a door on the first floor, and Duroy saw, wrapped in rugs and seated in an armchair near the window, a kind of living corpse, livid even under the red light of the setting sun, and looking towards him. He scarcely recognized, but rather guessed, that it was his friend. The room reeked of fever, medicated drinks, ether, tar, the nameless and oppressive odor of a consumptive's sick room. Forestier held out his hand slowly and with difficulty. "So here you are; you have come to see me die, then! Thanks."

Duroy affected to laugh. "To see you die? That would not be a very amusing sight, and I should not select such an occasion to visit Cannes. I came to give you a look in, and to rest myself a bit."

Forestier murmured, "Sit down," and then bent his head, as though lost in painful thoughts. He breathed hurriedly and pantingly, and from time to time gave a kind of groan, as if he wanted to remind the others how ill he was.

Seeing that he would not speak, his wife came and leaned against the window-sill, and indicating the view with a motion of her head, said, "Look! Is not that beautiful?"

Before them the hillside, dotted with villas, sloped downwards towards the town, which stretched in a half-circle along the shore with its head to the right in the direction of the pier, overlooked by the old city surmounted by its belfry, and its feet to the left towards the point of La Croisette, facing the Isles of Lerins. These two islands appeared like two green spots amidst the blue water. They seemed to be floating on it like two huge green leaves, so low and flat did they appear from this height. Afar off, bounding the view on the other side of the bay, beyond the pier and the belfry, a long succession of blue hills showed up against a dazzling sky, their strange and picturesque line of summits now rounded, now forked, now pointed, ending with a huge pyramidal mountain, its foot in the sea itself.

Madame Forestier pointed it out, saying: "This is L'Estherel."

The void beyond the dark hill tops was red, a glowing red that the eye would not fear, and Duroy, despite himself, felt the majesty of the close of the day. He murmured, finding no other term strong enough to express his admiration, "It is stunning."

Forestier raised his head, and turning to his wife, said: "Let me have some fresh air."

"Pray, be careful," was her reply. "It is late, and the sun is setting; you will catch a fresh cold, and you know how bad that is for you."

He made a feverish and feeble movement with his right hand that was almost meant for a blow, and murmured with a look of anger, the grin of a dying man that showed all the thinness of his lips, the hollowness of the cheeks, and the prominence of all the bones of the face: "I tell you I am stifling. What does it matter to you whether I die a day sooner or a day later, since I am done for?"

She opened the window quite wide. The air that entered surprised all three like a caress. It was a soft, warm breeze, a breeze of spring, already laden with the scents of the odoriferous shrubs and flowers which sprang up along this shore. A powerful scent of turpentine and the harsh savor of the eucalyptus could be distinguished.

Forestier drank it in with short and fevered gasps. He clutched the arm of his chair with his nails, and said in low, hissing, and savage tones: "Shut the window. It hurts me; I would rather die in a cellar."

His wife slowly closed the window, and then looked out in space, her forehead against the pane. Duroy, feeling very ill at ease, would have liked to have chatted with the invalid and reassured him. But he could think of nothing to comfort him. At length he said: "Then you have not got any better since you have been here?"

Forestier shrugged his shoulders with low-spirited impatience. "You see very well I have not," he replied, and again lowered his head.

Duroy went on: "Hang it all, it is ever so much nicer here than in Paris. We are still in the middle of winter there. It snows, it freezes, it rains, and it is dark enough for the lamps to be lit at three in the afternoon."

"Anything new at the paper?" asked Forestier.

"Nothing. They have taken on young Lacrin, who has left the *Voltaire*, to do your work, but he is not up to it. It is time that you came back."

The invalid muttered: "I—I shall do all my work six feet under the sod now."

This fixed idea recurred like a knell *apropos* of everything, continually cropping up in every idea, every sentence. There was a long silence, a deep and painful silence. The glow of the sunset was slowly fading, and the mountains were growing black against the red sky, which was getting duller. A colored shadow, a commencement of night, which yet retained the glow of an expiring furnace, stole into the room and seemed to tinge the furniture, the walls, the hangings, with mingled tints of sable and crimson. The chimney-glass, reflecting the horizon, seemed like a patch of blood. Madame Forestier did not stir, but remained standing with her back to the room, her face to the window pane.

Forestier began to speak in a broken, breathless voice, heartrending to listen to. "How many more sunsets shall I see? Eight, ten, fifteen, or twenty, perhaps thirty—no more. You have time before you; for me it is all over. And it will go on all the same, after I am gone, as if I was still here." He was silent for a few moments, and then continued: "All that I see reminds me that in a few days I shall see it no more. It is horrible. I shall see nothing—nothing of all that exists; not the smallest things one makes use of—the plates, the glasses, the beds in which one rests so comfortably, the carriages. How nice it is to drive out of an evening! How fond I was of all those things!"

He nervously moved the fingers of both hands, as though playing the piano on the arms of his chair. Each of his silences was more painful than his words, so evident was it that his thoughts must be fearful. Duroy suddenly recalled what Norbert de Varenne had said to him some weeks before, "I now see death so near that I often want to stretch out my arms to put it back. I see it everywhere. The insects crushed on the path, the falling leaves, the white hair in a friend's beard, rend my heart and cry to me, 'Behold!'"

He had not understood all this on that occasion; now, seeing Forestier, he did. An unknown pain assailed him, as if he himself was sensible of the presence of death, hideous death, hard by, within reach of his hand, on the chair in which his friend lay gasping. He longed to get up, to go away, to fly, to return to Paris at once. Oh! if he had known he would not have come.

Darkness had now spread over the room, like premature mourning for the dying man. The window alone remained still visible, showing, within the lighter square formed by it, the motionless outline of the young wife.

Forestier remarked, with irritation, "Well, are they going to bring in the lamp to-night? This is what they call looking after an invalid."

The shadow outlined against the window panes disappeared, and the sound of an electric bell rang through the house. A servant shortly entered and placed a lamp on the mantelpiece. Madame Forestier said to her husband, "Will you go to bed, or would you rather come down to dinner?"

He murmured: "I will come down."

Waiting for this meal kept them all three sitting still for nearly an hour, only uttering from time to time some needless commonplace remark, as if there had been some danger, some mysterious danger in letting silence endure too long, in letting the air congeal in this room where death was prowling.

At length dinner was announced. The meal seemed interminable to Duroy. They did not speak, but ate noiselessly, and then crumbled their bread with their fingers. The man servant who waited upon them went to and fro without the sound of his footsteps being heard, for as the creak of a boot-sole irritated Charles, he wore list slippers. The harsh tick of a wooden clock alone disturbed the calm with its mechanical and regular sound.

As soon as dinner was over Duroy, on the plea of fatigue, retired to his room, and leaning on the window-sill watched the full moon, in the midst of the sky like an immense lamp, casting its cold gleam upon the white walls of the villas, and scattering over the sea a soft and moving dappled light. He strove to find some reason to justify a swift departure, inventing plans, telegrams he was to receive, a recall from Monsieur Walter.

But his resolves to fly appeared more difficult to realize on awakening the next morning. Madame Forestier would not be taken in by his devices, and he would lose by his cowardice all the benefit of his self-devotion. He said to himself: "Bah! it is awkward; well so much the worse, there must be unpleasant situations in life, and, besides, it will perhaps be soon over."

It was a bright day, one of those bright Southern days that make the heart feel light, and Duroy walked down to the sea, thinking that it would be soon enough to see Forestier some time in course of the afternoon. When he returned to lunch, the servant remarked, "Master has already asked for you two or three times, sir. Will you please step up to his room, sir?"

He went upstairs. Forestier appeared to be dozing in his armchair. His wife was reading, stretched out on the sofa.

The invalid raised his head, and Duroy said, "Well, how do you feel? You seem quite fresh this morning."

"Yes, I am better, I have recovered some of my strength. Get through your lunch with Madeleine as soon as you can, for we are going out for a drive."

As soon as she was alone with Duroy, the young wife said to him, "There, to-day he thinks he is all right again. He has been making plans all the morning. We are going to the Golfe Juan now to buy some pottery for our rooms in Paris. He is determined to go out, but I am horribly afraid of some mishap. He cannot bear the shaking of the drive."

When the landau arrived, Forestier came down stairs a step at a time, supported by his servant. But as soon as he caught sight of the carriage, he ordered the hood to be taken off. His wife opposed this, saying, "You will catch cold. It is madness."

He persisted, repeating, "Oh, I am much better. I feel it."

They passed at first along some of those shady roads, bordered by gardens, which cause Cannes to resemble a kind of English Park, and then reached the highway to Antibes, running along the seashore. Forestier acted as guide. He had already pointed out the villa of the Court de Paris, and now indicated others. He was lively, with the forced and feeble gayety of a doomed man. He lifted his finger, no longer having strength to stretch out his arm, and said, "There is the Ile Sainte Marguerite, and the chateau from which Bazaine escaped. How they did humbug us over that matter!"

Then regimental recollections recurred to him, and he mentioned various officers whose names recalled incidents to them. But all at once, the road making a turn, they caught sight of the whole of the Golfe Juan, with the white village in the curve of the bay, and the point of Antibes at the further side of it. Forestier, suddenly seized upon by childish glee, exclaimed, "Ah! the squadron, you will see the squadron."

Indeed they could perceive, in the middle of the broad bay, half-a-dozen large ships resembling rocks covered with leafless trees. They were huge, strange, mis-shapen, with excrescences, turrets, rams, burying themselves in the water as though to take root beneath the waves. One could scarcely imagine how they could stir or move about, they seemed so heavy and so firmly fixed to the bottom. A floating battery, circular and high out of water, resembling the light-houses that are built on shoals. A tall three-master passed near them, with all its white sails set. It looked graceful and pretty beside these iron war monsters squatted on the water. Forestier tried to make them out. He pointed out the Colbert, the Suffren, the Admiral Duperre, the Redoubtable, the Devastation, and then checking himself, added, "No I made a mistake; that one is the Devastation."

They arrived opposite a species of large pavilion, on the front of which was the inscription, "Art Pottery of the Golfe Juan," and the carriage, driving up the sweep, stopped before the door. Forestier wanted to buy a couple of vases for his study. As he felt unequal to getting out of the carriage, specimens were brought out to him one after the other. He was a long time in making a choice, and consulted his wife and Duroy.

"You know," he said, "it is for the cabinet at the end of the study. Sitting in my chair, I have it before my eyes all the time. I want an antique form, a Greek outline." He examined the specimens, had others brought, and then turned again to the first ones. At length he made up his mind, and having paid, insisted upon the articles being sent on at once. "I shall be going back to Paris in a few days," he said.

They drove home, but as they skirted the bay a rush of cold air from one of the valleys suddenly met them, and the invalid began to cough. It was nothing at first, but it augmented and became an unbroken fit of coughing, and then a kind of gasping hiccough.

Forestier was choking, and every time he tried to draw breath the cough seemed to rend his chest. Nothing would soothe or check it. He had to be borne from the carriage to his room, and Duroy, who supported his legs, felt the jerking of his feet at each convulsion of his lungs. The warmth of the bed did not check the attack, which lasted till midnight, when, at length, narcotics lulled its deadly spasm. The sick man remained till morning sitting up in his bed, with his eyes open.

The first words he uttered were to ask for the barber, for he insisted on being shaved every morning. He got up for this operation, but had to be helped back into bed at once, and his breathing grew so short, so hard, and so difficult, that Madame Forestier, in alarm, had Duroy, who had just turned in, roused up again in order to beg him to go for the doctor.

He came back almost immediately with Dr. Gavaut, who prescribed a soothing drink and gave some advice; but when the journalist saw him to the door, in order to ask his real opinion, he said, "It is the end. He will be dead to-morrow morning. Break it to his poor wife, and send for a priest. I, for my part, can do nothing more. I am, however, entirely at your service."

Duroy sent for Madame Forestier. "He is dying," said he. "The doctor advises a priest being sent for. What would you like done?"

She hesitated for some time, and then, in slow tones, as though she had calculated everything, replied, "Yes, that will be best—in many respects. I will break it to him—tell him the vicar wants to see him, or something or other; I really don't know what. You would be very kind if you would go and find a priest for me and pick one out. Choose one who won't raise too many difficulties over the business. One who will be satisfied with confession, and will let us off with the rest of it all."

The young fellow returned with a complaisant old ecclesiastic, who accommodated himself to the state of affairs. As soon as he had gone into the dying man's room, Madame Forestier came out of it, and sat down with Duroy in the one adjoining.

"It has quite upset him," said she. "When I spoke to him about a priest his face assumed a frightful expression as if he had felt the breath—the breath of—you know. He understood that it was all over at last, and that his hours were numbered." She was very pale as she continued, "I shall never forget the expression of his face. He certainly saw death face to face at that moment. He saw him."

They could hear the priest, who spoke in somewhat loud tones, being slightly deaf, and who was saying, "No, no; you are not so bad as all that. You are ill, but in no danger. And the proof is that I have called in as a friend as a neighbor."

They could not make out Forestier's reply, but the old man went on, "No, I will not ask you to communicate. We will talk of that when you are better. If you wish to profit by my visit—to confess, for instance—I ask nothing better. I am a shepherd, you know, and seize on every occasion to bring a lamb back to the fold."

A long silence followed. Forestier must have been speaking in a faint voice. Then all at once the priest uttered in a different tone, the tone of one officiating at the altar. "The mercy of God is infinite. Repeat the Comfiteor, my son. You have perhaps forgotten it; I will help you. Repeat after me: 'Comfiteor Deo omnipotenti—Beata Maria semper virgini.'"

He paused from time to time to allow the dying man to catch him up. Then he said, "And now confess."

The young wife and Duroy sat still seized on by a strange uneasiness, stirred by anxious expectation. The invalid had murmured something. The priest repeated, "You have given way to guilty pleasures—of what kind, my son?"

Madeleine rose and said, "Let us go down into the garden for a short time. We must not listen to his secrets."

And they went and sat down on a bench before the door beneath a rose tree in bloom, and beside a bed of pinks, which shed their soft and powerful perfume abroad in the pure air. Duroy, after a few moments' silence, inquired, "Shall you be long before you return to Paris?"

"Oh, no," she replied. "As soon as it is all over I shall go back there."

"Within ten days?"

"Yes, at the most."

"He has no relations, then?"

"None except cousins. His father and mother died when he was quite young."

They both watched a butterfly sipping existence from the pinks, passing from one to another with a soft flutter of his wings, which continued to flap slowly when he alighted on a flower. They remained silent for a considerable time.

The servant came to inform them that "the priest had finished," and they went upstairs together.

Forestier seemed to have grown still thinner since the day before. The priest held out his hand to him, saying, "Good-day, my son, I shall call in again to-morrow morning," and took his departure.

As soon as he had left the room the dying man, who was panting for breath, strove to hold out his two hands to his wife, and gasped, "Save me—save me, darling, I don't want to die—I don't want to die. Oh! save me—tell me what I had better do; send for the doctor. I will take whatever you like. I won't die—I won't die."

He wept. Big tears streamed from his eyes down his fleshless cheeks, and the corners of his mouth contracted like those of a vexed child. Then his hands, falling back on the bed clothes, began a slow, regular, and continuous movement, as though trying to pick something off the sheet.

His wife, who began to cry too, said: "No, no, it is nothing. It is only a passing attack, you will be better to-morrow, you tired yourself too much going out yesterday."

Forestier's breathing was shorter than that of a dog who has been running, so quick that it could not be counted, so faint that it could scarcely be heard.

He kept repeating: "I don't want to die. Oh! God—God—God; what is to become of me? I shall no longer see anything—anything any more. Oh! God."

He saw before him some hideous thing invisible to the others, and his staring eyes reflected the terror it inspired. His two hands continued their horrible and wearisome action. All at once he started with a sharp shudder that could be seen to thrill the whole of his body, and jerked out the words, "The graveyard—I—Oh! God."

He said no more, but lay motionless, haggard and panting.

Time sped on, noon struck by the clock of a neighboring convent. Duroy left the room to eat a mouthful or two. He came back an hour later. Madame Forestier refused to take anything. The invalid had not stirred. He still continued to draw his thin fingers along the sheet as though to pull it up over his face.

His wife was seated in an armchair at the foot of the bed. Duroy took another beside her, and they waited in silence. A nurse had come, sent in by the doctor, and was dozing near the window.

Duroy himself was beginning to doze off when he felt that something was happening. He opened his eyes just in time to see Forestier close his, like two lights dying out. A faint rattle stirred in the throat of the dying man, and two streaks of blood appeared at the corners of his mouth, and then flowed down into his shirt. His hands ceased their hideous motion. He had ceased to breathe.

His wife understood this, and uttering a kind of shriek, she fell on her knees sobbing, with her face buried in the bed-clothes. George, surprised and scared, mechanically made the sign of the cross. The nurse awakened, drew near the bed. "It is all over," said she.

Duroy, who was recovering his self-possession, murmured, with a sigh of relief: "It was sooner over than I thought for."

When the first shock was over and the first tears shed, they had to busy themselves with all the cares and all the necessary steps a dead man exacts. Duroy was running about till nightfall. He was very hungry when he got back. Madame Forestier ate a little, and then they both installed themselves in the chamber of death to watch the body. Two candles burned on the night-table beside a plate filled with holy water, in which lay a sprig of mimosa, for they had not been able to get the necessary twig of consecrated box.

They were alone, the young man and the young wife, beside him who was no more. They sat without speaking, thinking and watching.

George, whom the darkness rendered uneasy in presence of the corpse, kept his eyes on this persistently. His eye and his mind were both attracted and fascinated by this fleshless visage, which the vacillating light caused to appear yet more hollow. That was his friend Charles Forestier, who was chatting with him only the day before! What a strange and fearful thing was this end of a human being! Oh! how he recalled the words of Norbert de Varenne haunted by the fear of death: "No one ever comes back." Millions on millions would be born almost identical, with eyes, a nose, a mouth, a skull and a mind within it, without he who lay there on the bed ever reappearing again.

For some years he had lived, eaten, laughed, loved, hoped like all the world. And it was all over for him all over for ever. Life; a few days, and then nothing. One is born, one grows up, one is happy, one waits, and then one dies. Farewell, man or woman, you will not return again to earth. Plants, beast, men, stars, worlds, all spring to life, and then die to be transformed anew. But never one of them comes back—insect, man, nor planet.

A huge, confused, and crushing sense of terror weighed down the soul of Duroy, the terror of that boundless and inevitable annihilation destroying all existence. He already bowed his head before its menace. He thought of the flies who live a few hours, the beasts who live a few days, the men who live a few years, the worlds which live a few centuries. What was the difference between one and the other? A few more days' dawn that was all.

He turned away his eyes in order no longer to have the corpse before them. Madame Forestier, with bent head, seemed also absorbed in painful thoughts. Her fair hair showed so prettily with her pale face, that a feeling, sweet as the touch of hope flitted through the young fellow's breast. Why grieve when he had still so many years before him? And he began to observe her. Lost in thought she did not notice him. He said to himself, "That, though, is the only good thing in life, to love, to hold the woman one loves in one's arms. That is the limit of human happiness."

What luck the dead man had had to meet such an intelligent and charming companion! How had they become acquainted? How ever had she agreed on her part to marry that poor and commonplace young fellow? How had she succeeded in making someone of him? Then he thought of all the hidden mysteries of people's lives. He remembered what had been whispered about the Count de Vaudrec, who had dowered and married her off it was said.

What would she do now? Whom would she marry? A deputy, as Madame de Marelle fancied, or some young fellow with a future before him, a higher class Forestier? Had she any projects, any plans, any settled ideas? How he would have liked to know that. But why this anxiety as to what she would do? He asked himself this, and perceived that his uneasiness was due to one of those half-formed and secret ideas which one hides from even one's self, and only discovers when fathoming one's self to the very bottom.

Yes, why should he not attempt this conquest himself? How strong and redoubtable he would be with her beside him!

How quick, and far, and surely he would fly! And why should he not succeed too? He felt that he pleased her, that she had for him more than mere sympathy; in fact, one of those affections which spring up between two kindred spirits and which partake as much of silent seduction as of a species of mute complicity. She knew him to be intelligent, resolute, and tenacious, she would have confidence in him.

Had she not sent for him under the present grave circumstances? And why had she summoned him? Ought he not to see in this a kind of choice, a species of confession. If she had thought of him just at the moment she was about to become a widow, it was perhaps that she had thought of one who was again to become her companion and ally? An impatient desire to know this, to question her, to learn her intentions, assailed him. He would have to leave on the next day but one, as he could not remain alone with her in the house. So it was necessary to be quick, it was necessary before returning to Paris to become acquainted, cleverly and delicately, with her projects, and not to allow her to go back on them, to yield perhaps to the solicitations of another, and pledge herself irrevocably.

The silence in the room was intense, nothing was audible save the regular and metallic tick of the pendulum of the clock on the mantelpiece.

He murmured: "You must be very tired?"

She replied: "Yes; but I am, above all, overwhelmed."

The sound of their own voices startled them, ringing strangely in this gloomy room, and they suddenly glanced at the dead man's face as though they expected to see it move on hearing them, as it had done some hours before.

Duroy resumed: "Oh! it is a heavy blow for you, and such a complete change in your existence, a shock to your heart and your whole life."

She gave a long sigh, without replying, and he continued, "It is so painful for a young woman to find herself alone as you will be."

He paused, but she said nothing, and he again went on, "At all events, you know the compact entered into between us. You can make what use of me you will. I belong to you."

She held out her hand, giving him at the same time one of those sweet, sad looks which stir us to the very marrow.

"Thank you, you are very kind," she said. "If I dared, and if I could do anything for you, I, too, should say, 'You may count upon me.'"

He had taken the proffered hand and kept it clasped in his, with a burning desire to kiss it. He made up his mind to this at last, and slowly raising it to his mouth, held the delicate skin, warm, slightly feverish and perfumed, to his lips for some time. Then, when he felt that his friendly caress was on the point of becoming too prolonged, he let fall the little hand. It sank back gently onto the knee of its mistress, who said, gravely: "Yes, I shall be very lonely, but I shall strive to be brave."

He did not know how to give her to understand that he would be happy, very happy, to have her for his wife in his turn. Certainly he could not tell her so at that hour, in that place, before that corpse; yet he might, it seemed to him, hit upon one of those ambiguous, decorous, and complicated phrases which have a hidden meaning under their words, and which express all one wants to by their studied reticence. But the corpse incommoded him, the stiffened corpse stretched out before them, and which he felt between them. For some time past, too, he fancied he detected in the close atmosphere of the room a suspicious odor, a fœtid breath exhaling from the decomposing chest, the first whiff of carrion which the dead lying on their bed throw out to the relatives watching them, and with which they soon fill the hollow of their coffin.

"Cannot we open the window a little?" said Duroy. "It seems to me that the air is tainted."

"Yes," she replied, "I have just noticed it, too."

He went to the window and opened it. All the perfumed freshness of night flowed in, agitating the flame of the two lighted candles beside the bed. The moon was shedding, as on the former evening, her full mellow light upon the white walls of the villas and the broad glittering expanse of the sea. Duroy, drawing in the air to the full depth of his lungs, felt himself suddenly seized with hope, and, as it were buoyed up by the approach of happiness. He turned round, saying: "Come and get a little fresh air. It is delightful."

She came quietly, and leant on the window-sill beside him. Then he murmured in a low tone: "Listen to me, and try to understand what I want to tell you. Above all, do not be indignant at my speaking to you of such a matter at such a moment, for I shall leave you the day after to-morrow, and when you return to Paris it may be too late. I am only a poor devil without fortune, and with a position yet to make, as you know. But I have a firm will, some brains I believe, and I am well on the right track. With a man who has made his position, one knows what one gets; with one who is starting, one never knows where he may finish. So much the worse, or so much the better. In short, I told you one day at your house that my brightest dream would have been to have married a woman like you. I repeat this wish to you now. Do not answer, let me continue. It is not a proposal I am making to you. The time and place would render that odious. I wish only not to leave you ignorant that you can make me happy with a word; that you can make me either a friend and brother, or a husband, at your will; that my heart and myself are yours. I do not want you to answer me now. I do not want us to speak any more about the matter here. When we meet again in Paris you will let me know what you have resolved upon. Until then, not a word. Is it not so?" He had uttered all this without looking at her, as though scattering his words abroad in the night before him. She seemed not to have heard them, so motionless had she remained, looking also straight before her with a fixed and vague stare at the vast landscape lit up by the moon. They remained for some time side by side, elbow touching elbow, silent and reflecting. Then she murmured: "It is rather cold," and turning round, returned towards the bed.

He followed her. When he drew near he recognized that Forestier's body was really beginning to smell, and drew his chair to a distance, for he could not have stood this odor of putrefaction long. He said: "He must be put in a coffin the first thing in the morning."

"Yes, yes, it is arranged," she replied. "The undertaker will be here at eight o'clock."

Duroy having sighed out the words, "Poor fellow," she, too, gave a long sigh of heartrending resignation.

They did not look at the body so often now, already accustomed to the idea of it, and beginning to mentally consent to the decease which but a short time back had shocked and angered them—them who were mortals, too. They no longer spoke, continuing to keep watch in befitting fashion without going to sleep. But towards midnight Duroy dozed off the first. When he woke up he saw that Madame Forestier was also slumbering, and having shifted to a more comfortable position, he reclosed his eyes, growling: "Confound it all, it is more comfortable between the sheets all the same."

A sudden noise made him start up. The nurse was entering the room. It was broad daylight. The young wife in the armchair in front of him seemed as surprised as himself. She was somewhat pale, but still pretty, fresh-looking, and nice, in spite of this night passed in a chair.

Then, having glanced at the corpse, Duroy started and exclaimed: "Oh, his beard!" The beard had grown in a few hours on this decomposing flesh as much as it would have in several days on a living face. And they stood scared by this life continuing in death, as though in presence of some fearful prodigy, some supernatural threat of resurrection, one of these startling and abnormal events which upset and confound the mind.

They both went and lay down until eleven o'clock. Then they placed Charles in his coffin, and at once felt relieved and soothed. They had sat down face to face at lunch with an aroused desire to speak of the livelier and more consolatory matters, to return to the things of life again, since they had done with the dead. Through the wide-open window the soft warmth of spring flowed in, bearing the perfumed breath of the bed of pinks in bloom before the door.

Madame Forestier suggested a stroll in the garden to Duroy, and they began to walk slowly round the little lawn, inhaling with pleasure the balmy air, laden with the scent of pine and eucalyptus. Suddenly she began to speak, without turning her head towards him, as he had done during the night upstairs. She uttered her words slowly, in a low and serious voice.

"Look here, my dear friend, I have deeply reflected already on what you proposed to me, and I do not want you to go away without an answer. Besides, I am neither going to say yes nor no. We will wait, we will see, we will know one another better. Reflect, too, on your side. Do not give way to impulse. But if I speak to you of this before even poor Charles is lowered into the tomb, it is because it is necessary, after what you have said to me, that you should thoroughly understand what sort of woman I am, in order that you may no longer cherish the wish you expressed to me, in case you are not of a—of a—disposition to comprehend and bear with me. Understand me well. Marriage for me is not a charm, but a partnership. I mean to be free, perfectly free as to my ways, my acts, my going and coming. I could neither tolerate supervision, nor jealousy, nor arguments as to my behavior. I should undertake, be it understood, never to compromise the name of the man who takes me as his wife, never to render him hateful and ridiculous. But this man must also undertake to see in me an equal, an ally, and not an inferior or an obedient and submissive wife. My notions, I know, are not those of every one, but I shall not change them. There you are. I will also add, do not answer me; it would be useless and unsuitable. We shall see one another again, and shall perhaps speak of all this again later on. Now, go for a stroll. I shall return to watch beside him. Till this evening."

He printed a long kiss on her hand, and went away without uttering a word. That evening they only saw one another at dinnertime. Then they retired to their rooms, both exhausted with fatigue.

Charles Forestier was buried the next day, without any funeral display, in the cemetery at Cannes. George Duroy wished to take the Paris express, which passed through the town at half-past one.

Madame Forestier drove with him to the station. They walked quietly up and down the platform pending the time for his departure, speaking of trivial matters.

The train rolled into the station. The journalist took his seat, and then got out again to have a few more moments' conversation with her, suddenly seized as he was with sadness and a strong regret at leaving her, as though he were about to lose her for ever.

A porter shouted, "Take your seats for Marseilles, Lyons, and Paris." Duroy got in and leant out of the window to say a few more words. The engine whistled, and the train began to move slowly on.

The young fellow, leaning out of the carriage, watched the woman standing still on the platform and following him with her eyes. Suddenly, as he was about to lose sight of her, he put his hand to his mouth and threw a kiss towards her. She returned it with a discreet and hesitating gesture.

IX

George Duroy had returned to all his old habits.

Installed at present in the little ground-floor suite of rooms in the Rue de Constantinople, he lived soberly, like a man preparing a new existence for himself.

Madame Forestier had not yet returned. She was lingering at Cannes. He received a letter from her merely announcing her return about the middle of April, without a word of allusion to their farewell. He was waiting, his mind was thoroughly made up now to employ every means in order to marry her, if she seemed to hesitate. But he had faith in his luck, confidence in that power of seduction which he felt within him, a vague and irresistible power which all women felt the influence of.

A short note informed him that the decisive hour was about to strike: "I am in Paris. Come and see me.—Madeleine Forestier."

Nothing more. He received it by the nine o'clock post. He arrived at her residence at three on the same day. She held out both hands to him smiling with her pleasant smile, and they looked into one another's eyes for a few seconds. Then she said: "How good you were to come to me there under those terrible circumstances."

"I should have done anything you told me to," he replied.

And they sat down. She asked the news, inquired about the Walters, about all the staff, about the paper. She had often thought about the paper.

"I miss that a great deal," she said, "really a very great deal. I had become at heart a journalist. What would you, I love the profession?"

Then she paused. He thought he understood, he thought he divined in her smile, in the tone of her voice, in her words themselves a kind of invitation, and although he had promised to himself not to precipitate matters, he stammered out: "Well, then—why—why should you not resume—this occupation—under—under the name of Duroy?"

She suddenly became serious again, and placing her hand on his arm, murmured: "Do not let us speak of that yet a while."

But he divined that she accepted, and falling at her knees began to passionately kiss her hands, repeating: "Thanks, thanks; oh, how I love you!"

She rose. He did so, too, and noted that she was very pale. Then he understood that he had pleased her, for a long time past, perhaps, and as they found themselves face to face, he clasped her to him and printed a long, tender, and decorous kiss on her forehead. When she had freed herself, slipping through his arms, she said in a serious tone: "Listen, I have not yet made up my mind to anything. However, it may be—yes. But you must promise me the most absolute secrecy till I give you leave to speak."

He swore this, and left, his heart overflowing with joy.

He was from that time forward very discreet as regards the visits he paid her, and did not ask for any more definite consent on her part, for she had a way of speaking of the future, of saying "by-and-by," and of shaping plans in which these two lives were blended, which answered him better and more delicately than a formal acceptation.

Duroy worked hard and spent little, trying to save money so as not to be without a penny at the date fixed for his marriage, and becoming as close as he had been prodigal. The summer went by, and then the autumn, without anyone suspecting anything, for they met very little, and only in the most natural way in the world.

One evening, Madeleine, looking him straight in the eyes said: "You have not yet announced our intentions to Madame de Marelle?"

"No, dear, having promised you to be secret, I have not opened my mouth to a living soul."

"Well, it is about time to tell her. I will undertake to inform the Walters. You will do so this week, will you not?"

He blushed as he said: "Yes, to-morrow."

She had turned away her eyes in order not to notice his confusion, and said: "If you like we will be married in the beginning of May. That will be a very good time."

"I obey you in all things with joy."

"The tenth of May, which is a Saturday, will suit me very nicely, for it is my birthday."

"Very well, the tenth of May."

"Your parents live near Rouen, do they not? You have told me so, at least."

"Yes, near Rouen, at Canteleu."

"What are they?"

"They are—they are small annuitants."

"Ah! I should very much like to know them."

He hesitated, greatly perplexed, and said: "But, you see, they are—" Then making up his mind, like a really clever man, he went on: "My dear, they are mere country folk, innkeepers, who have pinched themselves to the utmost to enable me to pursue my studies. For my part, I am not ashamed of them, but their—simplicity—their rustic manners—might, perhaps, render you uncomfortable."

She smiled, delightfully, her face lit up with gentle kindness as she replied: "No. I shall be very fond of them. We will go and see them. I want to. I will speak of this to you again. I, too, am a daughter of poor people, but I have lost my parents. I have no longer anyone in the world." She held out her hand to him as she added: "But you."

He felt softened, moved, overcome, as he had been by no other woman.

"I had thought about one matter," she continued, "but it is rather difficult to explain."

"What is it?" he asked.

"Well, it is this, my dear boy, I am like all women, I have my weaknesses, my pettinesses. I love all that glitters, that catches the ear. I should have so delighted to have borne a noble name. Could you not, on the occasion of your marriage, ennoble yourself a little?"

She had blushed in her turn, as if she had proposed something indelicate.

He replied simply enough: "I have often thought about it, but it did not seem to me so easy."

"Why so?"

He began to laugh, saying: "Because I was afraid of making myself look ridiculous."

She shrugged her shoulders. "Not at all, not at all Every one does it, and nobody laughs. Separate your name in two—Du Roy. That looks very well."

He replied at once like a man who understands the matter in question: "No, that will not do at all. It is too simple, too common, too well-known. I had thought of taking the name of my native place, as a literary pseudonym at first, then of adding it to my own by degrees, and then, later on, of even cutting my name in two, as you suggest."

"Your native place is Canteleu?" she queried.

"Yes."

She hesitated, saying: "No, I do not like the termination. Come, cannot we modify this word Canteleu a little?"

She had taken up a pen from the table, and was scribbling names and studying their physiognomy. All at once she exclaimed: "There, there it is!" and held out to him a paper, on which read—"Madame Duroy de Cantel."

He reflected a few moments, and then said gravely: "Yes, that does very well."

She was delighted, and kept repeating "Duroy de Cantel, Duroy de Cantel, Madame Duroy de Cantel. It is capital, capital." She went on with an air of conviction: "And you will see how easy it is to get everyone to accept it. But one must know how to seize the opportunity, for it will be too late afterwards. You must from to-morrow sign your descriptive articles D. de Cantel, and your 'Echoes' simply Duroy. It is done every day in the press, and no one will be astonished to see you take a pseudonym. At the moment of our marriage we can modify it yet a little more, and tell our friends that you had given up the 'Du' out of modesty on account of your position, or even say nothing about it. What is your father's Christian name?"

"Alexander."

She murmured: "Alexander, Alexander," two or three times, listening to the sonorous roll of the syllables, and then wrote on a blank sheet of paper:

"Monsieur and Madame Alexander Du Roy de Cantel have the honor to inform you of the marriage of Monsieur George Du Roy de Cantel, their son, to Madame Madeleine Forestier." She looked at her writing, holding it at a distance, charmed by the effect, and said: "With a little method we can manage whatever we wish."

When he found himself once more in the street, firmly resolved to call himself in future Du Roy, and even Du Roy de Cantel, it seemed to him that he had acquired fresh importance. He walked with more swagger, his head higher, his moustache fiercer, as a gentleman should walk. He felt in himself a species of joyous desire to say to the passers-by: "My name is Du Roy de Cantel."

But scarcely had he got home than the thought of Madame de Marelle made him feel uneasy, and he wrote to her at once to ask her to make an appointment for the next day.

"It will be a tough job," he thought. "I must look out for squalls."

Then he made up his mind for it, with the native carelessness which caused him to slur over the disagreeable side of life, and began to write a fancy article on the fresh taxes needed in order to make the Budget balance. He set down in this the nobiliary "De" at a hundred francs a year, and titles, from baron to prince, at from five hundred to five thousand francs. And he signed it "D. de Cantel."

He received a telegram from his mistress next morning saying that she would call at one o'clock. He waited for her somewhat feverishly, his mind made up to bring things to a point at once, to say everything right out, and then, when the first emotion had subsided, to argue cleverly in order to prove to her that he could not remain a bachelor for ever, and that as Monsieur de Marelle insisted on living, he had been obliged to think of another than herself as his legitimate companion. He felt moved, though, and when he heard her ring his heart began to beat.

She threw herself into his arms, exclaiming: "Good morning, Pretty-boy." Then, finding his embrace cold, looked at him, and said: "What is the matter with you?"

"Sit down," he said, "we have to talk seriously."

She sat down without taking her bonnet off, only turning back her veil, and waited.

He had lowered his eyes, and was preparing the beginning of his speech. He commenced in a low tone of voice: "My dear one, you see me very uneasy, very sad, and very much embarrassed at what I have to admit to you. I love you dearly. I really love you from the bottom of my heart, so that the fear of causing you pain afflicts me more than even the news I am going to tell you."

She grew pale, felt herself tremble, and stammered out: "What is the matter? Tell me at once."

He said in sad but resolute tones, with that feigned dejection which we make use of to announce fortunate misfortunes: "I am going to be married."

She gave the sigh of a woman who is about to faint, a painful sigh from the very depths of her bosom, and then began to choke and gasp without being able to speak.

Seeing that she did not say anything, he continued: "You cannot imagine how much I suffered before coming to this resolution. But I have neither position nor money. I am alone, lost in Paris. I needed beside me someone who above all would be an adviser, a consoler, and a stay. It is a partner, an ally, that I have sought, and that I have found."

He was silent, hoping that she would reply, expecting furious rage, violence, and insults. She had placed one hand on her heart as though to restrain its throbbings, and continued to draw her breath by painful efforts, which made her bosom heave spasmodically and her head nod to and fro. He took her other hand, which was resting on the arm of the chair, but she snatched it away abruptly. Then she murmured, as though in a state of stupefaction: "Oh, my God!"

He knelt down before her, without daring to touch her, however, and more deeply moved by this silence than he would have been by a fit of anger, stammered out: "Clo! my darling Clo! just consider my situation, consider what I am. Oh! if I had been able to marry you, what happiness it would have been. But you are married. What could I do? Come, think of it, now. I must take a place in society, and I cannot do it so long as I have not a home. If you only knew. There are days when I have felt a longing to kill your husband."

He spoke in his soft, subdued, seductive voice, a voice which entered the ear like music. He saw two tears slowly gather in the fixed and staring eyes of his mistress and then roll down her cheeks, while two more were already formed on the eyelids.

He murmured: "Do not cry, Clo; do not cry, I beg of you. You rend my very heart."

Then she made an effort, a strong effort, to be proud and dignified, and asked, in the quivering tone of a woman about to burst into sobs: "Who is it?"

He hesitated a moment, and then understanding that he must, said:

"Madeleine Forestier."

Madame de Marelle shuddered all over, and remained silent, so deep in thought that she seemed to have forgotten that he was at her feet. And two transparent drops kept continually forming in her eyes, falling and forming again.

She rose. Duroy guessed that she was going away without saying a word, without reproach or forgiveness, and he felt hurt and humiliated to the bottom of his soul. Wishing to stay her, he threw his arms about the skirt of her dress, clasping through the stuff her rounded legs, which he felt stiffen in resistance. He implored her, saying: "I beg of you, do not go away like that."

Then she looked down on him from above with that moistened and despairing eye, at once so charming and so sad, which shows all the grief of a woman's heart, and gasped out: "I—I have nothing to say. I have nothing to do with it. You—you are right. You—you have chosen well."

And, freeing herself by a backward movement, she left the room without his trying to detain her further.

Left to himself, he rose as bewildered as if he had received a blow on the head. Then, making up his mind, he muttered: "Well, so much the worse or the better. It is over, and without a scene; I prefer that," and relieved from an immense weight, suddenly feeling himself free, delivered, at ease as to his future life, he began to spar at the wall, hitting out with his fists in a kind of intoxication of strength and triumph, as if he had been fighting Fate.

When Madame Forestier asked: "Have you told Madame de Marelle?" he quietly answered, "Yes."

She scanned him closely with her bright eyes, saying: "And did it not cause her any emotion?"

"No, not at all. She thought it, on the contrary, a very good idea."

The news was soon known. Some were astonished, others asserted that they had foreseen it; others, again, smiled, and let it be understood that they were not surprised.

The young man who now signed his descriptive articles D. de Cantel, his "Echoes" Duroy, and the political articles which he was beginning to write from time to time Du Roy, passed half his time with his betrothed, who treated him with a fraternal familiarity into which, however, entered a real but hidden love, a species of desire concealed as a weakness. She had decided that the marriage should be quite private, only the witnesses being present, and that they should leave the same evening for Rouen. They would go the next day to see the journalist's parents, and remain with them some days. Duroy had striven to get her to renounce this project, but not having been able to do so, had ended by giving in to it.

So the tenth of May having come, the newly-married couple, having considered the religious ceremony useless since they had not invited anyone, returned to finish packing their boxes after a brief visit to the Town Hall. They took, at the Saint Lazare terminus, the six o'clock train, which bore them away towards Normandy. They had scarcely exchanged twenty words up to the time that they found themselves alone in the railway carriage. As soon as they felt themselves under way, they looked at one another and began to laugh, to hide a certain feeling of awkwardness which they did not want to manifest.

The train slowly passed through the long station of Batignolles, and then crossed the mangy-looking plain extending from the fortifications to the Seine. Duroy and his wife from time to time made a few idle remarks, and then turned again towards the windows. When they crossed the bridge of Asniéres, a feeling of greater liveliness was aroused in them at the sight of the river covered with boats, fishermen, and oarsmen. The sun, a bright May sun, shed its slanting rays upon the craft and upon the smooth stream, which seemed motionless, without current or eddy, checked, as it were, beneath the heat and brightness of the declining day. A sailing boat in the middle of the river having spread two large triangular sails of snowy canvas, wing and wing, to catch the faintest puffs of wind, looked like an immense bird preparing to take flight.

Duroy murmured: "I adore the neighborhood of Paris. I have memories of dinners which I reckon among the pleasantest in my life."

"And the boats," she replied. "How nice it is to glide along at sunset."

Then they became silent, as though afraid to continue their outpourings as to their past life, and remained so, already enjoying, perhaps, the poesy of regret.

Duroy, seated face to face with his wife, took her hand and slowly kissed it. "When we get back again," said he, "we will go and dine sometimes at Chatou."

She murmured: "We shall have so many things to do," in a tone of voice that seemed to imply, "The agreeable must be sacrificed to the useful."

He still held her hand, asking himself with some uneasiness by what transition he should reach the caressing stage. He would not have felt uneasy in the same way in presence of the ignorance of a young girl, but the lively and artful intelligence he felt existed in Madeleine, rendered his attitude an embarrassed one. He was afraid of appearing stupid to her, too timid or too brutal, too slow or too prompt. He kept pressing her hand gently, without her making any response to this appeal. At length he said: "It seems to me very funny for you to be my wife."

She seemed surprised as she said: "Why so?"

"I do not know. It seems strange to me. I want to kiss you, and I feel astonished at having the right to do so."

She calmly held out her cheek to him, which he kissed as he would have kissed that of a sister.

He continued: "The first time I saw you—you remember the dinner Forestier invited me to—I thought, 'Hang it all, if I could only find a wife like that.' Well, it's done. I have one."

She said, in a low tone: "That is very nice," and looked him straight in the face, shrewdly, and with smiling eyes.

He reflected, "I am too cold. I am stupid. I ought to get along quicker than this," and asked: "How did you make Forestier's acquaintance?"

She replied, with provoking archness: "Are we going to Rouen to talk about him?"

He reddened, saying: "I am a fool. But you frighten me a great deal."

She was delighted, saying: "I—impossible! How is it?"

He had seated himself close beside her. She suddenly exclaimed: "Oh! a stag."

The train was passing through the forest of Saint Germaine, and she had seen a frightened deer clear one of the paths at a bound. Duroy, leaning forward as she looked out of the open window, printed a long kiss, a lover's kiss, among the hair on her neck. She remained still for a few seconds, and then, raising her head, said: "You are tickling me. Leave off."

But he would not go away, but kept on pressing his curly moustache against her white skin in a long and thrilling caress.

She shook herself, saying: "Do leave off."

He had taken her head in his right hand, passed around her, and turned it towards him. Then he darted on her mouth like a hawk on its prey. She struggled, repulsed him, tried to free herself. She succeeded at last, and repeated: "Do leave off."

He remained seated, very red and chilled by this sensible remark; then, having recovered more self-possession, he said, with some liveliness: "Very well, I will wait, but I shan't be able to say a dozen words till we get to Rouen. And remember that we are only passing through Poissy."

"I will do the talking then," she said, and sat down quietly beside him.

She spoke with precision of what they would do on their return. They must keep on the suite of apartments that she had resided in with her first husband, and Duroy would also inherit the duties and salary of Forestier at the *Vie Francaise*. Before their union, besides, she had planned out, with the certainty of a man of business, all the financial details of their household. They had married under a settlement preserving to each of them their respective estates, and every incident that might arise—death, divorce, the birth of one or more children—was duly provided for. The young fellow contributed a capital of four thousand francs, he said, but of that sum he had borrowed fifteen hundred. The rest was due to savings effected during the year in view of the event. Her contribution was forty thousand francs, which she said had been left her by Forestier.

She returned to him as a subject of conversation. "He was a very steady, economical, hard-working fellow. He would have made a fortune in a very short time."

Duroy no longer listened, wholly absorbed by other thoughts. She stopped from time to time to follow out some inward train of ideas, and then went on: "In three or four years you can be easily earning thirty to forty thousand francs a year. That is what Charles would have had if he had lived."

George, who began to find the lecture rather a long one, replied: "I thought we were not going to Rouen to talk about him."

She gave him a slight tap on the cheek, saying, with a laugh: "That is so. I am in the wrong."

He made a show of sitting with his hands on his knees like a very good boy.

"You look very like a simpleton like that," said she.

He replied: "That is my part, of which, by the way, you reminded me just now, and I shall continue to play it."

"Why?" she asked.

"Because it is you who take management of the household, and even of me. That, indeed, concerns you, as being a widow."

She was amazed, saying: "What do you really mean?"

"That you have an experience that should enlighten my ignorance, and matrimonial practice that should polish up my bachelor innocence, that's all."

"That is too much," she exclaimed.

He replied: "That is so. I don't know anything about ladies; no, and you know all about gentlemen, for you are a widow. You must undertake my education—this evening—and you can begin at once if you like."

She exclaimed, very much amused: "Oh, indeed, if you reckon on me for that!"

He repeated, in the tone of a school boy stumbling through his lesson: "Yes, I do. I reckon that you will give me solid information—in twenty lessons. Ten for the elements, reading and grammar; ten for finishing accomplishments. I don't know anything myself."

She exclaimed, highly amused: "You goose."

He replied: "If that is the familiar tone you take, I will follow your example, and tell you, darling, that I adore you more and more every moment, and that I find Rouen a very long way off."

He spoke now with a theatrical intonation and with a series of changes of facial expression, which amused his companion, accustomed to the ways of literary Bohemia. She glanced at him out of the corner of her eye, finding him really charming, and experiencing the longing we have to pluck a fruit from the tree at once, and the check of reason which advises us to wait till dinner to eat it at the proper time. Then she observed, blushing somewhat at the thoughts which assailed her: "My dear little pupil, trust my experience, my great experience. Kisses in a railway train are not worth anything. They only upset one." Then she blushed still more as she murmured: "One should never eat one's corn in the ear."

He chuckled, kindling at the double meanings from her pretty mouth, and made the sign of the cross, with a movement of the lips, as though murmuring a prayer, adding aloud: "I have placed myself under the protection of St. Anthony, patron-saint of temptations. Now I am adamant."

Night was stealing gently on, wrapping in its transparent shadow, like a fine gauze, the broad landscape stretching away to the right. The train was running along the Seine, and the young couple began to watch the crimson reflections on the surface of the river, winding like a broad strip of polished metal alongside the line, patches fallen from the sky, which the departing sun had kindled into flame. These reflections slowly died out, grew deeper, faded sadly. The landscape became dark with that sinister thrill, that deathlike quiver, which each twilight causes to pass over the earth. This evening gloom, entering the open window, penetrated the two souls, but lately so lively, of the now silent pair.

They had drawn more closely together to watch the dying day. At Nantes the railway people had lit the little oil lamp, which shed its yellow, trembling light upon the drab cloth of the cushions. Duroy passed his arms round the waist of his wife, and clasped her to him. His recent keen desire had become a softened one, a longing for consoling little caresses, such as we lull children with.

He murmured softly: "I shall love you very dearly, my little Made."

The softness of his voice stirred the young wife, and caused a rapid thrill to run through her. She offered her mouth, bending towards him, for he was resting his cheek upon the warm pillow of her bosom, until the whistle of the train announced that they were nearing a station. She remarked, flattening the ruffled locks about her forehead with the tips of her fingers: "It was very silly. We are quite childish."

But he was kissing her hands in turn with feverish rapidity, and replied: "I adore you, my little Made."

Until they reached Rouen they remained almost motionless, cheek against cheek, their eyes turned to the window, through which, from time to time, the lights of houses could be seen in the darkness, satisfied with feeling themselves so close to one another, and with the growing anticipation of a freer and more intimate embrace.

They put up at a hotel overlooking the quay, and went to bed after a very hurried supper.

The chambermaid aroused them next morning as it was striking eight. When they had drank the cup of tea she had placed on the night-table, Duroy looked at his wife, then suddenly, with the joyful impulse of the fortunate man who has just found a treasure, he clasped her in his arms, exclaiming: "My little Made, I am sure that I love you ever so much, ever so much, ever so much."

She smiled with her confident and satisfied smile, and murmured, as she returned his kisses: "And I too—perhaps."

But he still felt uneasy about the visit of his parents. He had already forewarned his wife, had prepared and lectured her, but he thought fit to do so again.

"You know," he said, "they are only rustics—country rustics, not theatrical ones."

She laughed.

"But I know that: you have told me so often enough. Come, get up and let me get up."

He jumped out of bed, and said, as he drew on his socks:

"We shall be very uncomfortable there, very uncomfortable. There is only an old straw palliasse in my room. Spring mattresses are unknown at Canteleu."

She seemed delighted.

"So much the better. It will be delightful to sleep badly—beside—beside you, and to be woke up by the crowing of the cocks."

She had put on her dressing-gown—a white flannel dressing-gown—which Duroy at once recognized. The sight of it was unpleasant to him. Why? His wife had, he was aware, a round dozen of these morning garments. She could not destroy her trousseau in order to buy a new one. No matter, he would have preferred that her bed-linen, her night-linen, her under-clothing were not the same she had made use of with the other. It seemed to him that the soft, warm stuff must have retained something from its contact with Forestier.

He walked to the window, lighting a cigarette. The sight of the port, the broad stream covered with vessels with tapering spars, the steamers noisily unloading alongside the quay, stirred him, although he had been acquainted with it all for a long time past, and he exclaimed: "By Jove! it is a fine sight."

Madeleine approached, and placing both hands on one of her husband's shoulders, leaned against him with careless grace, charmed and delighted. She kept repeating: "Oh! how pretty, how pretty. I did not know that there were so many ships as that."

They started an hour later, for they were to lunch with the old people, who had been forewarned some days beforehand. A rusty open carriage bore them along with a noise of jolting ironmongery. They followed a long and rather ugly boulevard, passed between some fields through which flowed a stream, and began to ascend the slope. Madeleine, somewhat fatigued, had dozed off beneath the penetrating caress of the sun, which warmed her delightfully as she lay stretched back in the old carriage as though in a bath of light and country air.

Her husband awoke her, saying: "Look!"

They had halted two-thirds of the way up the slope, at a spot famous for the view, and to which all tourists drive. They overlooked the long and broad valley through which the bright river flowed in sweeping curves. It could be caught sight of in the distance, dotted with numerous islands, and describing a wide sweep before flowing through Rouen. Then the town appeared on the right bank, slightly veiled in the morning mist, but with rays of sunlight falling on its roofs; its thousand squat or pointed spires, light, fragile-looking, wrought like gigantic jewels; its round or square towers topped with heraldic crowns; its belfries; the numerous Gothic summits of its churches, overtopped by the sharp spire of the cathedral, that surprising spike of bronze—strange, ugly, and out of all proportion, the tallest in the world. Facing it, on the other side of the river, rose the factory chimneys of the suburb of Saint Serves—tall, round, and broadening at their summit. More numerous than their sister spires, they reared even in the distant country, their tall brick columns, and vomited into the blue sky their black and coaly breath. Highest of all, as high as the second of the summits reared by human labor, the pyramid of Cheops, almost level with its proud companion the cathedral spire, the great steam-pump of La Foudre seemed the queen of the busy, smoking factories, as the other was the queen of the sacred edifices. Further on, beyond the workmen's town, stretched a forest of pines, and the Seine, having passed between the two divisions of the city, continued its way, skirting a tall rolling slope, wooded at the summit, and showing here and there its bare bone of white stone. Then the river disappeared on the horizon, after again describing a long sweeping curve. Ships could be seen ascending and descending the stream, towed by tugs as big as flies and belching forth thick smoke. Islands were stretched along the water in a line, one close to the other, or with wide intervals between them, like the unequal beads of a verdant rosary.

The driver waited until the travelers' ecstasies were over. He knew from experience the duration of the admiration of all the breed of tourists. But when he started again Duroy suddenly caught sight of two old people advancing towards them some hundreds of yards further on, and jumped out, exclaiming: "There they are. I recognize them."

There were two country-folk, a man and a woman, walking with irregular steps, rolling in their gait, and sometimes knocking their shoulders together. The man was short and strongly built, high colored and inclined to stoutness, but powerful, despite his years. The woman was tall, spare, bent, careworn, the real hard-working country-woman who has toiled afield from childhood, and has never had time to amuse herself, while her husband has been joking and drinking with the customers. Madeleine had also alighted from the carriage, and she watched these two poor creatures coming towards them with a pain at her heart, a sadness she had not anticipated. They had not recognized their son in this fine gentleman and would never have guessed this handsome lady in the light dress to be their daughter-in-law. They were walking on quickly and in silence to meet their long-looked-for boy, without noticing these city folk followed by their carriage.

They passed by when George, who was laughing, cried out: "Good-day, Daddy Duroy!"

They both stopped short, amazed at first, then stupefied with surprise. The old woman recovered herself first, and stammered, without advancing a step: "Is't thou, boy?"

The young fellow answered: "Yes, it is I, mother," and stepping up to her, kissed her on both cheeks with a son's hearty smack. Then he rubbed noses with his father, who had taken off his cap, a very tall, black silk cap, made Rouen fashion, like those worn by cattle dealers.

Then George said: "This is my wife," and the two country people looked at Madeleine. They looked at her as one looks at a phenomenon, with an uneasy fear, united in the father with a species of approving satisfaction, in the mother with a kind of jealous enmity.

The man, who was of a joyous nature and inspired by a loveliness born of sweet cider and alcohol, grew bolder, and asked, with a twinkle in the corner of his eyes: "I may kiss her all the same?"

"Certainly," replied his son, and Madeleine, ill at ease, held out both cheeks to the sounding smacks of the rustic, who then wiped his lips with the back of his hand. The old woman, in her turn, kissed her daughter-in-law with a hostile reserve. No, this was not the daughter-in-law of her dreams; the plump, fresh housewife, rosy-cheeked as an apple, and round as a brood mare. She looked like a hussy, the fine lady with her furbelows and her musk. For the old girl all perfumes were musk.

They set out again, walking behind the carriage which bore the trunk of the newly-wedded pair. The old fellow took his son by the arm, and keeping him a little in the rear of the others, asked with interest: "Well, how goes business, lad?"

"Pretty fair."

"So much the better. Has thy wife any money?"

"Forty thousand francs," answered George.

His father gave vent to an admiring whistle, and could only murmur, "Dang it!" so overcome was he by the mention of the sum. Then he added, in a tone of serious conviction: "Dang it all, she's a fine woman!" For he found her to his taste, and he had passed for a good judge in his day.

Madeleine and her mother-in-law were walking side by side without exchanging a word. The two men rejoined them. They reached the village, a little roadside village formed of half-a-score houses on each side of the highway, cottages and farm buildings, the former of brick and the latter of clay, these covered with thatch and those with slates. Father Duroy's tavern, "The Bellevue," a bit of a house consisting of a ground floor and a garret, stood at the beginning of the village to the left. A pine branch above the door indicated, in ancient fashion, that thirsty folk could enter.

The things were laid for lunch, in the common room of the tavern, on two tables placed together and covered with two napkins. A neighbor, come in to help to serve the lunch, bowed low on seeing such a fine lady appear; and then, recognizing George, exclaimed: "Good Lord! is that the youngster?"

He replied gayly: "Yes, it is I, Mother Brulin," and kissed her as he had kissed his father and mother. Then turning to his wife, he said: "Come into our room and take your hat off."

He ushered her through a door to the right into a cold-looking room with tiled floor, white-washed walls, and a bed with white cotton curtains. A crucifix above a holy-water stoup, and two colored pictures, one representing Paul and Virginia under a blue palm tree, and the other Napoleon the First on a yellow horse, were the only ornaments of this clean and dispiriting apartment.

As soon as they were alone he kissed Madeleine, saying: "Thanks, Made. I am glad to see the old folks again. When one is in Paris one does not think about it; but when one meets again, it gives one pleasure all the same."

But his father, thumbing the partition with his fist, cried out: "Come along, come along, the soup is ready," and they had to sit down to table.

It was a long, countrified repast, with a succession of ill-assorted dishes, a sausage after a leg of mutton, and an omelette after a sausage. Father Duroy, excited by cider and some glasses of wine, turned on the tap of his choicest jokes—those he reserved for great occasions of festivity, smutty adventures that had happened, as he maintained, to friends of his. George, who knew all these stories, laughed, nevertheless, intoxicated by his native air, seized on by the innate love of one's birthplace and of spots familiar from childhood, by all the sensations and recollections once more renewed, by all the objects of yore seen again once more; by trifles, such as the mark of a knife on a door, a broken chair recalling some pretty event, the smell of the soil, the breath of the neighboring forest, the odors of the dwelling, the gutter, the dunghill.

Mother Duroy did not speak, but remained sad and grim, watching her daughter-in-law out of the corner of her eye, with hatred awakened in her heart—the hatred of an old toiler, an old rustic with fingers worn and limbs bent by hard work—for the city madame, who inspired her with the repulsion of an accursed creature, an impure being, created for idleness and sin. She kept getting up every moment to fetch the dishes or fill the glasses with cider, sharp and yellow from the decanter, or sweet, red, and frothing from the bottles, the corks of which popped like those of ginger beer.

Madeleine scarcely ate or spoke. She wore her wonted smile upon her lips, but it was a sad and resigned one. She was downcast. Why? She had wanted to come. She had not been unaware that she was going among country folk—poor country folk. What had she fancied them to be—she, who did not usually dream? Did she know herself? Do not women always hope for something that is not? Had she fancied them more poetical? No; but perhaps better informed, more noble, more affectionate, more ornamental. Yet she did not want them high-bred, like those in novels. Whence came it, then, that they shocked her by a thousand trifling, imperceptible details, by a thousand indefinable coarsenesses, by their very nature as rustics, by their words, their gestures, and their mirth? She recalled her own mother, of whom she never spoke to anyone—a governess, brought up at Saint Denis—seduced, and died from poverty and grief when she, Madeleine, was twelve years old. An unknown hand had had her brought up. Her father, no doubt. Who was he? She did not exactly know, although she had vague suspicions.

The lunch still dragged on. Customers were now coming in and shaking hands with the father, uttering exclamations of wonderment on seeing his son, and slyly winking as they scanned the young wife out of the corner of their eye, which was as much as to say: "Hang it all, she's not a duffer, George Duroy's wife." Others, less intimate, sat down at the wooden tables, calling for "A pot," "A jugful," "Two brandies," "A raspail," and began to play at dominoes, noisily rattling the little bits of black and white bone. Mother Duroy kept passing to and fro, serving the customers, with her melancholy air, taking money, and wiping the tables with the corner of her blue apron.

The smoke of clay pipes and sou cigars filled the room. Madeleine began to cough, and said: "Suppose we go out; I cannot stand it."

They had not quite finished, and old Duroy was annoyed at this. Then she got up and went and sat on a chair outside the door, while her father-in-law and her husband were finishing their coffee and their nip of brandy.

George soon rejoined her. "Shall we stroll down as far as the Seine?" said he.

She consented with pleasure, saying: "Oh, yes; let us go."

They descended the slope, hired a boat at Croisset, and passed the rest of the afternoon drowsily moored under the willows alongside an island, soothed to slumber by the soft spring weather, and rocked by the wavelets of the river. Then they went back at nightfall.

The evening's repast, eaten by the light of a tallow candle, was still more painful for Madeleine than that of the morning. Father Duroy, who was half drunk, no longer spoke. The mother maintained her dogged manner. The wretched light cast upon the gray walls the shadows of heads with enormous noses and exaggerated movements. A great hand was seen to raise a pitchfork to a mouth opening like a dragon's maw whenever any one of them, turning a little, presented a profile to the yellow, flickering flame.

As soon as dinner was over, Madeleine drew her husband out of the house, in order not to stay in this gloomy room, always reeking with an acrid smell of old pipes and spilt liquor. As soon as they were outside, he said: "You are tired of it already."

She began to protest, but he stopped her, saying: "No, I saw it very plainly. If you like, we will leave to-morrow."

"Very well," she murmured.

They strolled gently onward. It was a mild night, the deep, all-embracing shadow of which seemed filled with faint murmurings, rustlings, and breathings. They had entered a narrow path, overshadowed by tall trees, and running between two belts of underwood of impenetrable blackness.

"Where are we?" asked she.

"In the forest," he replied.

"Is it a large one?"

"Very large; one of the largest in France."

An odor of earth, trees, and moss—that fresh yet old scent of the woods, made up of the sap of bursting buds and the dead and moldering foliage of the thickets, seemed to linger in the path. Raising her head, Madeleine could see the stars through the tree-tops; and although no breeze stirred the boughs, she could yet feel around her the vague quivering of this ocean of leaves. A strange thrill shot through her soul and fleeted across her skin—a strange pain gripped her at the heart. Why, she did not understand. But it seemed to her that she was lost, engulfed, surrounded by perils, abandoned by everyone; alone, alone in the world beneath this living vault quivering there above her.

She murmured: "I am rather frightened. I should like to go back."

"Well, let us do so."

"And—we will leave for Paris to-morrow?"

"Yes, to-morrow."

"To-morrow morning?"

"To-morrow morning, if you like."

They returned home. The old folks had gone to bed. She slept badly, continually aroused by all the country sounds so new to her—the cry of the screech owl, the grunting of a pig in a sty adjoining the house, and the noise of a cock who kept on crowing from midnight. She was up and ready to start at daybreak.

When George announced to his parents that he was going back they were both astonished; then they understood the origin of his wish.

The father merely said: "Shall I see you again soon?"

"Yes, in the course of the summer."

"So much the better."

The old woman growled: "I hope you won't regret what you have done."

He left them two hundred francs as a present to assuage their discontent, and the carriage, which a boy had been sent in quest of, having made its appearance at about ten o'clock, the newly-married couple embraced the old country folk and started off once more.

As they were descending the hill Duroy began to laugh.

"There," he said, "I had warned you. I ought not to have introduced you to Monsieur and Madame du Roy de Cantel, Senior."

She began to laugh, too, and replied: "I am delighted now. They are good folk, whom I am beginning to like very well. I will send them some presents from Paris." Then she murmured: "Du Roy de Cantel, you will see that no one will be astonished at the terms of the notification of our marriage. We will say that we have been staying for a week with your parents on their estate." And bending towards him she kissed the tip of his moustache, saying: "Good morning, George."

He replied: "Good morning, Made," as he passed an arm around her waist.

In the valley below they could see the broad river like a ribbon of silver unrolled beneath the morning sun, the factory chimneys belching forth their clouds of smoke into the sky, and the pointed spires rising above the old town.

X

The Du Roys had been back in Paris a couple of days, and the journalist had taken up his old work pending the moment when he should definitely assume Forestier's duties, and give himself wholly up to politics. He was going home that evening to his predecessor's abode to dinner, with a light heart and a keen desire to embrace his wife, whose physical attractions and imperceptible domination exercised a powerful impulse over him. Passing by a florist's at the bottom of the Rue Notre Dame de Lorette, he was struck by the notion of buying a bouquet for Madeleine, and chose a large bunch of half-open roses, a very bundle of perfumed buds.

At each story of his new staircase he eyed himself complacently in the mirrors, the sight of which continually recalled to him his first visit to the house. He rang the bell, having forgotten his key, and the same man-servant, whom he had also kept on by his wife's advice, opened the door.

"Has your mistress come home?" asked George.

"Yes, sir."

But on passing through the dining-room he was greatly surprised to find the table laid for three, and the hangings of the drawing-room door being looped up, saw Madeleine arranging in a vase on the mantelpiece a bunch of roses exactly similar to his own. He was vexed and displeased; it was as though he had been robbed of his idea, his mark of attention, and all the pleasure he anticipated from it.

"You have invited some one to dinner, then?" he inquired, as he entered the room.

She answered without turning round, and while continuing to arrange the flowers: "Yes, and no. It is my old friend, the Count de Vaudrec, who has been accustomed to dine here every Monday, and who has come as usual."

George murmured: "Ah! very good."

He remained standing behind her, bouquet in hand, with a longing to hide it or throw it away. He said, however: "I have brought you some roses."

She turned round suddenly, smiling, and exclaimed: "Ah! how nice of you to have thought of that."

And she held out her arms and lips to him with an outburst of joy so real that he felt consoled. She took the flowers, smelt them, and with the liveliness of a delighted child, placed them in the vase that remained empty

- 150 -

opposite the other. Then she murmured, as she viewed the result: "How glad I am. My mantelpiece is furnished now." She added almost immediately, in a tone of conviction: "You know Vaudrec is awfully nice; you will be friends with him at once."

A ring announced the Count. He entered quietly, and quite at his ease, as though at home. After having gallantly kissed the young wife's fingers, he turned to the husband and cordially held out his hand, saying: "How goes it, my dear Du Roy?"

It was no longer his former stiff and starched bearing, but an affable one, showing that the situation was no longer the same. The journalist, surprised, strove to make himself agreeable in response to these advances. It might have been believed within five minutes that they had known and loved one another for ten years past.

Then Madeleine, whose face was radiant, said: "I will leave you together, I must give a look to my dinner." And she went out, followed by a glance from both men. When she returned she found them talking theatricals apropos of a new piece, and so thoroughly of the same opinion that a species of rapid friendship awoke in their eyes at the discovery of this absolute identity of ideas.

The dinner was delightful, so intimate and cordial, and the Count stayed on quite late, so comfortable did he feel in this nice little new household.

As soon as he had left Madeleine said to her husband: "Is he not perfect? He gains in every way by being known. He is a true friend—safe, devoted, faithful. Ah, without him—"

She did not finish the sentence, and George replied: "Yes, I find him very agreeable. I think that we shall get on very well together."

She resumed: "You do not know, but we have some work to do together before going to bed. I had not time to speak to you about it before dinner, because Vaudrec came in at once. I have had some important news, news from Morocco. It was Laroche-Mathieu, the deputy, the future minister, who brought it to me. We must work up an important article, a sensational one. I have the facts and figures. We will set to work at once. Bring the lamp."

He took it, and they passed into the study. The same books were ranged in the bookcase, which now bore on its summit the three vases bought at the Golfe Juan by Forestier on the eve of his death. Under the table the dead man's mat awaited the feet of Du Roy, who, on sitting down, took up an ivory penholder slightly gnawed at the end by the other's teeth. Madeleine leant against the mantelpiece, and having lit a cigarette related her news, and then explained her notions and the plan of the article she meditated. He listened attentively, scribbling notes as he did so, and when she had finished, raised objections, took up the question again, enlarged its bearing, and sketched in turn, not the plan of an article, but of a campaign against the existing Ministry. This attack would be its commencement. His wife had left off smoking, so strongly was her interest aroused, so vast was the vision that opened before her as she followed out George's train of thought.

She murmured, from time to time: "Yes, yes; that is very good. That is capital. That is very clever."

And when he had finished speaking in turn, she said: "Now let us write."

But he always found it hard to make a start, and with difficulty sought his expressions. Then she came gently, and, leaning over his shoulder, began to whisper sentences in his ear. From time to time she would hesitate, and ask: "Is that what you want to say?"

He answered: "Yes, exactly."

She had piercing shafts, the poisoned shafts of a woman, to wound the head of the Cabinet, and she blended jests about his face with others respecting his policy in a curious fashion, that made one laugh, and, at the same time, impressed one by their truth of observation.

Du Roy from time to time added a few lines which widened and strengthened the range of attack. He understood, too, the art of perfidious insinuation, which he had learned in sharpening up his "Echoes"; and when a fact put forward as certain by Madeleine appeared doubtful or compromising, he excelled in allowing it to be divined and in impressing it upon the mind more strongly than if he had affirmed it. When their article was finished, George read it aloud. They both thought it excellent, and smiled, delighted and surprised, as if they had just mutually revealed themselves to one another. They gazed into the depths of one another's eyes with yearnings of love and admiration, and they embraced one another with an ardor communicated from their minds to their bodies.

Du Roy took up the lamp again. "And now to bye-bye," said he, with a kindling glance.

She replied: "Go first, sir, since you light the way."

He went first, and she followed him into their bedroom, tickling his neck to make him go quicker, for he could not stand that.

The article appeared with the signature of George Duroy de Cantel, and caused a great sensation. There was an excitement about it in the Chamber.

Daddy Walter congratulated the author, and entrusted him with the political editorship of the *Vie Francaise*. The "Echoes" fell again to Boisrenard.

Then there began in the paper a violent and cleverly conducted campaign against the Ministry. The attack, now ironical, now serious, now jesting, and now virulent, but always skillful and based on facts, was delivered with a certitude and continuity which astonished everyone. Other papers continually cited the *Vie Francaise*, taking whole passages from it, and those in office asked themselves whether they could not gag this unknown and inveterate foe with the gift of a prefecture.

Du Roy became a political celebrity. He felt his influence increasing by the pressure of hands and the lifting of hats. His wife, too, filled him with stupefaction and admiration by the ingenuity of her mind, the value of her information, and the number of her acquaintances. Continually he would find in his drawing-room, on returning home, a senator, a deputy, a magistrate, a general, who treated Madeleine as an old friend, with serious familiarity. Where had she met all these people? In society, so she said. But how had she been able to gain their confidence and their affection? He could not understand it.

"She would make a terrible diplomatist," he thought.

She often came in late at meal times, out of breath, flushed, quivering, and before even taking off her veil would say: "I have something good to-day. Fancy, the Minister of Justice has just appointed two magistrates who formed a part of the mixed commission. We will give him a dose he will not forget in a hurry."

And they would give the minister a dose, and another the next day, and a third the day after. The deputy, Laroche-Mathieu, who dined at the Rue Fontaine every Tuesday, after the Count de Vaudrec, who began the week, would shake the hands of husband and wife with demonstrations of extreme joy. He never ceased repeating: "By Jove, what a campaign! If we don't succeed after all?"

He hoped, indeed, to succeed in getting hold of the portfolio of foreign affairs, which he had had in view for a long time.

He was one of those many-faced politicians, without strong convictions, without great abilities, without boldness, and without any depth of knowledge, a provincial barrister, a local dandy, preserving a cunning balance between all parties, a species of Republican Jesuit and Liberal mushroom of uncertain character, such as spring up by hundreds on the popular dunghill of universal suffrage. His village machiavelism caused him to be reckoned able among his colleagues, among all the adventurers and abortions who are made deputies. He was sufficiently well-dressed, correct, familiar, and amiable to succeed. He had his successes in society, in the mixed, perturbed, and somewhat rough society of the high functionaries of the day. It was said everywhere of him: "Laroche will be a minister," and he believed more firmly than anyone else that he would be. He was one of the chief shareholders in Daddy Walter's paper, and his colleague and partner in many financial schemes.

Du Roy backed him up with confidence and with vague hopes as to the future. He was, besides, only continuing the work begun by Forestier, to whom Laroche-Mathieu had promised the Cross of the Legion of Honor when the day of triumph should come. The decoration would adorn the breast of Madeleine's second husband, that was all. Nothing was changed in the main.

It was seen so well that nothing was changed that Du Roy's comrades organized a joke against him, at which he was beginning to grow angry. They no longer called him anything but Forestier. As soon as he entered the office some one would call out: "I say, Forestier."

He would pretend not to hear, and would look for the letters in his pigeon-holes. The voice would resume in louder tones, "Hi! Forestier." Some stifled laughs would be heard, and as Du Roy was entering the manager's room, the comrade who had called out would stop him, saying: "Oh, I beg your pardon, it is you I want to speak to. It is stupid, but I am always mixing you up with poor Charles. It is because your articles are so infernally like his. Everyone is taken in by them."

Du Roy would not answer, but he was inwardly furious, and a sullen wrath sprang up in him against the dead man. Daddy Walter himself had declared, when astonishment was expressed at the flagrant similarity in style and inspiration between the leaders of the new political editor and his predecessor: "Yes, it is Forestier, but a fuller, stronger, more manly Forestier."

Another time Du Roy, opening by chance the cupboard in which the cup and balls were kept, had found all those of his predecessor with crape round the handles, and his own, the one he had made use of when he practiced under the direction of Saint-Potin, ornamented with a pink ribbon. All had been arranged on the same shelf according to size, and a card like those in museums bore the inscription: "The Forestier-Du Roy (late Forestier and Co.) Collection." He quietly closed the cupboard, saying, in tones loud enough to be heard: "There are fools and envious people everywhere."

But he was wounded in his pride, wounded in his vanity, that touchy pride and vanity of the writer, which produce the nervous susceptibility ever on the alert, equally in the reporter and the genial poet. The word "Forestier" made his ears tingle. He dreaded to hear it, and felt himself redden when he did so. This name was to him a biting jest, more than a jest, almost an insult. It said to him: "It is your wife who does your work, as she did that of the other. You would be nothing without her."

He admitted that Forestier would have been no one without Madeleine; but as to himself, come now!

Then, at home, the haunting impression continued. It was the whole place now that recalled the dead man to him, the whole of the furniture, the whole of the knicknacks, everything he laid hands on. He had scarcely thought of this at the outset, but the joke devised by his comrades had caused a kind of mental wound, which a number of trifles, unnoticed up to the present, now served to envenom. He could not take up anything without at once fancying he saw the hand of Charles upon it. He only looked at it and made use of things the latter had made use of formerly; things that he had purchased, liked, and enjoyed. And George began even to grow irritated at the thought of the bygone relations between his friend and his wife. He was sometimes astonished at this revolt of his heart, which he did not understand, and said to himself, "How the deuce is it? I am not jealous of Madeleine's friends. I am never uneasy about what she is up to. She goes in and out as she chooses, and yet the recollection of that brute of a Charles puts me in a rage." He added, "At the bottom, he was only an idiot, and it is that, no doubt, that wounds me. I am vexed that Madeleine could have married such a fool." And he kept continually repeating, "How is it that she could have stomached such a donkey for a single moment?"

His rancor was daily increased by a thousand insignificant details, which stung him like pin pricks, by the incessant reminders of the other arising out of a word from Madeleine, from the man-servant, from the waiting-maid.

One evening Du Roy, who liked sweet dishes, said, "How is it we never have sweets at dinner?"

His wife replied, cheerfully, "That is quite true. I never think about them. It is all through Charles, who hated—"

He cut her short in a fit of impatience he was unable to control, exclaiming, "Hang it all! I am sick of Charles. It is always Charles here and Charles there, Charles liked this and Charles liked that. Since Charles is dead, for goodness sake leave him in peace."

Madeleine looked at her husband in amazement, without being able to understand his sudden anger. Then, as she was sharp, she guessed what was going on within him; this slow working of posthumous jealousy, swollen every moment by all that recalled the other. She thought it puerile, may be, but was flattered by it, and did not reply.

He was vexed with himself at this irritation, which he had not been able to conceal. As they were writing after dinner an article for the next day, his feet got entangled in the foot mat. He kicked it aside, and said with a laugh:

"Charles was always chilly about the feet, I suppose?"

She replied, also laughing: "Oh! he lived in mortal fear of catching cold; his chest was very weak."

Du Roy replied grimly: "He has given us a proof of that." Then kissing his wife's hand, he added gallantly: "Luckily for me."

But on going to bed, still haunted by the same idea, he asked: "Did Charles wear nightcaps for fear of the draughts?"

She entered into the joke, and replied: "No; only a silk handkerchief tied round his head."

George shrugged his shoulders, and observed, with contempt, "What a baby."

From that time forward Charles became for him an object of continual conversation. He dragged him in on all possible occasions, speaking of him as "Poor Charles," with an air of infinite pity. When he returned home from the office, where he had been accosted twice or thrice as Forestier, he avenged himself by bitter railleries against the dead man in his tomb. He recalled his defects, his absurdities, his littleness, enumerating them with enjoyment, developing and augmenting them as though he had wished to combat the influence of a dreaded rival over the heart of his wife. He would say, "I say, Made, do you remember the day when that duffer Forestier tried to prove to us that stout men were stronger than spare ones?"

Then he sought to learn a number of private and secret details respecting the departed, which his wife, ill at ease, refused to tell him. But he obstinately persisted, saying, "Come, now, tell me all about it. He must have been very comical at such a time?"

She murmured, "Oh! do leave him alone."

But he went on, "No, but tell me now, he must have been a duffer to sleep with?" And he always wound up with, "What a donkey he was."

One evening, towards the end of June, as he was smoking a cigarette at the window, the fineness of the evening inspired him with a wish for a drive, and he said, "Made, shall we go as far as the Bois de Boulogne?"

"Certainly."

They took an open carriage and drove up the Champs Elysées, and then along the main avenue of the Bois de Boulogne. It was a breezeless night, one of those stifling nights when the overheated air of Paris fills the chest like the breath of a furnace. A host of carriages bore along beneath the trees a whole population of lovers. They came one behind the other in an unbroken line. George and Madeleine amused themselves with watching all these couples, the woman in summer toilet and the man darkly outlined beside her. It was a huge flood of lovers towards the Bois, beneath the starry and heated sky. No sound was heard save the dull rumble of wheels. They kept passing by, two by two in each vehicle, leaning back on the seat, silent, clasped one against the other, lost in dreams of desire, quivering with the anticipation of coming caresses. The warm shadow seemed full of kisses. A sense of spreading lust rendered the air heavier and more suffocating. All the couples, intoxicated with the same idea, the same ardor, shed a fever about them.

George and Madeleine felt the contagion. They clasped hands without a word, oppressed by the heaviness of the atmosphere and the emotion that assailed them. As they reached the turning which follows the line of the fortification, they kissed one another, and she stammered somewhat confusedly, "We are as great babies as on the way to Rouen."

The great flood of vehicles divided at the entrance of the wood. On the road to the lake, which the young couple were following, they were now thinner, but the dark shadow of the trees, the air freshened by the leaves and by the dampness arising from the streamlets that could be heard flowing beneath them, and the coolness of the vast nocturnal vault bedecked with stars, gave to the kisses of the perambulating pairs a more penetrating charm.

George murmured, "Dear little Made," as he pressed her to him.

"Do you remember the forest close to your home, how gloomy it was?" said she. "It seemed to me that it was full of horrible creatures, and that there was no end to it, while here it is delightful. One feels caresses in the breeze, and I know that Sevres lies on the other side of the wood."

He replied, "Oh! in the forest at home there was nothing but deer, foxes, and wild boars, and here and there the hut of a forester."

This word, akin to the dead man's name, issuing from his mouth, surprised him just as if some one had shouted it out to him from the depths of a thicket, and he became suddenly silent, assailed anew by the strange and persistent uneasiness, and gnawing, invincible, jealous irritation that had been spoiling his existence for some time past. After a minute or so, he asked: "Did you ever come here like this of an evening with Charles?"

"Yes, often," she answered.

And all of a sudden he was seized with a wish to return home, a nervous desire that gripped him at the heart. But the image of Forestier had returned to his mind and possessed and laid hold of him. He could no longer speak or think of anything else and said in a spiteful tone, "I say, Made?"

"Yes, dear."

"Did you ever cuckold poor Charles?"

She murmured disdainfully, "How stupid you are with your stock joke."

But he would not abandon the idea.

"Come, Made, dear, be frank and acknowledge it. You cuckolded him, eh? Come, admit that you cuckolded him?"

She was silent, shocked as all women are by this expression.

He went on obstinately, "Hang it all, if ever anyone had the head for a cuckold it was he. Oh! yes. It would please me to know that he was one. What a fine head for horns." He felt that she was smiling at some recollection, perhaps, and persisted, saying, "Come out with it. What does it matter? It would be very comical to admit that you had deceived him, to me."

He was indeed quivering with hope and desire that Charles, the hateful Charles, the detested dead, had borne this shameful ridicule. And yet—yet—another emotion, less definite. "My dear little Made, tell me, I beg of you. He deserved it. You would have been wrong not to have given him a pair of horns. Come, Made, confess."

She now, no doubt, found this persistence amusing, for she was laughing a series of short, jerky laughs.

He had put his lips close to his wife's ear and whispered: "Come, come, confess."

She jerked herself away, and said, abruptly: "You are crazy. As if one answered such questions."

She said this in so singular a tone that a cold shiver ran through her husband's veins, and he remained dumbfounded, scared, almost breathless, as though from some mental shock.

The carriage was now passing along the lake, on which the sky seemed to have scattered its stars. Two swans, vaguely outlined, were swimming slowly, scarcely visible in the shadow. George called out to the driver: "Turn back!" and the carriage returned, meeting the others going at a walk, with their lanterns gleaming like eyes in the night.

What a strange manner in which she had said it. Was it a confession? Du Roy kept asking himself. And the almost certainty that she had deceived her first husband now drove him wild with rage. He longed to beat her, to strangle her, to tear her hair out. Oh, if she had only replied: "But darling, if I had deceived him, it would have been with yourself," how he would have kissed, clasped, worshiped her.

He sat still, his arms crossed, his eyes turned skyward, his mind too agitated to think as yet. He only felt within him the rancor fermenting and the anger swelling which lurk at the heart of all mankind in presence of the caprices of feminine desire. He felt for the first time that vague anguish of the husband who suspects. He was jealous at last, jealous on behalf of the dead, jealous on Forestier's account, jealous in a strange and poignant fashion, into which there suddenly entered a hatred of Madeleine. Since she had deceived the other, how could he have confidence in her himself? Then by degrees his mind became calmer, and bearing up against his pain, he thought: "All women are prostitutes. We must make use of them, and not give them anything of ourselves." The bitterness in his heart rose to his lips in words of contempt and disgust. He repeated to himself: "The victory in this world is to the strong. One must be strong. One must be above all prejudices."

The carriage was going faster. It repassed the fortifications. Du Roy saw before him a reddish light in the sky like the glow of an immense forge, and heard a vast, confused, continuous rumor, made up of countless different sounds, the breath of Paris panting this summer night like an exhausted giant.

George reflected: "I should be very stupid to fret about it. Everyone for himself. Fortune favors the bold. Egotism is everything. Egotism as regards ambition and fortune is better than egotism as regards woman and love."

The Arc de Triomphe appeared at the entrance to the city on its two tall supports like a species of shapeless giant ready to start off and march down the broad avenue open before him. George and Madeleine found themselves once more in the stream of carriages bearing homeward and bedwards the same silent and interlaced couples. It seemed that the whole of humanity was passing by intoxicated with joy, pleasure, and happiness. The young wife, who had divined something of what was passing through her husband's mind, said, in her soft voice: "What are you thinking of, dear? You have not said a word for the last half hour."

He answered, sneeringly: "I was thinking of all these fools cuddling one another, and saying to myself that there is something else to do in life."

She murmured: "Yes, but it is nice sometimes."

"It is nice—when one has nothing better to do."

George's thoughts were still hard at it, stripping life of its poesy in a kind of spiteful anger. "I should be very foolish to trouble myself, to deprive myself of anything whatever, to worry as I have done for some time past." Forestier's image crossed his mind without causing any irritation. It seemed to him that they had just been reconciled, that they had become friends again. He wanted to cry out: "Good evening, old fellow."

Madeleine, to whom this silence was irksome, said: "Suppose we have an ice at Tortoni's before we go in."

He glanced at her sideways. Her fine profile was lit up by the bright light from the row of gas jets of a café. He thought, "She is pretty. Well, so much the better. Jack is as good as his master, my dear. But if ever they catch me worrying again about you, it will be hot at the North Pole." Then he replied aloud: "Certainly, my dear," and in order that she should not guess anything, he kissed her.

It seemed to the young wife that her husband's lips were frozen. He smiled, however, with his wonted smile, as he gave her his hand to alight in front of the café.

XI

On reaching the office next day, Du Roy sought out Boisrenard.

"My dear fellow," said he, "I have a service to ask of you. It has been thought funny for some time past to call me Forestier. I begin to find it very stupid. Will you have the kindness to quietly let our friends know that I will smack the face of the first that starts the joke again? It will be for them to reflect whether it is worth risking a sword thrust for. I address myself to you because you are a calm-minded fellow, who can hinder matters from coming to painful extremities, and also because you were my second."

Boisrenard undertook the commission. Du Roy went out on business, and returned an hour later. No one called him Forestier.

When he reached home he heard ladies' voices in the drawing-room, and asked, "Who is there?"

"Madame Walter and Madame de Marelle," replied the servant.

His heart beat fast for a moment, and then he said to himself, "Well, let's see," and opened the door.

Clotilde was beside the fireplace, full in a ray of light from the window. It seemed to George that she grew slightly paler on perceiving him. Having first bowed to Madame Walter and her two daughters, seated like two sentinels on each side of their mother, he turned towards his late mistress. She held out her hand, and he took it and pressed it meaningly, as though to say, "I still love you." She responded to this pressure.

He inquired: "How have you been during the century that has elapsed since our last meeting?"

She replied with perfect ease: "Quite well; and you, Pretty-boy?" and turning to Madeleine, added: "You will allow me to call him Pretty-boy still?"

"Certainly, dear; I will allow whatever you please."

A shade of irony seemed hidden in these words.

Madame Walter spoke of an entertainment that was going to be given by Jacques Rival at his residence, a grand assault-at-arms, at which ladies of fashion were to be present, saying: "It will be very interesting. But I am so vexed we have no one to take us there, my husband being obliged to be away at that time."

Du Roy at once offered his services. She accepted, saying: "My daughters and I will be very much obliged to you."

He looked at the younger daughter, and thought: "She is not at all bad looking, this little Susan; not at all." She resembled a fair, fragile doll, too short but slender, with a small waist and fairly developed hips and bust, a face like a miniature, grayish-blue, enamel-like eyes, which seemed shaded by a careful yet fanciful painter, a polished, colorless skin, too white and too smooth, and fluffy, curly hair, in a charming aureola, like, indeed the hair of the pretty and expensive dolls we see in the arms of children much smaller than their plaything.

The elder sister, Rose, was ugly, dull-looking, and insignificant; one of those girls whom you do not notice, do not speak to, and do not talk about.

The mother rose, and, turning to George, said:

"Then I may reckon upon you for next Thursday, two o'clock?"

"You may reckon upon me, madame," he replied.

As soon as she had taken her departure, Madame de Marelle rose in turn, saying: "Good afternoon, Pretty-boy."

It was she who then clasped his hand firmly and for some time, and he felt moved by this silent avowal, struck again with a sudden caprice for this good-natured little, respectable Bohemian of a woman, who really loved him, perhaps.

As soon as he was alone with his wife, Madeleine broke out into a laugh, a frank, gay laugh, and, looking him fair in the face, said, "You know that Madame Walter is smitten with you."

"Nonsense," he answered, incredulously.

"It is so, I tell you; she spoke to me about you with wild enthusiasm. It is strange on her part. She would like to find two husbands such as you for her daughters. Fortunately, as regards her such things are of no moment."

He did not understand what she meant, and inquired, "How of no moment?"

She replied with the conviction of a woman certain of the soundness of her judgment, "Oh! Madame Walter is one of those who have never even had a whisper about them, never, you know, never. She is unassailable in every respect. Her husband you know as well as I do. But with her it is quite another thing. She has suffered enough through marrying a Jew, but she has remained faithful to him. She is an honest woman."

Du Roy was surprised. "I thought her a Jewess, too," said he.

"She, not at all. She is a lady patroness of all the good works of the Church of Madeleine. Her marriage, even, was celebrated religiously. I do not know whether there was a dummy baptism as regards the governor, or whether the Church winked at it."

George murmured: "Ah! so she fancied me."

"Positively and thoroughly. If you were not bespoken, I should advise you to ask for the hand of—Susan, eh? rather than that of Rose."

He replied, twisting his moustache: "Hum; their mother is not yet out of date."

Madeleine, somewhat out of patience, answered:

"Their mother! I wish you may get her, dear. But I am not alarmed on that score. It is not at her age that a woman is guilty of a first fault. One must set about it earlier."

George was reflecting: "If it were true, though, that I could have married Susan." Then he shrugged his shoulders. "Bah! it is absurd. As if her father would have ever have accepted me as a suitor."

He promised himself, though, to keep a more careful watch in the future over Madame Walter's bearing towards him, without asking whether he might ever derive any advantage from this. All the evening he was haunted by the recollection of his love passages with Clotilde, recollections at once tender and sensual. He recalled her drolleries, her pretty ways, and their adventures together. He repeated to himself, "She is really very charming. Yes, I will go and see her to-morrow."

As soon as he had lunched the next morning he indeed set out for the Rue de Verneuil. The same servant opened the door, and with the familiarity of servants of the middle-class, asked: "Are you quite well, sir?"

"Yes, thanks, my girl," he replied, and entered the drawing-room, in which an unskilled hand could be heard practicing scales on the piano. It was Laurine. He thought that she would throw her arms round his neck. But she rose gravely, bowed ceremoniously like a grown-up person, and withdrew with dignity. She had so much the bearing of an insulted woman that he remained in surprise. Her mother came in, and he took and kissed her hands.

"How I have thought of you," said he.

"And I," she replied.

They sat down and smiled at one another, looking into each other's eyes with a longing to kiss.

"My dear little Clo, I do love you."

"I love you, too."

"Then—then—you have not been so very angry with me?"

"Yes, and no. It hurt me a great deal, but I understood your reasons, and said to myself, 'He will come back to me some fine day or other.'"

"I dared not come back. I asked myself how I should be received. I did not dare, but I dearly wanted to. By the way, tell me what is the matter with Laurine. She scarcely said good-morning to me, and went out looking furious."

"I do not know. But we cannot speak of you to her since your marriage. I really believe she is jealous."

"Nonsense."

"It is so, dear. She no longer calls you Pretty-boy, but Monsieur Forestier."

Du Roy reddened, and then drawing close to her said:

"Kiss me."

She did so.

"Where can we meet again?" said he.

"Rue de Constantinople."

"Ah! the rooms are not let, then?"

"No, I kept them on."

"You kept them on?"

"Yes, I thought you would come back again."

A gush of joyful pride swelled his bosom. She loved him then, this woman, with a real, deep, constant love.

He murmured, "I love you," and then inquired, "Is your husband quite well?"

"Yes, very well. He has been spending a month at home, and was off again the day before yesterday."

Du Roy could not help laughing. "How lucky," said he.

She replied simply: "Yes, it is very lucky. But, all the same, he is not troublesome when he is here. You know that."

"That is true. Besides, he is a very nice fellow."

"And you," she asked, "how do you like your new life?"

"Not much one way or the other. My wife is a companion, a partner."

"Nothing more?"

"Nothing more. As to the heart—"

"I understand. She is pretty, though."

"Yes, but I do not put myself out about her."

He drew closer to Clotilde, and whispered. "When shall we see one another again?"

"To-morrow, if you like."

"Yes, to-morrow at two o'clock."

"Two o'clock."

He rose to take leave, and then stammered, with some embarrassment: "You know I shall take on the rooms in the Rue de Constantinople myself. I mean it. A nice thing for the rent to be paid by you."

It was she who kissed his hands adoringly, murmuring: "Do as you like. It is enough for me to have kept them for us to meet again there."

Du Roy went away, his soul filled with satisfaction. As he passed by a photographer's, the portrait of a tall woman with large eyes reminded him of Madame Walter. "All the same," he said to himself, "she must be still worth looking at. How is it that I never noticed it? I want to see how she will receive me on Thursday?"

He rubbed his hands as he walked along with secret pleasure, the pleasure of success in every shape, the egotistical joy of the clever man who is successful, the subtle pleasure made up of flattered vanity and satisfied sensuality conferred by woman's affection.

On the Thursday he said to Madeleine: "Are you not coming to the assault-at-arms at Rival's?"

"No. It would not interest me. I shall go to the Chamber of Deputies."

He went to call for Madame Walter in an open landau, for the weather was delightful. He experienced a surprise on seeing her, so handsome and young-looking did he find her. She wore a light-colored dress, the somewhat open bodice of which allowed the fullness of her bosom to be divined beneath the blonde lace. She had never seemed to him so well-looking. He thought her really desirable. She wore her calm and ladylike manner, a certain matronly bearing that caused her to pass almost unnoticed before the eyes of gallants. She scarcely spoke besides, save on well-known, suitable, and respectable topics, her ideas being proper, methodical, well ordered, and void of all extravagance.

Her daughter, Susan, in pink, looked like a newly-varnished Watteau, while her elder sister seemed the governess entrusted with the care of this pretty doll of a girl.

Before Rival's door a line of carriages were drawn up. Du Roy offered Madame Walter his arm, and they went in.

The assault-at-arms was given under the patronage of the wives of all the senators and deputies connected with the *Vie Francaise*, for the benefit of the orphans of the Sixth Arrondissement of Paris. Madame Walter had promised to come with her daughters, while refusing the position of lady patroness, for she only aided with her name works undertaken by the clergy. Not that she was very devout, but her marriage with a Jew obliged her, in her own opinion, to observe a certain religious attitude, and the gathering organized by the journalist had a species of Republican import that might be construed as anti-clerical.

In papers of every shade of opinion, during the past three weeks, paragraphs had appeared such as: "Our eminent colleague, Jacques Rival, has conceived the idea, as ingenious as it is generous, of organizing for the benefit of the orphans of the Sixth Arrondissement of Paris a grand assault-at-arms in the pretty fencing-room attached to his apartments. The invitations will be sent out by Mesdames Laloigue, Remontel, and Rissolin, wives of the senators bearing these names, and by Mesdames Laroche-Mathieu, Percerol, and Firmin, wives of the well-known deputies. A collection will take place during the interval, and the amount will at once be placed in the hands of the mayor of the Sixth Arrondissement, or of his representative."

It was a gigantic advertisement that the clever journalist had devised to his own advantage.

Jacques Rival received all-comers in the hall of his dwelling, where a refreshment buffet had been fitted up, the cost of which was to be deducted from the receipts. He indicated with an amiable gesture the little staircase leading to the cellar, saying: "Downstairs, ladies, downstairs; the assault will take place in the basement."

He darted forward to meet the wife of the manager, and then shaking Du Roy by the hand, said: "How are you, Pretty-boy?"

His friend was surprised, and exclaimed: "Who told you that—"

Rival interrupted him with: "Madame Walter, here, who thinks the nickname a very nice one."

Madame Walter blushed, saying: "Yes, I will admit that, if I knew you better, I would do like little Laurine and call you Pretty-boy, too. The name suits you very well."

Du Roy laughed, as he replied: "But I beg of you, madame, to do so."

She had lowered her eyes, and remarked: "No. We are not sufficiently intimate."

He murmured: "Will you allow me the hope that we shall be more so?"

"Well, we will see then," said she.

He drew on one side to let her precede him at the beginning of the narrow stairs lit by a gas jet. The abrupt transition from daylight to this yellow gleam had something depressing about it. A cellar-like odor rose up this winding staircase, a smell of damp heat and of moldy walls wiped down for the occasion, and also whiffs of incense recalling sacred offices and feminine emanations of vervain, orris root, and violets. A loud murmur of voices and the quivering thrill of an agitated crowd could also be heard down this hole.

The entire cellar was lit up by wreaths of gas jets and Chinese lanterns hidden in the foliage, masking the walls of stone. Nothing could be seen but green boughs. The ceiling was ornamented with ferns, the ground hidden by flowers and leaves. This was thought charming, and a delightful triumph of imagination. In the small cellar, at the end, was a platform for the fencers, between two rows of chairs for the judges. In the remaining space the front seats, ranged by tens to the right and to the left, would accommodate about two hundred people. Four hundred had been invited.

In front of the platform young fellows in fencing costume, with long limbs, erect figures, and moustaches curled up at the ends, were already showing themselves off to the spectators. People were pointing them out as notabilities of the art, professionals, and amateurs. Around them were chatting old and young gentlemen in frock coats, who bore a family resemblance to the fencers in fighting array. They were also seeking to be seen, recognized, and spoken of, being masters of the sword out of uniform, experts on foil play. Almost all the seats were occupied by ladies, who kept up a loud rustling of garments and a continuous murmur of voices. They were fanning themselves as though at a theater, for it was already as hot as an oven in this leafy grotto. A joker kept crying from time to time: "Orgeat, lemonade, beer."

Madame Walter and her daughters reached the seats reserved for them in the front row. Du Roy, having installed them there, was about to quit them, saying: "I am obliged to leave you; we men must not collar the seats."

But Madame Walter remarked, in a hesitating tone: "I should very much like to have you with us all the same. You can tell me the names of the fencers. Come, if you stand close to the end of the seat you will not be in anyone's way." She looked at him with her large mild eyes, and persisted, saying: "Come, stay with us, Monsieur—Pretty-boy. We have need of you."

He replied: "I will obey with pleasure, madame."

On all sides could be heard the remark: "It is very funny, this cellar; very pretty, too."

George knew it well, this vault. He recalled the morning he had passed there on the eve of his duel, alone in front of the little white carton target that had glared at him from the depths of the inner cellar like a huge and terrible eye.

The voice of Jacques Rival sounded from the staircase: "Just about to begin, ladies." And six gentlemen, in very tight-fitting clothes, to set off their chests, mounted the platform, and took their seats on the chairs reserved for the judges. Their names flew about. General de Reynaldi, the president, a short man, with heavy moustaches; the painter, Joséphin Roudet, a tall, ball-headed man, with a long beard; Matthéo de Ujar, Simon Ramoncel, Pierre de Carvin, three fashionable-looking young fellows; and Gaspard Merleron, a master. Two placards were hung up on the two sides of the vault. That on the right was inscribed "M. Crévecœur," and that on the left "M. Plumeau."

They were two professors, two good second-class masters. They made their appearance, both sparely built, with military air and somewhat stiff movements. Having gone through the salute with automatic action, they began to attack one another, resembling in their white costumes of leather and duck, two soldier pierrots fighting for fun. From time to time the word "Touched" was heard, and the six judges nodded with the air of connoisseurs. The public saw nothing but two living marionettes moving about and extending their arms; they understood nothing, but they were satisfied. These two men seemed to them, however, not over graceful, and vaguely ridiculous. They reminded them of the wooden wrestlers sold on the boulevards at the New Year's Fair.

The first couple of fencers were succeeded by Monsieur Planton and Monsieur Carapin, a civilian master and a military one. Monsieur Planton was very little, and Monsieur Carapin immensely stout. One would have thought that the first thrust would have reduced his volume like that of a balloon. People laughed. Monsieur Planton skipped about like a monkey: Monsieur Carapin, only moved his arm, the rest of his frame being paralyzed by fat. He lunged every five minutes with such heaviness and such effort that it seemed to need the most energetic resolution on his part to accomplish it, and then had great difficulty in recovering himself. The connoisseurs pronounced his play very steady and close, and the confiding public appreciated it as such.

Then came Monsieur Porion and Monsieur Lapalme, a master and an amateur, who gave way to exaggerated gymnastics; charging furiously at one another, obliging the judges to scuttle off with their chairs, crossing and re-crossing from one end of the platform to the other, one advancing and the other retreating, with vigorous and comic leaps and bounds. They indulged in little jumps backwards that made the ladies laugh, and long springs forward that caused them some emotion. This galloping assault was aptly criticized by some young rascal, who sang out: "Don't burst yourselves over it; it is a time job!" The spectators, shocked at this want of taste, cried "Ssh!" The judgment of the experts was passed around. The fencers had shown much vigor, and played somewhat loosely.

The first half of the entertainment was concluded by a very fine bout between Jacques Rival and the celebrated Belgian professor, Lebegue. Rival greatly pleased the ladies. He was really a handsome fellow, well made, supple, agile, and more graceful than any of those who had preceded him. He brought, even into his way of standing on guard and lunging, a certain fashionable elegance which pleased people, and contrasted with the energetic, but more commonplace style of his adversary. "One can perceive the well-bred man at once," was the remark. He scored the last hit, and was applauded.

But for some minutes past a singular noise on the floor above had disturbed the spectators. It was a loud trampling, accompanied by noisy laughter. The two hundred guests who had not been able to get down into the cellar were no doubt amusing themselves in their own way. On the narrow, winding staircase fifty men were packed. The heat down below was getting terrible. Cries of "More air," "Something to drink," were heard. The same joker kept on yelping in a shrill tone that rose above the murmur of conversation, "Orgeat, lemonade, beer." Rival made his appearance, very flushed, and still in his fencing costume. "I will have some refreshments brought," said he, and made his way to the staircase. But all communication with the ground floor was cut off. It would have been as easy to have pierced the ceiling as to have traversed the human wall piled up on the stairs.

Rival called out: "Send down some ices for the ladies." Fifty voices called out: "Some ices!" A tray at length made its appearance. But it only bore empty glasses, the refreshments having been snatched on the way.

A loud voice shouted: "We are suffocating down here. Get it over and let us be off." Another cried out: "The collection." And the whole of the public, gasping, but good-humored all the same, repeated: "The collection, the collection."

Six ladies began to pass along between the seats, and the sound of money falling into the collecting-bags could be heard.

Du Roy pointed out the celebrities to Madame Walter. There were men of fashion and journalists, those attached to the great newspapers, the old-established newspapers, which looked down upon the *Vie Francaise* with a certain reserve, the fruit of their experience. They had witnessed the death of so many of these politico-financial sheets, offspring of a suspicious partnership, and crushed by the fall of a ministry. There were also painters and sculptors, who are generally men with a taste for sport; a poet who was also a member of the Academy, and who was pointed out generally, and a number of distinguished foreigners.

Someone called out: "Good-day, my dear fellow." It was the Count de Vaudrec. Making his excuses to the ladies, Du Roy hastened to shake hands with him. On returning, he remarked: "What a charming fellow Vaudrec is! How thoroughly blood tells in him."

Madame Walter did not reply. She was somewhat fatigued, and her bosom rose with an effort every time she drew breath, which caught the eye of Du Roy. From time to time he caught her glance, a troubled, hesitating glance, which lighted upon him, and was at once averted, and he said to himself: "Eh! what! Have I caught her, too?"

The ladies who had been collecting passed to their seats, their bags full of gold and silver, and a fresh placard was hung in front of the platform, announcing a "surprising novelty." The judges resumed their seats, and the public waited expectantly.

Two women appeared, foil in hand and in fencing costume; dark tights, a very short petticoat half-way to the knee, and a plastron so padded above the bosom that it obliged them to keep their heads well up. They were both young and pretty. They smiled as they saluted the spectators, and were loudly applauded. They fell on guard, amidst murmured gallantries and whispered jokes. An amiable smile graced the lips of the judges, who approved the hits with a low "bravo." The public warmly appreciated this bout, and testified this much to the two combatants, who kindled desire among the men and awakened among the women the native taste of the Parisian for graceful indecency, naughty elegance, music hall singers, and couplets from operettas. Every time that one of the fencers lunged a thrill of pleasure ran through the public. The one who turned her back to the seats, a plump back, caused eyes and mouths to open, and it was not the play of her wrist that was most closely scanned. They were frantically applauded.

A bout with swords followed, but no one looked at it, for the attention of all was occupied by what was going on overhead. For some minutes they had heard the noise of furniture being dragged across the floor, as though moving was in progress. Then all at once the notes of a piano were heard, and the rhythmic beat of feet moving in cadence was distinctly audible. The people above had treated themselves to a dance to make up for not being able to see anything. A loud laugh broke out at first among the public in the fencing saloon, and then a wish for a dance being aroused among the ladies, they ceased to pay attention to what was taking place on the platform, and began to chatter out loud. This notion of a ball got up by the late-comers struck them as comical. They must be amusing themselves nicely, and it must be much better up there.

But two new combatants had saluted each other and fell on guard in such masterly style that all eyes followed their movements. They lunged and recovered themselves with such easy grace, such measured strength, such certainty, such sobriety in action, such correctness in attitude, such measure in their play, that even the ignorant were surprised and charmed. Their calm promptness, their skilled suppleness, their rapid motions, so nicely timed that they appeared slow, attracted and captivated the eye by their power of perfection. The public felt that they were looking at something good and rare; that two great artists in their own profession were showing them their best, all of skill, cunning, thought-out science and physical ability that it was possible for two masters to put forth. No one spoke now, so closely were they watched. Then, when they shook hands after the last hit, shouts of bravoes broke out. People stamped and yelled. Everyone knew their names—they were Sergent and Ravignac.

The excitable grew quarrelsome. Men looked at their neighbors with longings for a row. They would have challenged one another on account of a smile. Those who had never held a foil in their hand sketched attacks and parries with their canes.

But by degrees the crowd worked up the little staircase. At last they would be able to get something to drink. There was an outburst of indignation when they found that those who had got up the ball had stripped the refreshment buffet, and had then gone away declaring that it was very impolite to bring together two hundred people and not show them anything. There was not a cake, not a drop of champagne, syrup, or beer left; not a sweetmeat, not a fruit—nothing. They had sacked, pillaged, swept away everything. These details were related by the servants, who pulled long faces to hide their impulse to laugh right out. "The ladies were worse than the gentlemen," they asserted, "and ate and drank enough to make themselves ill." It was like the story of the survivors after the sack of a captured town.

There was nothing left but to depart. Gentlemen openly regretted the twenty francs given at the collection; they were indignant that those upstairs should have feasted without paying anything. The lady patronesses had collected upwards of three thousand francs. All expenses paid, there remained two hundred and twenty for the orphans of the Sixth Arrondissement.

Du Roy, escorting the Walter family, waited for his landau. As he drove back with them, seated in face of Madame Walter, he again caught her caressing and fugitive glance, which seemed uneasy. He thought: "Hang it all! I fancy she is nibbling," and smiled to recognize that he was really very lucky as regarded women, for Madame de Marelle, since the recommencement of their amour, seemed frantically in love with him.

He returned home joyously. Madeleine was waiting for him in the drawing-room.

"I have some news," said she. "The Morocco business is getting into a complication. France may very likely send out an expeditionary force within a few months. At all events, the opportunity will be taken of it to upset the Ministry, and Laroche-Mathieu will profit by this to get hold of the portfolio of foreign affairs."

Du Roy, to tease his wife, pretended not to believe anything of the kind. They would never be mad enough to recommence the Tunisian bungle over again. But she shrugged her shoulders impatiently, saying: "But I tell you yes, I tell you yes. You don't understand that it is a matter of money. Now-a-days, in political complications we must not ask: 'Who is the woman?' but 'What is the business?'"

He murmured "Bah!" in a contemptuous tone, in order to excite her, and she, growing irritated, exclaimed: "You are just as stupid as Forestier."

She wished to wound him, and expected an outburst of anger. But he smiled, and replied: "As that cuckold of a Forestier?"

She was shocked, and murmured: "Oh, George!"

He wore an insolent and chaffing air as he said: "Well, what? Did you not admit to me the other evening that Forestier was a cuckold?" And he added: "Poor devil!" in a tone of pity.

Madeleine turned her back on him, disdaining to answer; and then, after a moment's silence, resumed: "We shall have visitors on Tuesday. Madame Laroche-Mathieu is coming to dinner with the Viscountess de Percemur. Will you invite Rival and Norbert de Varenne? I will call to-morrow and ask Madame Walter and Madame de Marelle. Perhaps we shall have Madame Rissolin, too."

For some time past she had been strengthening her connections, making use of her husband's political influence to attract to her house, willy-nilly, the wives of the senators and deputies who had need of the support of the *Vie Francaise*.

George replied: "Very well. I will see about Rival and Norbert."

He was satisfied, and rubbed his hands, for he had found a good trick to annoy his wife and gratify the obscure rancor, the undefined and gnawing jealousy born in him since their drive in the Bois. He would never speak of Forestier again without calling him cuckold. He felt very well that this would end by enraging Madeleine. And half a score of times, in the course of the evening, he found means to mention with ironical good humor the name of "that cuckold of a Forestier." He was no longer angry with the dead! he was avenging him.

His wife pretended not to notice it, and remained smilingly indifferent.

The next day, as she was to go and invite Madame Walter, he resolved to forestall her, in order to catch the latter alone, and see if she really cared for him. It amused and flattered him. And then—why not—if it were possible?

He arrived at the Boulevard Malesherbes about two, and was shown into the drawing-room, where he waited till Madame Walter made her appearance, her hand outstretched with pleased eagerness, saying: "What good wind brings you hither?"

"No good wind, but the wish to see you. Some power has brought me here, I do not know why, for I have nothing to say to you. I came, here I am; will you forgive me this early visit and the frankness of this explanation?"

He uttered this in a gallant and jesting tone, with a smile on his lips. She was astonished, and colored somewhat, stammering: "But really—I do not understand—you surprise me."

He observed: "It is a declaration made to a lively tune, in order not to alarm you."

They had sat down in front of one another. She took the matter pleasantly, saying: "A serious declaration?"

"Yes. For a long time I have been wanting to utter it—for a very long time. But I dared not. They say you are so strict, so rigid."

She had recovered her assurance, and observed: "Why to-day, then?"

"I do not know." Then lowering his voice he added: "Or rather, because I have been thinking of nothing but you since yesterday."

She stammered, growing suddenly pale: "Come, enough of nonsense; let us speak of something else."

But he had fallen at her feet so suddenly that she was frightened. She tried to rise, but he kept her seated by the strength of his arms passed round her waist, and repeated in a voice of passion: "Yes, it is true that I have loved you madly for a long time past. Do not answer me. What would you have? I am mad. I love you. Oh! if you knew how I love you!"

She was suffocating, gasping, and strove to speak, without being able to utter a word. She pushed him away with her two hands, having seized him by the hair to hinder the approach of the mouth that she felt coming towards her own. She kept turning her head from right to left and from left to right with a rapid motion, closing her eyes, in order no longer to see him. He touched her through her dress, handled her, pressed her, and she almost fainted under his strong and rude caress. He rose suddenly and sought to clasp her to him, but, free for a moment, she had managed to escape by throwing herself back, and she now fled from behind one chair to another. He felt that pursuit was ridiculous, and he fell into a chair, his face hidden by his hands, feigning convulsive sobs. Then he got up, exclaimed "Farewell, farewell," and rushed away.

He quietly took his stick in the hall and gained the street, saying to himself: "By Jove, I believe it is all right there." And he went into a telegraph office to send a wire to Clotilde, making an appointment for the next day.

On returning home at his usual time, he said to his wife: "Well, have you secured all the people for your dinner?"

She answered: "Yes, there is only Madame Walter, who is not quite sure whether she will be free to come. She hesitated and talked about I don't know what—an engagement, her conscience. In short, she seemed very strange. No matter, I hope she will come all the same."

He shrugged his shoulders, saying: "Oh, yes, she'll come."

He was not certain, however, and remained anxious until the day of the dinner. That very morning Madeleine received a note from her: "I have managed to get free from my engagements with great difficulty, and shall be with you this evening. But my husband cannot accompany me."

Du Roy thought: "I did very well indeed not to go back. She has calmed down. Attention."

He, however, awaited her appearance with some slight uneasiness. She came, very calm, rather cool, and slightly haughty. He became humble, discreet, and submissive. Madame Laroche-Mathieu and Madame Rissolin accompanied their husbands. The Viscountess de Percemur talked society. Madame de Marelle looked charming in a strangely fanciful toilet, a species of Spanish costume in black and yellow, which set off her neat figure, her bosom, her rounded arms, and her bird-like head.

Du Roy had Madame Walter on his right hand, and during dinner only spoke to her on serious topics, and with an exaggerated respect. From time to time he glanced at Clotilde. "She is really prettier and fresher looking than ever," he thought. Then his eyes returned to his wife, whom he found not bad-looking either, although he retained towards her a hidden, tenacious, and evil anger.

But Madame Walter excited him by the difficulty of victory and by that novelty always desired by man. She wanted to return home early. "I will escort you," said he.

She refused, but he persisted, saying: "Why will not you permit me? You will wound me keenly. Do not let me think that you have not forgiven me. You see how quiet I am."

She answered: "But you cannot abandon your guests like that."

He smiled. "But I shall only be away twenty minutes. They will not even notice it. If you refuse you will cut me to the heart."

She murmured: "Well, then I agree."

But as soon as they were in the carriage he seized her hand, and, kissing it passionately, exclaimed: "I love you, I love you. Let me tell you that much. I will not touch you. I only want to repeat to you that I love you."

She stammered: "Oh! after what you promised me! This is wrong, very wrong."

He appeared to make a great effort, and then resumed in a restrained tone: "There, you see how I master myself. And yet—But let me only tell you that I love you, and repeat it to you every day; yes, let me come to your house and kneel down for five minutes at your feet to utter those three words while gazing on your beloved face."

She had yielded her hand to him, and replied pantingly: "No, I cannot, I will not. Think of what would be said, of the servants, of my daughters. No, no, it is impossible."

He went on: "I can no longer live without seeing you. Whether at your house or elsewhere, I must see you, if only for a moment, every day, to touch your hand, to breathe the air stirred by your dress, to gaze on the outline of your form, and on your great calm eyes that madden me."

She listened, quivering, to this commonplace love-song, and stammered: "No, it is out of the question."

He whispered in her ear, understanding that he must capture her by degrees, this simple woman, that he must get her to make appointments with him, where she would at first, where he wished afterwards. "Listen, I must see you; I shall wait for you at your door like a beggar; but I will see you, I will see you to-morrow."

She repeated: "No, do not come. I shall not receive you. Think of my daughters."

"Then tell me where I shall meet you—in the street, no matter where, at whatever hour you like, provided I see you. I will bow to you; I will say 'I love you,' and I will go away."

She hesitated, bewildered. And as the brougham entered the gateway of her residence she murmured hurriedly: "Well, then, I shall be at the Church of the Trinity to-morrow at half-past three." Then, having alighted, she said to her coachman: "Drive Monsieur Du Roy back to his house."

As he re-entered his home, his wife said: "Where did you get to?"

He replied, in a low tone: "I went to the telegraph office to send off a message."

Madame de Marelle approached them. "You will see me home, Pretty-boy?" said she. "You know I only came such a distance to dinner on that condition." And turning to Madeleine, she added: "You are not jealous?"

Madame Du Roy answered slowly: "Not over much."

The guests were taking their leave. Madame Laroche-Mathieu looked like a housemaid from the country. She was the daughter of a notary, and had been married to the deputy when he was only a barrister of small standing. Madame Rissolin, old and stuck-up, gave one the idea of a midwife whose fashionable education had been acquired through a circulating library. The

Viscountess de Percemur looked down upon them. Her "Lily Fingers" touched these vulgar hands with repugnance.

Clotilde, wrapped in lace, said to Madeleine as she went out: "Your dinner was perfection. In a little while you will have the leading political drawing-room in Paris."

As soon as she was alone with George she clasped him in her arms, exclaiming: "Oh, my darling Pretty-boy, I love you more and more every day!"

XII

The Place de la Trinité lay, almost deserted, under a dazzling July sun. An oppressive heat was crushing Paris. It was as though the upper air, scorched and deadened, had fallen upon the city—a thick, burning air that pained the chests inhaling it. The fountains in front of the church fell lazily. They seemed weary of flowing, tired out, limp, too; and the water of the basins, in which leaves and bits of paper were floating, looked greenish, thick and glaucous. A dog having jumped over the stone rim, was bathing in the dubious fluid. A few people, seated on the benches of the little circular garden skirting the front of the church, watched the animal curiously.

Du Roy pulled out his watch. It was only three o'clock. He was half an hour too soon. He laughed as he thought of this appointment. "Churches serve for anything as far as she is concerned," said he to himself. "They console her for having married a Jew, enable her to assume an attitude of protestation in the world of politics and a respectable one in that of fashion, and serve as a shelter to her gallant rendezvous. So much for the habit of making use of religion as an umbrella. If it is fine it is a walking stick; if sunshiny, a parasol; if it rains, a shelter; and if one does not go out, why, one leaves it in the hall. And there are hundreds like that who care for God about as much as a cherry stone, but who will not hear him spoken against. If it were suggested to them to go to a hotel, they would think it infamous, but it seems to them quite simple to make love at the foot of the altar."

He walked slowly along the edge of the fountain, and then again looked at the church clock, which was two minutes faster than his watch. It was five minutes past three. He thought that he would be more comfortable inside, and entered the church. The coolness of a cellar assailed him, he breathed it with pleasure, and then took a turn round the nave to reconnoiter the place. Other regular footsteps, sometimes halting and then beginning anew, replied from the further end of the vast pile to the sound of his own, which rang sonorously beneath the vaulted roof. A curiosity to know who this other promenader was seized him. It was a stout, bald-headed gentleman who was strolling about with his nose in the air, and his hat behind his back. Here and there an old woman was praying, her face hidden in her hands. A sensation of solitude and rest stole over the mind. The light, softened by the stained-glass windows, was refreshing to the eyes. Du Roy thought that it was "deucedly comfortable" inside there.

He returned towards the door and again looked at his watch. It was still only a quarter-past three. He sat down at the entrance to the main aisle, regretting that one could not smoke a cigarette. The slow footsteps of the stout gentleman could still be heard at the further end of the church, near the choir.

Someone came in, and George turned sharply round. It was a poor woman in a woolen skirt, who fell on her knees close to the first chair, and remained motionless, with clasped hands, her eyes turned to heaven, her soul absorbed in prayer. Du Roy watched her with interest, asking himself what grief, what pain, what despair could have crushed her heart. She was worn out by poverty, it was plain. She had, perhaps, too, a husband who was beating her to death, or a dying child. He murmured mentally: "Poor creatures. How some of them do suffer." Anger rose up in him against pitiless Nature. Then he reflected that these poor wretches believed, at any rate, that they were taken into consideration up above, and that they were duly entered in the registers of heaven with a debtor and creditor balance. Up above! And Du Roy, whom the silence of the church inclined to sweeping reflections, judging creation at a bound, muttered contemptuously: "What bosh all that sort of thing is!"

The rustle of a dress made him start. It was she.

He rose, and advanced quickly. She did not hold out her hand, but murmured in a low voice: "I have only a few moments. I must get back home. Kneel down near me, so that we may not be noticed." And she advanced up the aisle, seeking a safe and suitable spot, like a woman well acquainted with the place. Her face was hidden by a thick veil, and she walked with careful footsteps that could scarcely be heard.

When she reached the choir she turned, and muttered, in that mysterious tone of voice we always assume in church: "The side aisles will be better. We are too much in view here."

She bowed low to the high altar, turned to the right, and returned a little way towards the entrance; then, making up her mind, she took a chair and knelt down. George took possession of the next one to her, and as soon as they were in an attitude of prayer, began: "Thanks; oh, thanks; I adore you! I should like to be always telling you so, to tell you how I began to love you, how I was captivated the first time I saw you. Will you allow me some day to open my heart to tell you all this?"

She listened to him in an attitude of deep meditation, as if she heard nothing. She replied between her fingers: "I am mad to allow you to speak to me like this, mad to have come here, mad to do what I am doing, mad to let you believe that—that—this adventure can have any issue. Forget all this; you must, and never speak to me again of it."

She paused. He strove to find an answer, decisive and passionate words, but not being able to join action to words, was partially paralyzed. He replied: "I expect nothing, I hope for nothing. I love you. Whatever you may do, I will repeat it to you so often, with such power and ardor, that you will end by understanding it. I want to make my love penetrate you, to pour it into your soul, word by word, hour by hour, day by day, so that at length it impregnates you like a liquid, falling drop by drop; softens you, mollifies you, and obliges you later on to reply to me: 'I love you, too.'"

He felt her shoulder trembling against him and her bosom throbbing, and she stammered, abruptly: "I love you, too!"

He started as though he had received a blow, and sighed: "Good God."

She replied, in panting tones: "Ought I to have told you that? I feel I am guilty and contemptible. I, who have two daughters, but I cannot help it, I cannot help it. I could not have believed, I should never have thought—but it is stronger than I. Listen, listen: I have never loved anyone but you; I swear it. And I have loved you for a year past in secret, in my secret heart. Oh! I have suffered and struggled till I can do so no more. I love you."

She was weeping, with her hands crossed in front of her face, and her whole frame was quivering, shaken by the violence of her emotion.

George murmured: "Give me your hand, that I may touch it, that I may press it."

She slowly withdrew her hand from her face. He saw her cheek quite wet and a tear ready to fall on her lashes. He had taken her hand and was pressing it, saying: "Oh, how I should like to drink your tears!"

She said, in a low and broken voice, which resembled a moan: "Do not take advantage of me; I am lost."

He felt an impulse to smile. How could he take advantage of her in that place? He placed the hand he held upon his heart, saying: "Do you feel it beat?" For he had come to the end of his passionate phrases.

For some moments past the regular footsteps of the promenader had been coming nearer. He had gone the round of the altars, and was now, for the second time at least, coming down the little aisle on the right. When Madame Walter heard him close to the pillar which hid her, she snatched her fingers from George's grasp, and again hid her face. And both remained motionless, kneeling as though they had been addressing fervent supplications to heaven together. The stout gentleman passed close to them, cast an indifferent look upon them, and walked away to the lower end of the church, still holding his hat behind his back.

Du Roy, who was thinking of obtaining an appointment elsewhere than at the Church of the Trinity, murmured: "Where shall I see you to-morrow?"

She did not answer. She seemed lifeless—turned into a statue of prayer. He went on: "To-morrow, will you let me meet you in the Parc Monseau?"

She turned towards him her again uncovered face, a livid face, contracted by fearful suffering, and in a jerky voice ejaculated: "Leave me, leave me now; go away, go away, only for five minutes! I suffer too much beside you. I want to pray, and I cannot. Go away, let me pray alone for five minutes. I cannot. Let me implore God to pardon me—to save me. Leave me for five minutes."

Her face was so upset, so full of pain, that he rose without saying a word, and then, after a little hesitation, asked: "Shall I come back presently?"

She gave a nod, which meant, "Yes, presently," and he walked away towards the choir. Then she strove to pray. She made a superhuman effort to invoke the Deity, and with quivering frame and bewildering soul appealed for mercy to heaven. She closed her eyes with rage, in order no longer to see him who just left her. She sought to drive him from her mind, she struggled against him, but instead of the celestial apparition awaited in the distress of her heart, she still perceived the young fellow's curly moustache. For a year past she had been struggling thus every day, every night, against the growing possession, against this image which haunted her dreams, haunted her flesh, and disturbed her nights. She felt caught like a beast in a net, bound, thrown into the arms of this man, who had vanquished, conquered her, simply by the hair on his lip and the color of his eyes. And now in this church, close to God, she felt still weaker, more abandoned, and more lost than at home. She could no longer pray, she could only think of him. She suffered already that he had quitted her. She struggled, however, despairingly, resisted, implored help with all the strength of her soul. She would liked to have died rather than fall thus, she who had never faltered in her duty. She murmured wild words of supplication, but she was listening to George's footsteps dying away in the distance.

She understood that it was all over, that the struggle was a useless one. She would not yield, however; and she was seized by one of those nervous crises that hurl women quivering, yelling, and writhing on the ground. She trembled in every limb, feeling that she was going to fall and roll among the chairs, uttering shrill cries. Someone approached with rapid steps. It was a priest. She rose and rushed towards him, holding out her clasped hands, and stammering: "Oh! save me, save me!"

He halted in surprise, saying: "What is it you wish, madame?"

"I want you to save me. Have pity on me. If you do not come to my assistance, I am lost."

He looked at her, asking himself whether she was not mad, and then said: "What can I do for you?"

He was a tall, and somewhat stout young man, with full, pendulous cheeks, dark, with a carefully shaven face, a good-looking city curate belonging to a wealthy district, and accustomed to rich penitents.

"Hear my confession, and advise me, sustain me, tell me what I am to do."

He replied: "I hear confessions every Saturday, from three to six o'clock."

Having seized his arm, she gripped it tightly as she repeated: "No, no, no; at once, at once! You must. He is here, in the church. He is waiting for me."

"Who is waiting for you?" asked the priest.

"A man who will ruin me, who will carry me off, if you do not save me. I cannot flee from him. I am too weak—too weak! Oh, so weak, so weak!" She fell at his feet sobbing: "Oh, have pity on me, father! Save me, in God's name, save me!"

She held him by his black gown lest he should escape, and he with uneasiness glanced around, lest some malevolent or devout eye should see this woman fallen at his feet. Understanding at length that he could not escape, he said: "Get up; I have the key of the confessional with me."

And fumbling in his pocket he drew out a ring full of keys, selected one, and walked rapidly towards the little wooden cabin, dust holes of the soul into which believers cast their sins. He entered the center door, which he closed behind him, and Madame Walter, throwing herself into the narrow recess at the side, stammered fervently, with a passionate burst of hope: "Bless me father, for I have sinned."

Du Roy, having taken a turn round the choir, was passing down the left aisle. He had got half-way when he met the stout, bald gentleman still walking quietly along, and said to himself: "What the deuce is that customer doing here?"

The promenader had also slackened his pace, and was looking at George with an evident wish to speak to him. When he came quite close he bowed, and said in a polite fashion: "I beg your pardon, sir, for troubling you, but can you tell me when this church was built?"

Du Roy replied: "Really, I am not quite certain. I think within the last twenty or five-and-twenty years. It is, besides, the first time I ever was inside it."

"It is the same with me. I have never seen it."

The journalist, whose interest was awakened, remarked: "It seems to me that you are going over it very carefully. You are studying it in detail."

The other replied, with resignation: "I am not examining it; I am waiting for my wife, who made an appointment with me here, and who is very much behind time." Then, after a few moments' silence, he added: "It is fearfully hot outside."

Du Roy looked at him, and all at once fancied that he resembled Forestier.

"You are from the country?" said he, inquiringly.

"Yes, from Rennes. And you, sir, is it out of curiosity that you entered this church?"

"No, I am expecting a lady," and bowing, the journalist walked away, with a smile on his lips.

Approaching the main entrance, he saw the poor woman still on her knees, and still praying. He thought: "By Jove! she keeps hard at it." He was no longer moved, and no longer pitied her.

He passed on, and began quietly to walk up the right-hand aisle to find Madame Walter again. He marked the place where he had left her from a distance, astonished at not seeing her. He thought he had made a mistake in the pillar; went on as far as the end one, and then returned. She had gone, then. He was surprised and enraged. Then he thought she might be looking for him, and made the circuit of the church again. Not finding her, he returned, and sat down on the chair she had occupied, hoping she would rejoin him there, and waited. Soon a low murmur of voices aroused his attention. He had not seen anyone in that part of the church. Whence came this whispering? He rose to see, and perceived in the adjacent chapel the doors of the confessional. The skirt of a dress issuing from one of these trailed on the pavement. He approached to examine the woman. He recognized her. She was confessing.

He felt a violent inclination to take her by the shoulders and to pull her out of the box. Then he thought: "Bah! it is the priest's turn now; it will be mine to-morrow." And he sat down quietly in front of the confessional, biding his time, and chuckling now over the adventure. He waited a long time. At length Madame Walter rose, turned round, saw him, and came up to him. Her expression was cold and severe, "Sir," said she, "I beg of you not to accompany me, not to follow me, and not to come to my house alone. You will not be received. Farewell."

And she walked away with a dignified bearing. He let her depart, for one of his principles was never to force matters. Then, as the priest, somewhat upset, issued in turn from his box, he walked up to him, and, looking him straight in the eyes, growled to his face: "If you did not wear a petticoat, what a smack you would get across your ugly chops." After which he turned on his heels and went out of the church, whistling between his teeth. Standing under the porch, the stout gentleman, with the hat on his head and his hands behind his back, tired of waiting, was scanning the broad squares and all the streets opening onto it. As Du Roy passed him they bowed to one another.

The journalist, finding himself at liberty, went to the office of the *Vie Francaise*. As soon as he entered he saw by the busy air of the messengers that something out of the common was happening, and at once went into the manager's room. Daddy Walter, in a state of nervous excitement, was standing up dictating an article in broken sentences; issuing orders to the reporters, who surrounded him, between two paragraphs; giving instructions to Boisrenard; and opening letters.

As Du Roy came in, the governor uttered a cry of joy: "Ah! how lucky; here is Pretty-boy!" He stopped short, somewhat confused, and excused himself: "I beg your pardon for speaking like that, but I am very much disturbed by certain events. And then I hear my wife and daughter speaking of you as Pretty-boy from morning till night, and have ended by falling into the habit myself. You are not offended?"

"Not at all!" said George, laughingly; "there is nothing in that nickname to displease me."

Daddy Walter went on: "Very well, then, I christen you Pretty-boy, like everyone else. Well, the fact is, great things are taking place. The Ministry has been overthrown by a vote of three hundred and ten to a hundred and two. Our prorogation is again postponed—postponed to the Greek calends, and here we are at the twenty-eighth of July. Spain is angry about the Morocco business, and it is that which has overthrown Durand de l'Aine and his following. We are right in the swim. Marrot is entrusted with the formation of a new Cabinet. He takes General Boutin d'Acre as minister of war, and our friend Laroche-Mathieu for foreign affairs. We are going to become an official organ. I am writing a leader, a simple declaration of our principles, pointing out the line to be followed by the Ministry." The old boy smiled, and continued: "The line they intend following, be it understood. But I want something interesting about

Morocco; an actuality; a sensational article; something or other. Find one for me."

Du Roy reflected for a moment, and then replied: "I have the very thing for you. I will give you a study of the political situation of the whole of our African colony, with Tunis on the left, Algeria in the middle, and Morocco on the right; the history of the races inhabiting this vast extent of territory; and the narrative of an excursion on the frontier of Morocco to the great oasis of Figuig, where no European has penetrated, and which is the cause of the present conflict. Will that suit you?"

"Admirably!" exclaimed Daddy Walter. "And the title?"

"From Tunis to Tangiers."

"Splendid!"

Du Roy went off to search the files of the *Vie Francaise* for his first article, "The Recollections of a Chasseur d'Afrique," which, rebaptized, touched up, and modified, would do admirably, since it dealt with colonial policy, the Algerian population, and an excursion in the province of Oran. In three-quarters of an hour it was rewritten, touched up, and brought to date, with a flavor of realism, and praises of the new Cabinet. The manager, having read the article, said: "It is capital, capital, capital! You are an invaluable fellow. I congratulate you."

And Du Roy went home to dinner delighted with his day's work, despite the check at the Church of the Trinity, for he felt the battle won. His wife was anxiously waiting for him. She exclaimed, as soon as she saw him: "Do you know that Laroche-Mathieu is Minister for Foreign Affairs?"

"Yes; I have just written an article on Algeria, in connection with it."

"What?"

"You know, the first we wrote together, 'The Recollections of a Chasseur d'Afrique,' revised and corrected for the occasion."

She smiled, saying: "Ah, that is very good!" Then, after a few moments' reflection, she continued: "I was thinking—that continuation you were to have written then, and that you—put off. We might set to work on it now. It would make a nice series, and very appropriate to the situation."

He replied, sitting down to table: "Exactly, and there is nothing in the way of it now that cuckold of a Forestier is dead."

She said quietly, in a dry and hurt tone: "That joke is more than out of place, and I beg of you to put an end to it. It has lasted too long already."

He was about to make an ironical answer, when a telegram was brought him, containing these words: "I had lost my senses. Forgive me, and come at four o'clock to-morrow to the Parc Monceau."

He understood, and with heart suddenly filled with joy, he said to his wife, as he slipped the message into his pocket: "I will not do so any more, darling; it was stupid, I admit."

And he began his dinner. While eating he kept repeating to himself the words: "I had lost my senses. Forgive me, and come at four o'clock to-morrow to the Parc Monceau." So she was yielding. That meant: "I surrender, I am yours when you like and where you like." He began to laugh, and Madeleine asked: "What is it?"

"Nothing," he answered; "I was thinking of a priest I met just now, and who had a very comical mug."

Du Roy arrived to the time at the appointed place next day. On the benches of the park were seated citizens overcome by heat, and careless nurses, who seemed to be dreaming while their children were rolling on the gravel of the paths. He found Madame Walter in the little antique ruins from which a spring flows. She was walking round the little circle of columns with an uneasy and unhappy air. As soon as he had greeted her, she exclaimed: "What a number of people there are in the garden."

He seized the opportunity: "It is true; will you come somewhere else?"

"But where?"

"No matter where; in a cab, for instance. You can draw down the blind on your side, and you will be quite invisible."

"Yes, I prefer that; here I am dying with fear."

"Well, come and meet me in five minutes at the gate opening onto the outer boulevard. I will have a cab."

And he darted off.

As soon as she had rejoined him, and had carefully drawn down the blind on her side, she asked: "Where have you told the driver to take us?"

George replied: "Do not trouble yourself, he knows what to do."

He had given the man his address in the Rue de Constantinople.

She resumed: "You cannot imagine what I suffer on account of you, how I am tortured and tormented. Yesterday, in the church, I was cruel, but I wanted to flee from you at any cost. I was so afraid to find myself alone with you. Have you forgiven me?"

He squeezed her hands: "Yes, yes, what would I not forgive you, loving you as I do?"

She looked at him with a supplicating air: "Listen, you must promise to respect me—not to—not to—otherwise I cannot see you again."

He did not reply at once; he wore under his moustache that keen smile that disturbed women. He ended by murmuring: "I am your slave."

Then she began to tell him how she had perceived that she was in love with him on learning that he was going to marry Madeleine Forestier. She gave details, little details of dates and the like. Suddenly she paused. The cab had stopped. Du Roy opened the door.

"Where are we?" she asked.

"Get out and come into this house," he replied. "We shall be more at ease there."

"But where are we?"

"At my rooms," and here we will leave them to their *tête-à-tête*.

XIII

Autumn had come. The Du Roys had passed the whole of the summer in Paris, carrying on a vigorous campaign in the *Vie Francaise* during the short vacation of the deputies.

Although it was only the beginning of October, the Chambers were about to resume their sittings, for matters as regarded Morocco were becoming threatening. No one at the bottom believed in an expedition against Tangiers, although on the day of the prorogation of the Chamber, a deputy of the Right, Count de Lambert-Serrazin, in a witty speech, applauded even by the Center had offered to stake his moustache, after the example of a celebrated Viceroy of the Indies, against the whiskers of the President of the Council, that the new Cabinet could not help imitating the old one, and sending an army to Tangiers, as a pendant to that of Tunis, out of love of symmetry, as one puts two vases on a fireplace.

He had added: "Africa is indeed, a fireplace for France, gentleman—a fireplace which consumes our best wood; a fireplace with a strong draught, which is lit with bank notes. You have had the artistic fancy of ornamenting the left-hand corner with a Tunisian knick-knack which had cost you dear. You will see that Monsieur Marrot will want to imitate his predecessor, and ornament the right-hand corner with one from Morocco."

This speech, which became famous, served as a peg for Du Roy for a half a score of articles upon the Algerian colony—indeed, for the entire series broken short off after his *début* on the paper. He had energetically supported the notion of a military expedition, although convinced that it would not take place. He had struck the chord of patriotism, and bombarded Spain with the entire arsenal of contemptuous arguments which we make use of against nations whose interests are contrary to our own. The *Vie Francaise* had gained considerable importance through its own connection with the party in office. It published political intelligence in advance of the most important papers, and hinted discreetly the intentions of its friends the Ministry, so that all the papers of Paris and the provinces took their news from it. It was quoted and feared, and people began to respect it. It was no longer the suspicious organ of a knot of political jugglers, but the acknowledged one of the Cabinet. Laroche-Mathieu was the soul of the paper, and Du Roy his mouthpiece. Daddy Walter, a silent member and a crafty manager, knowing when to keep in the background, was busying himself on the quiet, it is said, with an extensive transaction with some copper mines in Morocco.

Madeleine's drawing-room had been an influential center, in which several members of the Cabinet met every week. The President of the Council had even dined twice at her house, and the wives of the statesmen who had formerly hesitated to cross her threshold now boasted of being her friends, and paid her more visits than were returned by her. The Minister for Foreign Affairs reigned almost as a master in the household. He called at all hours, bringing dispatches, news, items of information, which he dictated either to the husband or the wife, as if they had been his secretaries.

When Du Roy, after the minister's departure, found himself alone with Madeleine, he would break out in a menacing tone with bitter insinuations against the goings-on of this commonplace parvenu.

But she would shrug her shoulders contemptuously, repeating: "Do as much as he has done yourself. Become a minister, and you can have your own way. Till then, hold your tongue."

He twirled his moustache, looking at her askance: "People do not know of what I am capable," he said, "They will learn it, perhaps, some day."

She replied, philosophically: "Who lives long enough will see it."

The morning on which the Chambers reassembled the young wife, still in bed, was giving a thousand recommendations to her husband, who was dressing himself in order to lunch with M. Laroche-Mathieu, and receive his instructions prior to the sitting for the next day's political leader in the *Vie Francaise*, this leader being meant to be a kind of semi-official declaration of the real objects of the Cabinet.

Madeleine was saying: "Above all, do not forget to ask him whether General Belloncle is to be sent to Oran, as has been reported. That would mean a great deal."

George replied irritably: "But I know just as well as you what I have to do. Spare me your preaching."

She answered quietly: "My dear, you always forget half the commissions I entrust you with for the minister."

He growled: "He worries me to death, that minister of yours. He is a nincompoop."

She remarked quietly: "He is no more my minister than he is yours. He is more useful to you than to me."

He turned half round towards her, saying, sneeringly: "I beg your pardon, but he does not pay court to me."

She observed slowly: "Nor to me either; but he is making our fortune."

He was silent for a few moments, and then resumed: "If I had to make a choice among your admirers, I should still prefer that old fossil De Vaudrec. What has become of him, I have not seen him for a week?"

"He is unwell," replied she, unmoved. "He wrote to me that he was even obliged to keep his bed from an attack of gout. You ought to call and ask how he is. You know he likes you very well, and it would please him."

George said: "Yes, certainly; I will go some time to-day."

He had finished his toilet, and, hat on head, glanced at himself in the glass to see if he had neglected anything. Finding nothing, he came up to the bed and kissed his wife on the forehead, saying: "Good-bye, dear, I shall not be in before seven o'clock at the earliest."

And he went out. Monsieur Laroche-Mathieu was awaiting him, for he was lunching at ten o'clock that morning, the Council having to meet at noon, before the opening of Parliament. As soon as they were seated at table alone with the minister's private secretary, for Madame Laroche-Mathieu had been unwilling to change her own meal times, Du Roy spoke of his article, sketched out the line he proposed to take, consulting notes scribbled on visiting cards, and when he had finished, said: "Is there anything you think should be modified, my dear minister?"

"Very little, my dear fellow. You are perhaps a trifle too strongly affirmative as regards the Morocco business. Speak of the expedition as if it were going to take place; but, at the same time, letting it be understood that it will not take place, and that you do not believe in it in the least in the world. Write in such a way that the public can easily read between the lines that we are not going to poke our noses into that adventure."

"Quite so. I understand, and I will make myself thoroughly understood. My wife commissioned me to ask you, on this point, whether General Belloncle will be sent to Oran. After what you have said, I conclude he will not."

The statesman answered, "No."

Then they spoke of the coming session. Laroche-Mathieu began to spout, rehearsing the phrases that he was about to pour forth on his colleagues a few hours later. He waved his right hand, raising now his knife, now his fork, now a bit of bread, and without looking at anyone, addressing himself to the invisible assembly, he poured out his dulcet eloquence, the eloquence of a good-looking, dandified fellow. A tiny, twisted moustache curled up at its two ends above his lip like scorpion's tails, and his hair, anointed with brilliantine and parted in the middle, was puffed out like his temples, after the fashion of a provincial lady-killer. He was a little too stout, puffy, though still young, and his stomach stretched his waistcoat.

The private secretary ate and drank quietly, no doubt accustomed to these floods of loquacity; but Du Roy, whom jealousy of achieved success cut to the quick, thought: "Go on you proser. What idiots these political jokers are." And comparing his own worth to the frothy importance of the minister, he said to himself, "By Jove! if I had only a clear hundred thousand francs to offer myself as a candidate at home, near Rouen, and dish my sunning dullards of Normandy folk in their own sauce, what a statesman I should make beside these short-sighted rascals!"

Monsieur Laroche-Mathieu went on spouting until coffee was served; then, seeing that he was behind hand, he rang for his brougham, and holding out his hand to the journalist, said: "You quite understand, my dear fellow?"

"Perfectly, my dear minister; you may rely upon me."

And Du Roy strolled leisurely to the office to begin his article, for he had nothing to do till four o'clock. At four o'clock he was to meet, at the Rue de Constantinople, Madame de Marelle, whom he met there regularly twice a week—on Mondays and Fridays. But on reaching the office a telegram was handed to him. It was from Madame Walter, and ran as follows: "I must see you to-day. Most important. Expect me at two o'clock, Rue de Constantinople. Can render you a great service. Till death.—Virginie."

He began to swear: "Hang it all, what an infernal bore!" And seized with a fit of ill-temper, he went out again at once too irritated to work.

For six weeks he had been trying to break off with her, without being able to wear out her eager attachment. She had had, after her fall, a frightful fit of remorse, and in three successive rendezvous had overwhelmed her lover with reproaches and maledictions. Bored by these scenes and already tired of this mature and melodramatic conquest, he had simply kept away, hoping to put an end to the adventure in that way. But then she had distractedly clutched on to him, throwing herself into this amour as a man throws himself into a river with a stone about his neck. He had allowed himself to be recaptured out of weakness and consideration for her, and she had enwrapt him in an unbridled and fatiguing passion, persecuting him with her affection. She insisted on seeing him every day, summoning him at all hours to a hasty meeting at a street corner, at a shop, or in a public garden. She would then repeat to him in a few words, always the same, that she worshiped and idolized him, and leave him, vowing that she felt so happy to have seen him. She showed herself quite another creature than he had fancied her, striving to charm him with puerile glances, a childishness in love affairs ridiculous at her age. Having remained up till then strictly honest, virgin in heart, inaccessible to all sentiment, ignorant of sensuality, a strange outburst of youthful tenderness, of ardent, naive and tardy love, made up of unlooked-for outbursts, exclamations of a girl of sixteen, graces grown old without ever having been young, had taken place in this staid woman. She wrote him ten letters a day, maddeningly foolish letters, couched in a style at once poetic and ridiculous, full of the pet names of birds and beasts.

As soon as they found themselves alone together she would kiss him with the awkward prettiness of a great tomboy, pouting of the lips that were grotesque, and bounds that made her too full bosom shake beneath her bodice. He was above all, sickened with hearing her say, "My pet," "My doggie," "My jewel," "My birdie," "My treasure," "My own," "My precious," and to see her offer herself to him every time with a little comedy of infantile modesty, little movements of alarm that she thought pretty, and the tricks of a depraved schoolgirl. She would ask, "Whose mouth is this?" and when he did not reply "Mine," would persist till she made him grow pale with nervous irritability. She ought to have felt, it seemed to him, that in love extreme tact, skill, prudence, and exactness are requisite; that having given herself to him, she, a woman of mature years, the mother of a family, and holding a position in society, should yield herself gravely, with a kind of restrained eagerness, with tears, perhaps, but with those of Dido, not of Juliet.

She kept incessantly repeating to him, "How I love you, my little pet. Do you love me as well, baby?"

He could no longer bear to be called "my little pet," or "baby," without an inclination to call her "old girl."

She would say to him, "What madness of me to yield to you. But I do not regret it. It is so sweet to love."

All this seemed to George irritating from her mouth. She murmured, "It is so sweet to love," like the village maiden at a theater.

Then she exasperated him by the clumsiness of her caresses. Having become all at once sensual beneath the kisses of this young fellow who had so warmed her blood, she showed an unskilled ardor and a serious application that made Du Roy laugh and think of old men trying to learn to read. When she would have gripped him in her embrace, ardently gazing at him with the deep and terrible glance of certain aging women, splendid in their last loves, when she should have bitten him with silent and quivering mouth, crushing him beneath her warmth and weight, she would wriggle about like a girl, and lisp with the idea of being pleasant: "Me love 'ou so, ducky, me love 'ou so. Have nice lovey-lovey with 'ittle wifey."

He then would be seized with a wild desire to take his hat and rush out, slamming the door behind him.

They had frequently met at the outset at the Rue de Constantinople; but Du Roy, who dreaded a meeting there with Madame de Marelle, now found a thousand pretexts for refusing such appointments. He had then to call on her almost every day at her home, now to lunch, now to dinner. She squeezed his hand under the table, held out her mouth to him behind the doors. But he, for his part, took pleasure above all in playing with Susan, who amused him with her whimsicalities. In her doll-like frame was lodged an active, arch, sly, and startling wit, always ready to show itself off. She joked at everything and everybody with biting readiness. George stimulated her imagination, excited it to irony and they understood one another marvelously. She kept appealing to him every moment, "I say, Pretty-boy. Come here, Pretty-boy."

He would at once leave the mother and go to the daughter, who would whisper some bit of spitefulness, at which they would laugh heartily.

However, disgusted with the mother's love, he began to feel an insurmountable repugnance for her; he could no longer see, hear, or think of her without anger. He ceased, therefore, to visit her, to answer her letters, or to yield to her appeals. She understood at length that he no longer loved her, and suffered terribly. But she grew insatiable, kept watch on him, followed him, waited for him in a cab with the blinds drawn down, at the door of the office, at the door of his dwelling, in the streets through which she hoped he might pass. He longed to ill-treat her, swear at her, strike her, say to her plainly, "I have had enough of it, you worry my life out." But he observed some circumspection on account of the *Vie Francaise*, and strove by dint of coolness, harshness, tempered by attention, and even rude words at times, to make her understand that there must be an end to it. She strove, above all, to devise schemes to allure him to a meeting in the Rue de Constantinople, and he was in a perpetual state of alarm lest the two women should find themselves some day face to face at the door.

His affection for Madame de Marelle had, on the contrary, augmented during the summer. He called her his "young rascal," and she certainly charmed him. Their two natures had kindred links; they were both members of the adventurous race of vagabonds, those vagabonds in society who so strongly resemble, without being aware of it, the vagabonds of the highways. They had had a summer of delightful love-making, a summer of students on the spree, bolting off to lunch or dine at Argenteuil, Bougival, Maisons, or Poissy, and passing hours in a boat gathering flowers from the bank. She adored the fried fish served on the banks of the Seine, the stewed rabbits, the arbors in the tavern gardens, and the shouts of the boating men. He liked to start off with her on a bright day on a suburban line, and traverse the ugly environs of Paris, sprouting with tradesmen's hideous boxes, talking lively nonsense. And when he had to return to dine at

Madame Walter's he hated the eager old mistress from the mere recollection of the young one whom he had left, and who had ravished his desires and harvested his ardor among the grass by the water side.

He had fancied himself at length pretty well rid of Madame Walter, to whom he had expressed, in a plain and almost brutal fashion, his intentions of breaking off with her, when he received at the office of the paper the telegram summoning him to meet her at two o'clock at the Rue de Constantinople. He re-read it as he walked along, "Must see you to-day. Most important. Expect me two o'clock, Rue de Constantinople. Can render you a great service. Till death.—Virginie."

He thought, "What does this old screech-owl want with me now? I wager she has nothing to tell me. She will only repeat that she adores me. Yet I must see what it means. She speaks of an important affair and a great service; perhaps it is so. And Clotilde, who is coming at four o'clock! I must get the first of the pair off by three at the latest. By Jove, provided they don't run up against one another! What bothers women are."

And he reflected that, after all, his own wife was the only one who never bothered him at all. She lived in her own way, and seemed to be very fond of him during the hours destined to love, for she would not admit that the unchangeable order of the ordinary occupations of life should be interfered with.

He walked slowly towards the rendezvous, mentally working himself up against Madame Walter. "Ah! I will just receive her nicely if she has nothing to tell me. Cambronne's language will be academical compared to mine. I will tell her that I will never set foot in her house again, to begin with."

He went in to wait for Madame Walter. She arrived almost immediately, and as soon as she caught sight of him, she exclaimed, "Ah, you have had my telegram! How fortunate."

He put on a grumpy expression, saying: "By Jove, yes; I found it at the office just as I was going to start off to the Chamber. What is it you want now?"

She had raised her veil to kiss him, and drew nearer with the timid and submissive air of an oft-beaten dog.

"How cruel you are towards me! How harshly you speak to me! What have I done to you? You cannot imagine how I suffer through you."

He growled: "Don't go on again in that style."

She was standing close to him, only waiting for a smile, a gesture, to throw herself into his arms, and murmured: "You should not have taken me to treat me thus, you should have left me sober-minded and happy as I was. Do you remember what you said to me in the church, and how you forced me into this house? And now, how do you speak to me? how do you receive me? Oh, God! oh, God! what pain you give me!"

He stamped his foot, and exclaimed, violently: "Ah, bosh! That's enough of it! I can't see you a moment without hearing all that foolery. One would really think that I had carried you off at twelve years of age, and that you were as ignorant as an angel. No, my dear, let us put things in their proper light; there was no seduction of a young girl in the business. You gave yourself to me at full years of discretion. I thank you. I am infinitely grateful to you, but I am not bound to be tied till death to your petticoat strings. You have a husband and I a wife. We are neither of us free. We indulged in a mutual caprice, and it is over."

"Oh, you are brutal, coarse, shameless," she said; "I was indeed no longer a young girl, but I had never loved, never faltered."

He cut her short with: "I know it. You have told me so twenty times. But you had had two children."

She drew back, exclaiming: "Oh, George, that is unworthy of you," and pressing her two hands to her heart, began to choke and sob.

When he saw the tears come he took his hat from the corner of the mantelpiece, saying: "Oh, you are going to cry, are you? Good-bye, then. So it was to show off in this way that you came here, eh?"

She had taken a step forward in order to bar the way, and quickly pulling out a handkerchief from her pocket, wiped her eyes with an abrupt movement. Her voice grew firmer by the effort of her will, as she said, in tones tremulous with pain, "No—I came to—to tell you some news—political news—to put you in the way of gaining fifty thousand francs—or even more—if you like."

He inquired, suddenly softening, "How so? What do you mean?"

"I caught, by chance, yesterday evening, some words between my husband and Laroche-Mathieu. They do not, besides, trouble themselves to hide much from me. But Walter recommended the Minister not to let you into the secret, as you would reveal everything."

Du Roy had put his hat down on a chair, and was waiting very attentively.

"What is up, then?" said he.

"They are going to take possession of Morocco."

"Nonsense! I lunched with Laroche-Mathieu, who almost dictated to me the intention of the Cabinet."

"No, darling, they are humbugging you, because they were afraid lest their plan should be known."

"Sit down," said George, and sat down himself in an armchair. Then she drew towards him a low stool, and sitting down on it between his knees, went on in a coaxing tone, "As I am always thinking about you, I pay attention now to everything that is whispered around me."

And she began quietly to explain to him how she had guessed for some time past that something was being hatched unknown to him; that they were making use of him, while dreading his co-operation. She said, "You know, when one is in love, one grows cunning."

At length, the day before, she had understood it all. It was a business transaction, a thumping affair, worked out on the quiet. She smiled now, happy in her dexterity, and grew excited, speaking like a financier's wife accustomed to see the market rigged, used to rises and falls that ruin, in two hours of speculation, thousands of little folk who have placed their savings in undertakings guaranteed by the names of men honored and respected in the world of politics of finance.

She repeated, "Oh, it is very smart what they have been up to! Very smart. It was Walter who did it all, though, and he knows all about such things. Really, it is a first-class job."

He grew impatient at these preliminaries, and exclaimed, "Come, tell me what it is at once."

"Well, then, this is what it is. The Tangiers expedition was decided upon between them on the day that Laroche-Mathieu took the ministry of foreign affairs, and little by little they have bought up the whole of the Morocco loan, which had fallen to sixty-four or sixty-five francs. They have bought it up very cleverly by means of shady brokers, who did not awaken any mistrust. They have even sold the Rothschilds, who grew astonished to find Morocco stock always asked for, and who were astonished by having agents pointed out to them—all lame ducks. That quieted the big financiers. And now the expedition is to take place, and as soon as we are there the French Government will guarantee the debt. Our friends will gain fifty or sixty millions. You understand the matter? You understand, too, how afraid they have been of everyone, of the slightest indiscretion?"

She had leaned her head against the young fellow's waistcoat, and with her arms resting on his legs, pressed up against him, feeling that she was interesting him now, and ready to do anything for a caress, for a smile.

"You are quite certain?" he asked.

"I should think so," she replied, with confidence.

"It is very smart indeed. As to that swine of a Laroche-Mathieu, just see if I don't pay him out one of these days. Oh, the scoundrel, just let him look out for himself! He shall go through my hands." Then he began to reflect, and went on, "We ought, though, to profit by all this."

"You can still buy some of the loan," said she; "it is only at seventy-two francs."

He said, "Yes, but I have no money under my hand."

She raised her eyes towards him, eyes full of entreaty, saying, "I have thought of that, darling, and if you were very nice, very nice, if you loved me a little, you would let me lend you some."

He answered, abruptly and almost harshly, "As to that, no, indeed."

She murmured, in an imploring voice: "Listen, there is something that you can do without borrowing money. I wanted to buy ten thousand francs' worth of the loan to make a little nest-egg. Well, I will take twenty thousand, and you shall stand in for half. You understand that I am not going to hand the money over to Walter. So there is nothing to pay for the present. If it all succeeds, you gain seventy thousand francs. If not, you will owe me ten thousand, which you can pay when you please."

He remarked, "No, I do not like such pains."

Then she argued, in order to get him to make up his mind. She proved to him that he was really pledging his word for ten thousand francs, that he was running risks, and that she was not advancing him anything, since the actual outlay was made by Walter's bank. She pointed out to him, besides, that it was he who had carried on in the *Vie Francaise* the whole of the political campaign that had rendered the scheme possible. He would be very foolish not to profit by it. He still hesitated, and she added, "But just reflect that in reality it is Walter who is advancing you these ten thousand Francs, and that you have rendered him services worth a great deal more than that."

"Very well, then," said he, "I will go halves with you. If we lose, I will repay you the ten thousand francs."

She was so pleased that she rose, took his head in both her hands, and began to kiss him eagerly. He did not resist at first, but as she grew bolder, clasping him to her and devouring him with caresses, he reflected that the other would be there shortly, and that if he yielded he would lose time and exhaust in the arms of the old woman an ardor that he had better reserve for the young one. So he repulsed her gently, saying, "Come, be good now."

She looked at him disconsolately, saying, "Oh, George, can't I even kiss you?"

He replied, "No, not to-day. I have a headache, and it upsets me."

She sat down again docilely between his knees, and asked, "Will you come and dine with us to-morrow? You would give me much pleasure."

He hesitated, but dared not refuse, so said, "Certainly."

"Thanks, darling."

She rubbed her cheek slowly against his breast with a regular and coaxing movement, and one of her long black hairs caught in his waistcoat. She noticed it, and a wild idea crossed her mind, one of those superstitious notions which are often the whole of a woman's reason. She began to twist this hair gently round a button. Then she fastened another hair to the next button, and a third to the next. One to every button. He would tear them out of her head presently when he rose, and hurt her. What happiness! And he would carry away something of her without knowing it; he would carry away a tiny lock of her hair which he had never yet asked for. It was a tie by which she attached him to her, a secret, invisible bond, a talisman she left with him. Without willing it he would think of her, dream of her, and perhaps love her a little more the next day.

He said, all at once, "I must leave you, because I am expected at the Chamber at the close of the sitting. I cannot miss attending to-day."

She sighed, "Already!" and then added, resignedly, "Go, dear, but you will come to dinner to-morrow."

And suddenly she drew aside. There was a short and sharp pain in her head, as though needles had been stuck into the skin. Her heart throbbed; she was pleased to have suffered a little by him. "Good-bye," said she.

He took her in his arms with a compassionate smile, and coldly kissed her eyes. But she, maddened by this contact, again murmured, "Already!" while her suppliant glance indicated the bedroom, the door of which was open.

He stepped away from her, and said in a hurried tone, "I must be off; I shall be late."

Then she held out her lips, which he barely brushed with his, and having handed her her parasol, which she was forgetting, he continued, "Come, come, we must be quick, it is past three o'clock."

She went out before him, saying, "To-morrow, at seven," and he repeated, "To-morrow, at seven."

They separated, she turning to the right and he to the left. Du Roy walked as far as the outer boulevard. Then he slowly strolled back along the Boulevard Malesherbes. Passing a pastry cook's, he noticed some *marrons glacés* in a glass jar, and thought, "I will take in a pound for Clotilde."

He bought a bag of these sweetmeats, which she was passionately fond of, and at four o'clock returned to wait for his young mistress. She was a little late, because her husband had come home for a week, and said, "Can you come and dine with us to-morrow? He will be so pleased to see you."

"No, I dine with the governor. We have a heap of political and financial matters to talk over."

She had taken off her bonnet, and was now laying aside her bodice, which was too tight for her. He pointed out the bag on the mantel-shelf, saying, "I have bought you some *marrons glacés*."

She clapped her hands, exclaiming: "How nice; what a dear you are."

She took one, tasted them, and said: "They are delicious. I feel sure I shall not leave one of them." Then she added, looking at George with sensual merriment: "You flatter all my vices, then."

She slowly ate the sweetmeats, looking continually into the bag to see if there were any left. "There, sit down in the armchair," said she, "and I will squat down between your knees and nibble my bon-bons. I shall be very comfortable."

He smiled, sat down, and took her between his knees, as he had had Madame Walter shortly before. She raised her head in order to speak to him, and said, with her mouth full: "Do you know, darling, I dreamt of you? I dreamt that we were both taking a long journey together on a camel. He had two humps, and we were each sitting astride on a hump, crossing the desert. We had taken some sandwiches in a piece of paper and some wine in a bottle, and were dining on our humps. But it annoyed me because we could not do anything else; we were too far off from one another, and I wanted to get down."

He answered: "I want to get down, too."

He laughed, amused at the story, and encouraged her to talk nonsense, to chatter, to indulge in all the child's play of conversation which lovers utter. The nonsense which he thought delightful in the mouth of Madame de Marelle would have exasperated him in that of Madame Walter. Clotilde, too, called him "My darling," "My pet," "My own." These words seemed sweet and caressing. Said by the other woman shortly before, they had irritated and sickened him. For words of love, which are always the same, take the flavor of the lips they come from.

But he was thinking, even while amusing himself with this nonsense, of the seventy thousand francs he was going to gain, and suddenly checked the gabble of his companion by two little taps with his finger on her head. "Listen, pet," said he.

"I am going to entrust you with a commission for your husband. Tell him from me to buy to-morrow ten thousand francs' worth of the Morocco loan, which is quoted at seventy-two, and I promise him that he will gain from sixty to eighty thousand francs before three months are over. Recommend the most positive silence to him. Tell him from me that the expedition to Tangiers is decided on, and that the French government will guarantee the debt of Morocco. But do not let anything out about it. It is a State secret that I am entrusting to you."

She listened to him seriously, and murmured: "Thank you, I will tell my husband this evening. You can reckon on him; he will not talk. He is a very safe man, and there is no danger."

But she had eaten all the sweetmeats. She crushed up the bag between her hands and flung it into the fireplace. Then she said, "Let us go to bed," and without getting up, began to unbutton George's waistcoat. All at once she stopped, and pulling out between two fingers a long hair, caught in a buttonhole, began to laugh. "There, you have brought away one of Madeleine's hairs. There is a faithful husband for you."

Then, becoming once more serious, she carefully examined on her head the almost imperceptible thread she had found, and murmured: "It is not Madeleine's, it is too dark."

He smiled, saying: "It is very likely one of the maid's."

But she was inspecting the waistcoat with the attention of a detective, and collected a second hair rolled round a button; then she perceived a third, and pale and somewhat trembling, exclaimed: "Oh, you have been sleeping with a woman who has wrapped her hair round all your buttons."

He was astonished, and gasped out: "No, you are mad."

All at once he remembered, understood it all, was uneasy at first, and then denied the charge with a chuckle, not vexed at the bottom that she should suspect him of other loves. She kept on searching, and still found hairs, which she rapidly untwisted and threw on the carpet. She had guessed matters with her artful woman's instinct, and stammered out, vexed, angry, and ready to cry: "She loves you, she does—and she wanted you to take away something belonging to her. Oh, what a traitor you are!" But all at once she gave a cry, a shrill cry of nervous joy. "Oh! oh! it is an old woman—here is a white hair. Ah, you go in for old women now! Do they pay you, eh—do they pay you? Ah, so you have come to old women, have you? Then you have no longer any need of me. Keep the other one."

She rose, ran to her bodice thrown onto a chair, and began hurriedly to put it on again. He sought to retain her, stammering confusedly: "But, no, Clo, you are silly. I do not know anything about it. Listen now—stay here. Come, now—stay here."

She repeated: "Keep your old woman—keep her. Have a ring made out of her hair—out of her white hair. You have enough of it for that."

With abrupt and swift movements she had dressed herself and put on her bonnet and veil, and when he sought to take hold of her, gave him a smack with all her strength. While he remained bewildered, she opened the door and fled.

As soon as he was alone he was seized with furious anger against that old hag of a Mother Walter. Ah, he would send her about her business, and pretty roughly, too! He bathed his reddened cheek and then went out, in turn meditating vengeance. This time he would not forgive her. Ah, no! He walked down as far as the boulevard, and sauntering along stopped in front of a jeweler's shop to look at a chronometer he had fancied for a long time back, and which was ticketed eighteen hundred francs. He thought all at once, with a thrill of joy at his heart, "If I gain my seventy thousand francs I can afford it."

And he began to think of all the things he would do with these seventy thousand francs. In the first place, he would get elected deputy. Then he would buy his chronometer, and would speculate on the Bourse, and would—

He did not want to go to the office, preferring to consult Madeleine before seeing Walter and writing his article, and started for home. He had reached the Rue Druot, when he stopped short. He had forgotten to ask after the Count de Vaudrec, who lived in the Chaussee d'Antin. He therefore turned back, still sauntering, thinking of a thousand things, mainly pleasant, of his coming fortune, and also of that scoundrel of a Laroche-Mathieu, and that old stickfast of a Madame Walter. He was not uneasy about the wrath of Clotilde, knowing very well that she forgave quickly.

He asked the doorkeeper of the house in which the Count de Vaudrec resided: "How is Monsieur de Vaudrec? I hear that he has been unwell these last few days."

The man replied: "The Count is very bad indeed, sir. They are afraid he will not live through the night; the gout has mounted to his heart."

Du Roy was so startled that he no longer knew what he ought to do. Vaudrec dying! Confused and disquieting ideas shot through his mind that he dared not even admit to himself. He stammered: "Thank you; I will call again," without knowing what he was saying.

Then he jumped into a cab and was driven home. His wife had come in. He went into her room breathless, and said at once: "Have you heard? Vaudrec is dying."

She was sitting down reading a letter. She raised her eyes, and repeating thrice: "Oh! what do you say, what do you say, what do you say?"

"I say that Vaudrec is dying from a fit of gout that has flown to the heart." Then he added: "What do you think of doing?"

She had risen livid, and with her cheeks shaken by a nervous quivering, then she began to cry terribly, hiding her face in her hands. She stood shaken by sobs and torn by grief. But suddenly she mastered her sorrow, and wiping her eyes, said: "I—I am going there—don't bother about me—I don't know when I shall be back—don't wait for me."

He replied: "Very well, dear." They shook hands, and she went off so hurriedly that she forgot her gloves.

George, having dined alone, began to write his article. He did so exactly in accordance with the minister's instructions, giving his readers to understand that the expedition to Morocco would not take place. Then he took it to the office, chatted for a few minutes with the governor, and went out smoking, light-hearted, though he knew not why. His wife had not come home, and he went to bed and fell asleep.

Madeleine came in towards midnight. George, suddenly roused, sat up in bed. "Well?" he asked.

He had never seen her so pale and so deeply moved. She murmured: "He is dead."

"Ah!—and he did not say anything?"

"Nothing. He had lost consciousness when I arrived."

George was thinking. Questions rose to his lips that he did not dare to put. "Come to bed," said he.

She undressed rapidly, and slipped into bed beside him, when he resumed: "Were there any relations present at his death-bed?"

"Only a nephew."

"Ah! Did he see this nephew often?"

"Never. They had not met for ten years."

"Had he any other relatives?"

"No, I do not think so."

"Then it is his nephew who will inherit?"

"I do not know."

"He was very well off, Vaudrec?"

"Yes, very well off."

"Do you know what his fortune was?"

"No, not exactly. One or two millions, perhaps."

He said no more. She blew out the light, and they remained stretched out, side by side, in the darkness—silent, wakeful, and reflecting. He no longer felt inclined for sleep. He now thought the seventy thousand francs promised by Madame Walter insignificant. Suddenly he fancied that Madeleine was crying. He inquired, in order to make certain: "Are you asleep?"

"No."

Her voice was tearful and quavering, and he said: "I forgot to tell you when I came in that your minister has let us in nicely."

"How so?"

He told her at length, with all details, the plan hatched between Laroche-Mathieu and Walter. When he had finished, she asked: "How do you know this?"

He replied: "You will excuse me not telling you. You have your means of information, which I do not seek to penetrate. I have mine, which I wish to keep to myself. I can, in any case, answer for the correctness of my information."

Then she murmured: "Yes, it is quite possible. I fancied they were up to something without us."

But George, who no longer felt sleepy, had drawn closer to his wife, and gently kissed her ear. She repulsed him sharply. "I beg of you to leave me alone. I am not in a mood to romp." He turned resignedly towards the wall, and having closed his eyes, ended by falling asleep.

XIV

The church was draped with black, and over the main entrance a huge scutcheon, surmounted by a coronet, announced to the passers-by that a gentleman was being buried. The ceremony was just over, and those present at it were slowly dispersing, defiling past the coffin and the nephew of the Count de Vaudrec, who was shaking extended hands and returning bows. When George Du Roy and his wife came out of the church they began to walk homeward side by side, silent and preoccupied. At length George said, as though speaking to himself: "Really, it is very strange."

"What, dear?" asked Madeleine.

"That Vaudrec should not have left us anything."

She blushed suddenly, as though a rosy veil had been cast over her white skin, and said: "Why should he have left us anything? There was no reason for it." Then, after a few moments' silence, she went on: "There is perhaps a will in the hands of some notary. We know nothing as yet."

He reflected for a short time, and then murmured: "Yes, it is probable, for, after all, he was the most intimate friend of us both. He dined with us twice a week, called at all hours, and was at home at our place, quite at home in every respect. He loved you like a father, and had no children, no brothers and sisters, nothing but a nephew, and a nephew he never used to see. Yes, there must be a will. I do not care for much, only a remembrance to show that he thought of us, that he loved us, that he recognized the affection we felt for him. He certainly owed us some such mark of friendship."

She said in a pensive and indifferent manner: "It is possible, indeed, that there may be a will."

As they entered their rooms, the man-servant handed a letter to Madeleine. She opened it, and then held it out to her husband. It ran as follows:

> "Office of Maitre Lamaneur, Notary,
> "17 Rue des Vosges.
>
> "MADAME: I have the honor to beg you to favor me with a call here on Tuesday, Wednesday, or Thursday between the hours of two and four, on business concerning you.—I am, etc.—LAMANEUR."

George had reddened in turn. "That is what it must be," said he. "It is strange, though, that it is you who are summoned, and not myself, who am legally the head of the family."

She did not answer at once, but after a brief period of reflection, said: "Shall we go round there by and by?"

"Yes, certainly."

They set out as soon as they had lunched. When they entered Maitre Lamaneur's office, the head clerk rose with marked attention and ushered them in to his master. The notary was a round, little man, round all over. His head looked like a ball nailed onto another ball, which had legs so short that they almost resembled balls too. He bowed, pointed to two chairs, and turning towards Madeleine, said: "Madame, I have sent for you in order to acquaint you with the will of the Count de Vaudrec, in which you are interested."

George could not help muttering: "I thought so."

The notary went on: "I will read to you the document, which is very brief."

He took a paper from a box in front of him, and read as follows:

"I, the undersigned, Paul Emile Cyprien Gontran, Count de Vaudrec, being sound in body and mind, hereby express my last wishes. As death may overtake us at any moment, I wish, in provision of his attacks, to take the precaution of making my will, which will be placed in the hands of Maitre Lamaneur. Having no direct heirs, I leave the whole of my fortune, consisting of stock to the amount of six hundred thousand francs, and landed property worth about five hundred thousand francs, to Madame Claire Madeleine Du Roy without any charge or condition. I beg her to accept this gift of a departed friend as a proof of a deep, devoted, and respectful affection."

The notary added: "That is all. This document is dated last August, and replaces one of the same nature, written two years back, with the name of Madame Claire Madeleine Forestier. I have this first will, too, which would prove, in the case of opposition on the part of the family, that the wishes of Count de Vaudrec did not vary."

Madeleine, very pale, looked at her feet. George nervously twisted the end of his moustache between his fingers. The notary continued after a moment of silence: "It is, of course, understood, sir, that your wife cannot accept the legacy without your consent."

Du Roy rose and said, dryly: "I must ask time to reflect."

The notary, who was smiling, bowed, and said in an amiable tone: "I understand the scruples that cause you to hesitate, sir. I should say that the nephew of Monsieur de Vaudrec, who became acquainted this very morning with his uncle's last wishes, stated that he was prepared to respect them, provided the sum of a hundred thousand francs was allowed him. In my opinion the will is unattackable, but a law-suit would cause a stir, which it may perhaps suit you to avoid. The world often judges things ill-naturedly. In any case, can you give me your answer on all these points before Saturday?"

George bowed, saying: "Yes, sir."

Then he bowed again ceremoniously, ushered out his wife, who had remained silent, and went out himself with so stiff an air that the notary no longer smiled.

As soon as they got home, Du Roy abruptly closed the door, and throwing his hat onto the bed, said: "You were Vaudrec's mistress."

Madeleine, who was taking off her veil, turned round with a start, exclaiming: "I? Oh!"

"Yes, you. A man does not leave the whole of his fortune to a woman, unless—"

She was trembling, and was unable to remove the pins fastening the transparent tissue. After a moment's reflection she stammered, in an agitated tone: "Come, come—you are mad—you are—you are. Did not you, yourself, just now have hopes that he would leave us something?"

George remained standing beside her, following all her emotions like a magistrate seeking to note the least faltering on the part of an accused. He said, laying stress on every word: "Yes, he might have left something to me, your husband—to me, his friend—you understand, but not to you—my wife. The distinction is capital, essential from the point of propriety and of public opinion."

Madeleine in turn looked at him fixedly in the eyes, in profound and singular fashion, as though seeking to read something there, as though trying to discover that unknown part of a human being which we never fathom, and of which we can scarcely even catch rapid glimpses in those moments of carelessness or inattention, which are like doors left open, giving onto the mysterious depths of the mind. She said slowly: "It seems to me, however, that a legacy of this importance would have been looked on as at least equally strange left to you."

He asked abruptly: "Why so?"

She said: "Because—" hesitated, and then continued: "Because you are my husband, and have only known him for a short time, after all—because I have been his friend for a very long while—and because his first will, made during Forestier's lifetime, was already in my favor."

George began to stride up and down. He said: "You cannot accept."

She replied in a tone of indifference: "Precisely so; then it is not worth while waiting till Saturday, we can let Maitre Lamaneur know at once."

He stopped short in front of her, and they again stood for some moments with their eyes riveted on one another, striving to fathom the impenetrable secret of their hearts, to cut down to the quick of their thoughts. They tried to see one another's conscience unveiled in an ardent and mute interrogation; the struggle of two beings who, living side by side, were always ignorant of one another, suspecting, sniffing round, watching, but never understanding one another to the muddy depths of their souls. And suddenly he murmured to her face, in a low voice: "Come, admit that you were De Vaudrec's mistress."

She shrugged her shoulders, saying: "You are ridiculous. Vaudrec was very fond of me, very—but there was nothing more—never."

He stamped his foot. "You lie. It is not possible."

She replied, quietly: "It is so, though."

He began to walk up and down again, and then, halting once more, said: "Explain, then, how he came to leave the whole of his fortune to you."

She did so in a careless and disinterested tone, saying: "It is quite simple. As you said just now, he had only ourselves for friends, or rather myself, for he has known me from a child. My mother was a companion at the house of some relatives of his. He was always coming here, and as he had no natural heirs he thought of me. That there was a little love for me in the matter is possible. But where is the woman who has not been loved thus? Why should not such secret, hidden affection have placed my name at the tip of his pen when he thought of expressing his last wishes? He brought me flowers every Monday. You were not at all astonished at that, and yet he did not bring you any, did he? Now he has given me his fortune for the same reason, and because he had no one to offer it to. It would have been, on the contrary, very surprising for him to have left it to you. Why should he have done so? What were you to him?"

She spoke so naturally and quietly that George hesitated. He said, however: "All the same, we cannot accept this inheritance under such conditions. The effect would be deplorable. All the world would believe it; all the world would gossip about it, and laugh at me. My fellow journalists are already only too disposed to feel jealous of me and to attack me. I should have, before anyone, a care for my honor and my reputation. It is impossible for me to allow my wife to accept a legacy of this kind from a man whom public report has already assigned to her as a lover. Forestier might perhaps have tolerated it, but not me."

She murmured, mildly: "Well, dear, do not let us accept it. It will be a million the less in our pockets, that is all."

He was still walking up and down, and began to think aloud, speaking for his wife's benefit without addressing himself directly to her: "Yes, a million, so much the worse. He did not understand, in making his will, what a fault in tact, what a breach of propriety he was committing. He did not see in what a false, a ridiculous position he would place me. Everything is a matter of detail in this life. He should have left me half; that would have settled everything."

He sat down, crossed his legs, and began to twist the end of his moustache, as he did in moments of boredom, uneasiness, and difficult reflection. Madeleine took up some embroidery at which she worked from time to time, and said, while selecting her wools: "I have only to hold my tongue. It is for you to reflect."

He was a long time without replying, and then said, hesitatingly: "The world will never understand that Vaudrec made you his sole heiress, and that I allowed it. To receive his fortune in that way would be an acknowledgment on your part of a guilty connection, and on mine of a shameful complaisance. Do you understand now how our acceptance of it would be interpreted? It would be necessary to find a side issue, some clever way of palliating matters. To let it go abroad, for instance, that he had divided the money between us, leaving half to the husband and half to the wife."

She observed: "I do not see how that can be done, since the will is plain."

"Oh, it is very simple. You could leave me half the inheritance by a deed of gift. We have no children, so it is feasible. In that way the mouth of public malevolence would be closed."

She replied, somewhat impatiently: "I do not see any the more how the mouth of public malevolence is to be closed, since the will is there, signed by Vaudrec?"

He said, angrily: "Have we any need to show it and to paste it up on all the walls? You are really stupid. We will say that the Count de Vaudrec left his fortune between us. That is all. But you cannot accept this legacy without my authorization. I will only give it on condition of a division, which will hinder me from becoming a laughing stock."

She looked at him again with a penetrating glance, and said: "As you like. I am agreeable."

Then he rose, and began to walk up and down again. He seemed to be hesitating anew, and now avoided his wife's penetrating glance. He was saying: "No, certainly not. Perhaps it would be better to give it up altogether. That is more worthy, more correct, more honorable. And yet by this plan nothing could be imagined against us—absolutely nothing. The most unscrupulous people could only admit things as they were." He paused in front of Madeleine. "Well, then, if you like, darling, I will go back alone to Maitre Lamaneur to explain matters to him and consult him. I will tell him of my scruples, and add that we have arrived at the notion of a division to prevent gossip. From the moment that I accept half this inheritance, it is plain that no one has the right to smile. It is equal to saying aloud: 'My wife accepts because I accept—I, her husband, the best judge of what she may do without compromising herself. Otherwise a scandal would have arisen.'"

Madeleine merely murmured: "Just as you like."

He went on with a flow of words: "Yes, it is all as clear as daylight with this arrangement of a division in two. We inherit from a friend who did not want to make any difference between us, any distinction; who did not wish to appear to say: 'I prefer one or the other after death, as I did during life.' He liked the wife best, be it understood, but in leaving the fortune equally to both, he wished plainly to express that his preference was purely platonic. And you may be sure that, if he had thought of it, that is what he would have done. He did not reflect. He did not foresee the consequences. As you said very appropriately just now, it was you to whom he offered flowers every week, it is to you he wished to leave his last remembrance, without taking into consideration that—"

She checked him, with a shade of irritation: "All right; I understand. You have no need to make so many explanations. Go to the notary's at once."

He stammered, reddening: "You are right. I am off."

He took his hat, and then, at the moment of going out, said: "I will try to settle the difficulty with the nephew for fifty thousand francs, eh?"

She replied, with dignity: "No. Give him the hundred thousand francs he asks. Take them from my share, if you like."

He muttered, shamefacedly: "Oh, no; we will share that. Giving up fifty thousand francs apiece, there still remains to us a clear million." He added: "Good-bye, then, for the present, Made." And he went off to explain to the notary the plan which he asserted had been imagined by his wife.

They signed the next day a deed of gift of five hundred thousand francs, which Madeleine Du Roy abandoned to her husband. On leaving the notary's office, as the day was fine, George suggested that they should walk as far as the boulevards. He showed himself pleasant and full of attention and affection. He laughed, pleased at everything, while she remained thoughtful and somewhat severe.

It was a somewhat cool autumn day. The people in the streets seemed in a hurry, and walked rapidly. Du Roy led his wife to the front of the shop in which he had so often gazed at the longed-for chronometer. "Shall I stand you some jewelry?" said he.

She replied, indifferently: "Just as you like."

They went in, and he asked: "What would you prefer—a necklace, a bracelet, or a pair of earrings?"

The sight of the trinkets in gold, and precious stones overcame her studied coolness, and she scanned with kindling and inquisitive eyes the glass cases filled with jewelry. And, suddenly moved by desire, said: "That is a very pretty bracelet."

It was a chain of quaint pattern, every link of which had a different stone set in it.

George inquired: "How much is this bracelet?"

"Three thousand francs, sir," replied the jeweler.

"If you will let me have it for two thousand five hundred, it is a bargain."

The man hesitated, and then replied: "No, sir; that is impossible."

Du Roy went on: "Come, you can throw in that chronometer for fifteen hundred; that will make four thousand, which I will pay at once. Is it agreed? If not, I will go somewhere else."

The jeweler, in a state of perplexity, ended by agreeing, saying: "Very good, sir."

And the journalist, after giving his address, added: "You will have the monogram, G. R. C., engraved on the chronometer under a baron's coronet."

Madeleine, surprised, began to smile, and when they went out, took his arm with a certain affection. She found him really clever and capable. Now that he had an income, he needed a title. It was quite right.

The jeweler bowed them out, saying: "You can depend upon me; it will be ready on Thursday, Baron."

They paused before the Vaudeville, at which a new piece was being played.

"If you like," said he, "we will go to the theater this evening. Let us see if we can have a box."

They took a box, and he continued: "Suppose we dine at a restaurant."

"Oh, yes; I should like that!"

He was as happy as a king, and sought what else they could do. "Suppose we go and ask Madame de Marelle to spend the evening with us. Her husband is at home, I hear, and I shall be delighted to see him."

They went there. George, who slightly dreaded the first meeting with his mistress, was not ill-pleased that his wife was present to prevent anything like an explanation. But Clotilde did not seem to remember anything against him, and even obliged her husband to accept the invitation.

The dinner was lovely, and the evening pleasant. George and Madeleine got home late. The gas was out, and to light them upstairs, the journalist struck a wax match from time to time. On reaching the first-floor landing the flame, suddenly starting forth as he struck, caused their two lit-up faces to show in the glass standing out against the darkness of the staircase. They resembled phantoms, appearing and ready to vanish into the night.

Du Roy raised his hand to light up their reflections, and said, with a laugh of triumph: "Behold the millionaires!"

XV

The conquest of Morocco had been accomplished two months back. France, mistress of Tangiers, held the whole of the African shore of the Mediterranean as far as Tripoli, and had guaranteed the debt of the newly annexed territory. It was said that two ministers had gained a score of millions over the business, and Laroche-Mathieu was almost openly named. As to Walter, no one in Paris was ignorant of the fact that he had brought down two birds with one stone, and made thirty or forty millions out of the loan and eight to ten millions out of the copper and iron mines, as well as out of a large stretch of territory bought for almost nothing prior to the conquest, and sold after the French occupation to companies formed to promote colonization. He had become in a few days one of the lords of creation, one of those omnipotent financiers more powerful than monarchs who cause heads to bow, mouths to stammer, and all that is base, cowardly, and envious, to well up from the depths of the human heart. He was no longer the Jew Walter, head of a shady bank, manager of a fishy paper, deputy suspected of illicit jobbery. He was Monsieur Walter, the wealthy Israelite.

He wished to show himself off. Aware of the monetary embarrassments of the Prince de Carlsbourg, who owned one of the finest mansions in the Rue de Faubourg, Saint Honoré, with a garden giving onto the Champs Elysées, he proposed to him to buy house and furniture, without shifting a stick, within twenty-four hours. He offered three millions, and the prince, tempted by the amount, accepted. The following day Walter installed himself in his new domicile. Then he had another idea, the idea of a conqueror who wishes to conquer Paris, the idea of a Bonaparte. The whole city was flocking at that moment to see a great painting by the Hungarian artist, Karl Marcowitch, exhibited at a dealer's named Jacques Lenoble, and representing Christ walking on the water. The art critics, filled with enthusiasm, declared the picture the most superb masterpiece of the century. Walter bought it for four hundred thousand francs, and took it away, thus cutting suddenly short a flow of public curiosity, and forcing the whole of Paris to speak of him in terms of envy, blame, or approbation. Then he had it announced in the papers that he would invite everyone known in Parisian society to view at his house some evening this triumph of the foreign master, in order that it might not be said that he had hidden away a work of art. His house would be open; let those who would, come. It would be enough to show at the door the letter of invitation.

This ran as follows: "Monsieur and Madame Walter beg of you to honor them with your company on December 30th, between 9 and 12 p. m., to view the picture by Karl Marcowitch, 'Jesus Walking on the Waters,' lit up by electric light." Then, as a postscript, in small letters: "Dancing after midnight." So those who wished to stay could, and out of these the Walters would recruit their future acquaintances. The others would view the picture, the mansion, and their owners with worldly curiosity, insolent and indifferent, and would then go away as they came. But Daddy Walter knew very well that they would return later on, as they had come to his Israelite brethren grown rich like himself. The first thing was that they should enter his house, all these titled paupers who were mentioned in the papers, and they would enter it to see the face of a man who had gained fifty millions in six weeks; they would enter it to see and note who else came there; they would also enter it because he had had the good taste and dexterity to summon them to admire a Christian picture at the home of a child of Israel. He seemed to say to them: "You see I have given five hundred thousand francs for the religious masterpiece of Marcowitch, 'Jesus Walking on the Waters.' And this masterpiece will always remain before my eyes in the house of the Jew, Walter."

In society there had been a great deal of talk over these invitations, which, after all, did not pledge one in any way. One could go there as one went to see watercolors at Monsieur Petit's. The Walters owned a masterpiece, and threw open their doors one evening so that everyone could admire it. Nothing could be better. The *Vie Francaise* for a fortnight past had published every morning a note on this coming event of the 30th December, and had striven to kindle public curiosity.

Du Roy was furious at the governor's triumph. He had thought himself rich with the five hundred thousand francs extorted from his wife, and now he held himself to be poor, fearfully poor, when comparing his modest fortune with the shower of millions that had fallen around him, without his being able to pick any of it up. His envious hatred waxed daily. He was angry with everyone—with the Walters, whom he had not been to see at their new home; with his wife, who, deceived by Laroche-Mathieu, had persuaded him not to invest in the Morocco loan; and, above all, with the minister who had tricked him, who had made use of him, and who dined at his table twice a week. George was his agent, his secretary, his mouthpiece, and when he was writing from his dictation felt wild longings to strangle this triumphant foe. As a minister, Laroche-Mathieu had shown modesty in mien, and in order to retain his portfolio, did not let it be seen that he was gorged with gold. But Du Roy felt the presence of this gold in the haughtier tone of the parvenu barrister, in his more insolent gestures, his more daring affirmation, his perfect self-confidence. Laroche-Mathieu now reigned in the Du Roy household, having taken the place and the days of the Count de Vaudrec, and spoke to the servants like a second master. George tolerated him with a quiver running through him like a dog who wants to bite, and dares not. But he was often harsh and brutal towards Madeleine, who shrugged her shoulders and treated him like a clumsy child. She was, besides, astonished at his continual ill-humor, and repeated: "I cannot make you out. You are always grumbling, and yet your position is a splendid one."

He would turn his back without replying.

He had declared at first that he would not go to the governor's entertainment, and that he would never more set foot in the house of that dirty Jew. For two months Madame Walter had been writing to him daily, begging him to come, to make an appointment with her whenever he liked, in order, she said, that she might hand over the seventy thousand francs she had gained for him. He did not reply, and threw these despairing letters into the fire. Not that he had renounced receiving his share of their profits, but he wanted to madden her, to treat her with contempt, to trample her under feet. She was too rich. He wanted to show his pride. The very day of the exhibition of the picture, as Madeleine pointed out to him that he was very wrong not to go, he replied: "Hold your tongue. I shall stay at home."

Then after dinner he suddenly said: "It will be better after all to undergo this affliction. Get dressed at once."

She was expecting this, and said: "I will be ready in a quarter of an hour." He dressed growling, and even in the cab he continued to spit out his spleen.

The court-yard of the Carlsbourg mansion was lit up by four electric lights, looking like four small bluish moons, one at each corner. A splendid carpet was laid down the high flight of steps, on each of which a footman in livery stood motionless as a statue.

Du Roy muttered: "Here's a fine show-off for you," and shrugged his shoulders, his heart contracted by jealousy.

His wife said: "Be quiet and do likewise."

They went in and handed their heavy outer garments to the footmen who advanced to meet them. Several ladies were also there with their husbands, freeing themselves from their furs. Murmurs of: "It is very beautiful, very beautiful," could be heard. The immense entrance hall was hung with tapestry, representing the adventures of Mars and Venus. To the right and left were the two branches of a colossal double staircase, which met on the first floor. The banisters were a marvel of wrought-iron work, the dull old gilding of which glittered with discreet luster beside the steps of pink marble. At the entrance to the reception-rooms two little girls, one in a pink folly costume, and the other in a blue one, offered a bouquet of flowers to each lady. This was held to be charming.

The reception-rooms were already crowded. Most of the ladies were in outdoor dress, showing that they came there as to any other exhibition. Those who intended remaining for the ball were bare armed and bare necked. Madame Walter, surrounded by her friends, was in the second room acknowledging the greetings of the visitors. Many of these did not know her, and walked about as though in a museum, without troubling themselves about the masters of the house.

When she perceived Du Roy she grew livid, and made a movement as though to advance towards him. Then she remained motionless, awaiting him. He greeted her ceremoniously, while Madeleine overwhelmed her with affection and compliments. Then George left his wife with her and lost himself in the crowd, to listen to the spiteful things that assuredly must be said.

Five reception-rooms opened one into the other, hung with costly stuffs, Italian embroideries, or oriental rugs of varying shades and styles, and bearing on their walls pictures by old masters. People stopped, above all, to admire a small room in the Louis XVI style, a kind of boudoir, lined with silk, with bouquets of roses on a pale blue ground. The furniture, of gilt wood, upholstered in the same material, was admirably finished.

George recognized some well-known people—the Duchess de Ferraciné, the Count and Countess de Ravenal, General Prince d'Andremont, the beautiful Marchioness des Dunes, and all those folk who are seen at first performances. He was suddenly seized by the arm, and a young and pleased voice murmured in his ear: "Ah! here you are at last, you naughty Pretty-boy. How is it one no longer sees you?"

It was Susan Walter, scanning him with her enamel-like eyes from beneath the curly cloud of her fair hair. He was delighted to see her again, and frankly pressed her hand. Then, excusing himself, he said: "I have not been able to come. I have had so much to do during the past two months that I have not been out at all."

She said, with her serious air: "That is wrong, very wrong. You have caused us a great deal of pain, for we adore you, mamma and I. As to myself, I cannot get on without you. When you are not here I am bored to death. You see I tell you so plainly, so that you may no longer have the right of disappearing like that. Give me your arm, I will show you 'Jesus Walking on the Waters' myself; it is right away at the end, beyond the conservatory.

Papa had it put there so that they should be obliged to see everything before they could get to it. It is astonishing how he is showing off this place."

They went on quietly among the crowd. People turned round to look at this good-looking fellow and this charming little doll. A well-known painter said: "What a pretty pair. They go capitally together."

George thought: "If I had been really clever, this is the girl I should have married. It was possible. How is it I did not think of it? How did I come to take that other one? What a piece of stupidity. We always act too impetuously, and never reflect sufficiently."

And envy, bitter envy, sank drop by drop into his mind like a gall, embittering all his pleasures, and rendering existence hateful.

Susan was saying: "Oh! do come often, Pretty-boy; we will go in for all manner of things now, papa is so rich. We will amuse ourselves like madcaps."

He answered, still following up his idea: "Oh! you will marry now. You will marry some prince, a ruined one, and we shall scarcely see one another."

She exclaimed, frankly: "Oh! no, not yet. I want someone who pleases me, who pleases me a great deal, who pleases me altogether. I am rich enough for two."

He smiled with a haughty and ironical smile, and began to point out to her people that were passing, very noble folk who had sold their rusty titles to the daughters of financiers like herself, and who now lived with or away from their wives, but free, impudent, known, and respected. He concluded with: "I will not give you six months before you are caught with that same bait. You will be a marchioness, a duchess or a princess, and will look down on me from a very great height, miss."

She grew indignant, tapped him on the arm with her fan, and vowed that she would marry according to the dictates of her heart.

He sneered: "We shall see about all that, you are too rich."

She remarked: "But you, too, have come in for an inheritance."

He uttered in a tone of contempt: "Oh! not worth speaking about. Scarcely twenty thousand francs a year, not much in these days."

"But your wife has also inherited."

"Yes. A million between us. Forty thousand francs' income. We cannot even keep a carriage on it."

They had reached the last of the reception-rooms, and before them lay the conservatory—a huge winter garden full of tall, tropical trees, sheltering clumps of rare flowers. Penetrating beneath this somber greenery, through which the light streamed like a flood of silver, they breathed the warm odor of damp earth, and an air heavy with perfumes. It was a strange sensation, at once sweet, unwholesome, and pleasant, of a nature that was artificial, soft, and enervating. They walked on carpets exactly like moss, between two thick clumps of shrubs. All at once Du Roy noticed on his left, under a wide dome of palms, a broad basin of white marble, large enough to bathe in, and on the edge of which four large Delft swans poured forth water through their open beaks. The bottom of the basin was strewn with golden sand, and swimming about in it were some enormous goldfish, quaint Chinese monsters, with projecting eyes and scales edged with blue, mandarins of the waters, who recalled, thus suspended above this gold-colored ground, the embroideries of the Flowery Land. The journalist halted with beating heart. He said to himself: "Here is luxury. These are the houses in which one ought to live. Others have arrived at it. Why should not I?"

He thought of means of doing so; did not find them at once, and grew irritated at his powerlessness. His companion, somewhat thoughtful, did not speak. He looked at her in sidelong fashion, and again thought: "To marry this little puppet would suffice."

But Susan all at once seemed to wake up. "Attention!" said she; and pushing George through a group which barred their way, she made him turn sharply to the right.

In the midst of a thicket of strange plants, which extended in the air their quivering leaves, opening like hands with slender fingers, was seen the motionless figure of a man standing on the sea. The effect was surprising. The picture, the sides of which were hidden in the moving foliage, seemed a black spot upon a fantastic and striking horizon. It had to be carefully looked at in order to understand it. The frame cut the center of the ship in which were the apostles, scarcely lit up by the oblique rays from a lantern, the full light of which one of them, seated on the bulwarks, was casting upon the approaching Savior. Jesus was advancing with his foot upon a wave, which flattened itself submissively and caressingly beneath the divine tread. All was dark about him. Only the stars shone in the sky. The faces of the apostles, in the vague light of the lantern, seemed convulsed with surprise. It was a wonderful and unexpected work of a master; one of those works which agitate the mind and give you something to dream of for years. People who look at such things at the outset remain silent, and then go thoughtfully away, and only speak later on of the worth of the painting.

Du Roy, having contemplated it for some time, said: "It is nice to be able to afford such trifles."

But as he was pushed against by others coming to see it, he went away, still keeping on his arm Susan's little hand, which he squeezed slightly. She said: "Would you like a glass of champagne? Come to the refreshment buffet. We shall find papa there."

And they slowly passed back through the saloons, in which the crowd was increasing, noisy and at home, the fashionable crowd of a public fête. George all at once thought he heard a voice say: "It is Laroche-Mathieu and Madame Du Roy." These words flitted past his ear like those distant sounds borne by the wind. Whence came they? He looked about on all sides, and indeed saw his wife passing by on the minister's arm. They were chatting intimately in a low tone, smiling, and with their eyes fixed on one another's. He fancied he noticed that people whispered as they looked at them, and he felt within him a stupid and brutal desire to spring upon them, these two creatures, and smite them down. She was making him ridiculous. He thought of Forestier. Perhaps they were saying: "That cuckold Du Roy." Who was she? A little parvenu sharp enough, but really not over-gifted with parts. People visited him because they feared him, because they felt his strength, but they must speak in unrestrained fashion of this little journalistic household. He would never make any great way with this woman, who would always render his home a suspected one, who would always compromise herself, whose very bearing betrayed the woman of intrigue. She would now be a cannon ball riveted to his ankle. Ah! if he had only known, if he had only guessed. What a bigger game he would have played. What a fine match he might have won with this little Susan for stakes. How was it he had been blind enough not to understand that?

They reached the dining-room—an immense apartment, with marble columns, and walls hung with old tapestry. Walter perceived his descriptive writer, and darted forward to take him by the hands. He was intoxicated with joy. "Have you seen everything? Have you shown him everything, Susan? What a lot of people, eh, Pretty-boy! Did you see the Prince de Guerche? He came and drank a glass of punch here just now," he exclaimed.

Then he darted towards the Senator Rissolin, who was towing along his wife, bewildered, and bedecked like a stall at a fair. A gentleman bowed to Susan, a tall, thin fellow, slightly bald, with yellow whiskers, and that air of good breeding which is everywhere recognizable. George heard his name mentioned, the Marquis de Cazolles, and became suddenly jealous of him. How long had she known him? Since her accession to wealth, no doubt. He divined a suitor.

He was taken by the arm. It was Norbert de Varenne. The old poet was airing his long hair and worn dress-coat with a weary and indifferent air. "This is what they call amusing themselves," said he. "By and by they will dance, and then they will go bed, and the little girls will be delighted. Have some champagne. It is capital."

He had a glass filled for himself, and bowing to Du Roy, who had taken another, said: "I drink to the triumph of wit over wealth." Then he added softly: "Not that wealth on the part of others hurts me; or that I am angry at it. But I protest on principle."

George no longer listened to him. He was looking for Susan, who had just disappeared with the Marquis de Cazolles, and abruptly quitting Norbert de Varenne, set out in pursuit of the young girl. A dense crowd in quest of refreshments checked him. When he at length made his way through it, he found himself face to face with the de Marelles. He was still in the habit of meeting the wife, but he had not for some time past met the husband, who seized both his hands, saying: "How can I thank you, my dear fellow, for the advice you gave me through Clotilde. I have gained close on a hundred thousand francs over the Morocco loan. It is to you I owe them. You are a valuable friend."

Several men turned round to look at the pretty and elegant brunette. Du Roy replied: "In exchange for that service, my dear fellow, I am going to take your wife, or rather to offer her my arm. Husband and wife are best apart, you know."

Monsieur de Marelle bowed, saying: "You are quite right. If I lose you, we will meet here in an hour."

"Exactly."

The pair plunged into the crowd, followed by the husband. Clotilde kept saying: "How lucky these Walters are! That is what it is to have business intelligence."

George replied: "Bah! Clever men always make a position one way or another."

She said: "Here are two girls who will have from twenty to thirty millions apiece. Without reckoning that Susan is pretty."

He said nothing. His own idea, coming from another's mouth, irritated him. She had not yet seen the picture of "Jesus Walking on the Water," and he proposed to take her to it. They amused themselves by talking scandal of the people they recognized, and making fun of those they did not. Saint-Potin passed by, bearing on the lapel of his coat a number of decorations, which greatly amused them. An ex-ambassador following him showed far fewer.

Du Roy remarked: "What a mixed salad of society."

Boisrenard, who shook hands with him, had also adorned his buttonhole with the green and yellow ribbon worn on the day of the duel. The Viscountess de Percemur, fat and bedecked, was chatting with a duke in the little Louis XVI boudoir.

George whispered: "An amorous *tête-à-tête*."

But on passing through the greenhouse, he noticed his wife seated beside Laroche-Mathieu, both almost hidden behind a clump of plants. They seemed to be asserting: "We have appointed a meeting here, a meeting in public. For we do not care a rap what people think."

Madame de Marelle agreed that the Jesus of Karl Marcowitch was astounding, and they retraced their steps. They had lost her husband. George inquired: "And Laurine, is she still angry with me?"

"Yes, still so as much as ever. She refuses to see you, and walks away when you are spoken of."

He did not reply. The sudden enmity of this little girl vexed and oppressed him. Susan seized on them as they passed through a doorway, exclaiming: "Ah! here you are. Well, Pretty-boy, you must remain alone. I am going to take away Clotilde to show her my room."

The two moved rapidly away, gliding through the throng with that undulating snake-like motion women know how to adopt in a crowd. Almost immediately a voice murmured: "George."

It was Madame Walter, who went on in a low tone: "Oh! how ferociously cruel you are. How you do make me suffer without reason. I told Susan to get your companion away in order to be able to say a word to you. Listen, I must speak to you this evening, I must, or you don't know what I will do. Go into the conservatory. You will find a door on the left leading into the garden. Follow the path in front of it. At the end of it you will find an arbor. Wait for me there in ten minutes' time. If you won't, I declare to you that I will create a scene here at once."

He replied loftily: "Very well. I will be at the spot you mention within ten minutes."

And they separated. But Jacques Rival almost made him behindhand. He had taken him by the arm and was telling him a lot of things in a very excited manner. He had no doubt come from the refreshment buffet. At length Du Roy left him in the hands of Monsieur de Marelle, whom he had come across, and bolted. He still had to take precautions not to be seen by his wife or Laroche-Mathieu. He succeeded, for they seemed deeply interested in something, and found himself in the garden. The cold air struck him like an ice bath. He thought: "Confound it, I shall catch cold," and tied his pocket-handkerchief round his neck. Then he slowly went along the walk, seeing his way with difficulty after coming out of the bright light of the reception-rooms. He could distinguish to the right and left leafless shrubs, the branches of which were quivering. Light filtered through their branches, coming from the windows of the mansion. He saw something white in the middle of the path in front of him, and Madame Walter, with bare arms and bosom, said in a quivering voice; "Ah here you are; you want to kill me, then?"

He answered quickly: "No melodramatics, I beg of you, or I shall bolt at once."

She had seized him round the neck, and with her lips close to his, said: "But what have I done to you? You are behaving towards me like a wretch. What have I done to you?"

He tried to repulse her. "You wound your hair round every one of my buttons the last time I saw you, and it almost brought about a rupture between my wife and myself."

She was surprised for a moment, and then, shaking her head, said: "Oh! your wife would not mind. It was one of your mistresses who had made a scene over it."

"I have no mistresses."

"Nonsense. But why do you no longer ever come to see me? Why do you refuse to come to dinner, even once a week, with me? What I suffer is fearful. I love you to that degree that I no longer have a thought that is not for you; that I see you continually before my eyes; that I can no longer say a word without being afraid of uttering your name. You cannot understand that, I know. It seems to me that I am seized in some one's clutches, tied up in a sack, I don't know what. Your remembrance, always with me, clutches my throat, tears my chest, breaks my legs so as to no longer leave me strength to walk. And I remain like an animal sitting all day on a chair thinking of you."

He looked at her with astonishment. She was no longer the big frolicsome tomboy he had known, but a bewildered despairing woman, capable of anything. A vague project, however, arose in his mind. He replied: "My dear, love is not eternal. We take and we leave one another. But when it drags on, as between us two, it becomes a terrible drag. I will have no more of it. That is the truth. However, if you can be reasonable, and receive and treat me as a friend, I will come as I used to. Do you feel capable of that?"

She placed her two bare arms on George's coat, and murmured: "I am capable of anything in order to see you."

"Then it is agreed on," said he; "we are friends, and nothing more."

She stammered: "It is agreed on;" and then, holding out her lips to him: "One more kiss; the last."

He refused gently, saying: "No, we must keep to our agreement."

She turned aside, wiping away a couple of tears, and then, drawing from her bosom a bundle of papers tied with pink silk ribbon, offered it to Du Roy, saying: "Here; it is your share of the profit in the Morocco affair. I was so pleased to have gained it for you. Here, take it."

He wanted to refuse, observing: "No, I will not take that money."

Then she grew indignant. "Ah! so you won't take it now. It is yours, yours, only. If you do not take it, I will throw it into the gutter. You won't act like that, George?"

He received the little bundle, and slipped it into his pocket.

"We must go in," said he, "you will catch cold."

She murmured: "So much the better, if I could die."

She took one of his hands, kissed it passionately, with rage and despair, and fled towards the mansion. He returned, quietly reflecting. Then he re-entered the conservatory with haughty forehead and smiling lip. His wife and Laroche-Mathieu were no longer there. The crowd was thinning. It was becoming evident that they would not stay for the dance. He perceived Susan arm-in-arm with her sister. They both came towards him to ask him to dance the first quadrille with the Count de Latour Yvelin.

He was astonished, and asked: "Who is he, too?"

Susan answered maliciously: "A new friend of my sister's." Rose blushed, and murmured: "You are very spiteful, Susan; he is no more my friend than yours."

Susan smiled, saying: "Oh! I know all about it."

Rose annoyed, turned her back on them and went away. Du Roy familiarly took the elbow of the young girl left standing beside him, and said in his caressing voice: "Listen, my dear, you believe me to be your friend?"

"Yes, Pretty-boy."

"You have confidence in me?" "Quite."

"You remember what I said to you just now?"

"What about?"

"About your marriage, or rather about the man you are going to marry." "Yes."

"Well, then, you will promise me one thing?"

"Yes; but what is it?"

"To consult me every time that your hand is asked for, and not to accept anyone without taking my advice."

"Very well."

"And to keep this a secret between us two. Not a word of it to your father or your mother."

"Not a word."

"It is a promise, then?" "It is a promise."

Rival came up with a bustling air. "Mademoiselle, your papa wants you for the dance."

She said: "Come along, Pretty-boy."

But he refused, having made up his mind to leave at once, wishing to be alone in order to think. Too many new ideas had entered his mind, and he began to look for his wife. In a short time he saw her drinking chocolate at the buffet with two gentlemen unknown to him. She introduced her husband without mentioning their names to him. After a few moments, he said, "Shall we go?"

"When you like."

She took his arm, and they walked back through the reception-rooms, in which the public were growing few. She said: "Where is Madame Walter, I should like to wish her good-bye?"

"It is better not to. She would try to keep us for the ball, and I have had enough of this."

"That is so, you are quite right."

All the way home they were silent. But as soon as they were in their room Madeleine said smilingly, before even taking off her veil. "I have a surprise for you."

He growled ill-temperedly: "What is it?"

"Guess." "I will make no such effort."

"Well, the day after to-morrow is the first of January."

"Yes."

"The time for New Year's gifts."

"Yes."

"Here's one for you that Laroche-Mathieu gave me just now."

She gave him a little black box resembling a jewel-case. He opened it indifferently, and saw the cross of the Legion of Honor. He grew somewhat pale, then smiled, and said: "I should have preferred ten millions. That did not cost him much."

She had expected an outburst of joy, and was irritated at this coolness. "You are really incredible. Nothing satisfies you now," said she.

He replied, tranquilly: "That man is only paying his debt, and he still owes me a great deal."

She was astonished at his tone, and resumed: "It is though, a big thing at your age."

He remarked: "All things are relative. I could have something bigger now."

He had taken the case, and placing it on the mantel-shelf, looked for some moments at the glittering star it contained. Then he closed it and went to bed, shrugging his shoulders.

The *Journal Officiel* of the first of January announced the nomination of Monsieur Prosper George Du Roy, journalist, to the dignity of chevalier of the Legion of Honor, for special services. The name was written in two words, which gave George more pleasure than the derivation itself.

An hour after having read this piece of news he received a note from Madame Walter begging him to come and dine with her that evening with his wife, to celebrate his new honors. He hesitated for a few moments, and then throwing this note, written in ambiguous terms, into the fire, said to Madeleine:

"We are going to dinner at the Walter's this evening."

She was astonished. "Why, I thought you never wanted to set foot in the house again."

He only remarked: "I have changed my mind."

When they arrived Madame Walter was alone in the little Louis XVI. boudoir she had adopted for the reception of personal friends. Dressed in black, she had powdered her hair, which rendered her charming. She had the air at a distance of an old woman, and close at hand, of a young one, and when one looked at her well, of a pretty snare for the eyes.

"You are in mourning?" inquired Madeleine.

She replied, sadly: "Yes, and no. I have not lost any relative. But I have reached the age when one wears the mourning of one's life. I wear it to-day to inaugurate it. In future I shall wear it in my heart."

Du Roy thought: "Will this resolution hold good?"

The dinner was somewhat dull. Susan alone chattered incessantly. Rose seemed preoccupied. The journalist was warmly congratulated. During the evening they strolled chatting through the saloons and the conservatory. As Du Roy was walking in the rear with Madame Walter, she checked him by the arm.

"Listen," said she, in a low voice, "I will never speak to you of anything again, never. But come and see me, George. It is impossible for me to live without you, impossible. It is indescribable torture. I feel you, I cherish you before my eyes, in my heart, all day and all night. It is as though you had caused me to drink a poison which was eating me away within. I cannot bear it, no, I cannot bear it. I am willing to be nothing but an old woman for you. I have made my hair white to show you so, but come here, only come here from time to time as a friend."

She had taken his hand and was squeezing it, crushing it, burying her nails in his flesh.

He answered, quietly: "It is understood, then. It is useless to speak of all that again. You see I came to-day at once on receiving your letter."

Walter, who had walked on in advance with his two daughters and Madeleine, was waiting for Du Roy beside the picture of "Jesus Walking on the Waters."

"Fancy," said he, laughing, "I found my wife yesterday on her knees before this picture, as if in a chapel. She was paying her devotions. How I did laugh."

Madame Walter replied in a firm voice—a voice thrilling with secret exultation: "It is that Christ who will save my soul. He gives me strength and courage every time I look at Him." And pausing in front of the Divinity standing amidst the waters, she murmured: "How handsome he is. How afraid of Him those men are, and yet how they love Him. Look at His head, His eyes—how simple yet how supernatural at the same time."

Susan exclaimed, "But He resembles you, Pretty-boy. I am sure He resembles you. If you had a beard, or if He was clean shaven, you would be both alike. Oh, but it is striking!"

She insisted on his standing beside the picture, and they all, indeed, recognized that the two faces resembled one another. Everyone was astonished. Walter thought it very singular. Madeleine, smiling, declared that Jesus had a more manly air. Madame Walter stood motionless, gazing fixedly at the face of her lover beside the face of Christ, and had become as white as her hair.

XVI

During the remainder of the winter the Du Roys often visited the Walters. George even dined there by himself continually, Madeleine saying she was tired, and preferring to remain at home. He had adopted Friday as a fixed day, and Madame Walter never invited anyone that evening; it belonged to Pretty-boy, to him alone. After dinner they played cards, and fed the goldfish, amusing themselves like a family circle. Several times behind a door or a clump of shrubs in the conservatory, Madame Walter had suddenly clasped George in her arms, and pressing him with all her strength to her breast, had whispered in his ear, "I love you, I love you till it is killing me." But he had always coldly repulsed her, replying, in a dry tone: "If you begin that business once again, I shall not come here any more."

Towards the end of March the marriage of the two sisters was all at once spoken about. Rose, it was said, was to marry the Count de Latour-Yvelin, and Susan the Marquis de Cazolles. These two gentlemen had become familiars of the household, those familiars to whom special favors and marked privileges are granted. George and Susan continued to live in a species of free and fraternal intimacy, romping for hours, making fun of everyone, and seeming greatly to enjoy one another's company. They had never spoken again of the possible marriage of the young girl, nor of the suitors who offered themselves.

The governor had brought George home to lunch one morning. Madame Walter was called away immediately after the repast to see one of the tradesmen, and the young fellow said to Susan: "Let us go and feed the goldfish."

They each took a piece of crumb of bread from the table and went into the conservatory. All along the marble brim cushions were left lying on the ground, so that one could kneel down round the basin, so as to be nearer the fish. They each took one of these, side by side, and bending over the water, began to throw in pellets of bread rolled between the fingers. The fish, as soon as they caught sight of them, flocked round, wagging their tails, waving their fins, rolling their great projecting eyes, turning round, diving to catch the bait as it sank, and coming up at once to ask for more. They had a funny action of the mouth, sudden and rapid movements, a strangely monstrous appearance, and against the sand of the bottom stood out a bright red, passing like flames through the transparent water, or showing, as soon as they halted, the blue edging to their scales. George and Susan saw their own faces looking up in the water, and smiled at them. All at once he said in a low voice: "It is not kind to hide things from me, Susan."

"What do you mean, Pretty-boy?" asked she.

"Don't you remember, what you promised me here on the evening of the fête?"

"No."

"To consult me every time your hand was asked for."

"Well?"

"Well, it has been asked for."

"By whom?"

"You know very well."

"No. I swear to you."

"Yes, you do. That great fop, the Marquis de Cazolles."

"He is not a fop, in the first place."

"It may be so, but he is stupid, ruined by play, and worn out by dissipation. It is really a nice match for you, so pretty, so fresh, and so intelligent."

She inquired, smiling: "What have you against him?"

"I, nothing."

"Yes, you have. He is not all that you say."

"Nonsense. He is a fool and an intriguer."

She turned round somewhat, leaving off looking into the water, and said: "Come, what is the matter with you?"

He said, as though a secret was being wrenched from the bottom of his heart: "I—I—am jealous of him."

She was slightly astonished, saying: "You?"

"Yes, I."

"Why so?"

"Because I am in love with you, and you know it very well, you naughty girl."

She said, in a severe tone: "You are mad, Pretty-boy."

He replied; "I know very well that I am mad. Ought I to have admitted that—I, a married man, to you, a young girl? I am more than mad, I am guilty. I have no possible hope, and the thought of that drives me out of my senses. And when I hear it said that you are going to be married, I have fits of rage enough to kill someone. You must forgive me this, Susan."

He was silent. The whole of the fish, to whom bread was no longer being thrown, were motionless, drawn up in line like English soldiers, and looking at the bent heads of those two who were no longer troubling themselves about them. The young girl murmured, half sadly, half gayly: "It is a pity that you are married. What would you? Nothing can be done. It is settled."

He turned suddenly towards her, and said right in her face: "If I were free, would you marry me?"

She replied, in a tone of sincerity: "Yes, Pretty-boy, I would marry you, for you please me far better than any of the others."

He rose, and stammered: "Thanks, thanks; do not say 'yes' to anyone yet, I beg of you; wait a little longer, I entreat you. Will you promise me this much?"

She murmured, somewhat uneasily, and without understanding what he wanted: "Yes, I promise you."

Du Roy threw the lump of bread he still held in his hand into the water, and fled as though he had lost his head, without wishing her good-bye. All the fish rushed eagerly at this lump of crumb, which floated, not having been kneaded in the fingers, and nibbled it with greedy mouths. They dragged it away to the other end of the basin, and forming a moving cluster, a kind of animated and twisting flower, a live flower fallen into the water head downwards.

Susan, surprised and uneasy, got up and returned slowly to the dining-room. The journalist had left.

He came home very calm, and as Madeleine was writing letters, said to her: "Are you going to dine at the Walters' on Friday? I am going."

She hesitated, and replied: "No. I do not feel very well. I would rather stay at home."

He remarked: "Just as you like."

Then he took his hat and went out again at once. For some time past he had been keeping watch over her, following her about, knowing all her movements. The hour he had been awaiting was at length at hand. He had not been deceived by the tone in which she had said: "I would rather stay at home."

He was very amiable towards her during the next few days. He even appeared lively, which was not usual, and she said: "You are growing quite nice again."

He dressed early on the Friday, in order to make some calls before going to the governor's, he said. He started just before six, after kissing his wife, and went and took a cab at the Place Notre Dame de Lorette. He said to the driver: "Pull up in front of No. 17, Rue Fontaine, and stay there till I tell you to go on again. Then drive to the Cock Pheasant restaurant in the Rue Lafayette."

The cab started at a slow trot, and Du Roy drew down the blinds. As soon as he was opposite the door he did not take his eyes off it. After waiting ten minutes he saw Madeleine come out and go in the direction of the outer boulevards. As soon as she had got far enough off he put his head through the window, and said to the driver: "Go on." The cab started again, and landed him in front of the Cock Pheasant, a well-known middle-class restaurant. George went into the main dining-room and ate slowly, looking at his watch from time to time. At half-past seven, when he had finished his coffee, drank two liqueurs of brandy, and slowly smoked a good cigar, he went out, hailed another cab that was going by empty, and was driven to the Rue La Rochefoucauld. He ascended without making any inquiry of the doorkeeper, to the third story of the house he had told the man to drive to, and when a servant opened the door to him, said: "Monsieur Guibert de Lorme is at home, is he not?"

"Yes sir."

He was ushered into the drawing-room, where he waited for a few minutes. Then a gentleman came in, tall, and with a military bearing, gray-haired though still young, and wearing the ribbon of the Legion of Honor. Du Roy bowed, and said: "As I foresaw, Mr. Commissionary, my wife is now dining with her lover in the furnished rooms they have hired in the Rue des Martyrs."

The commissary of police bowed, saying: "I am at your service, sir."

George continued: "You have until nine o'clock, have you not? That limit of time passed, you can no longer enter a private dwelling to prove adultery."

"No, sir; seven o'clock in winter, nine o'clock from the 31st March. It is the 5th of April, so we have till nine o'clock.

"Very well, Mr. Commissionary, I have a cab downstairs; we can take the officers who will accompany you, and wait a little before the door. The later we arrive the best chance we have of catching them in the act."

"As you like, sir."

The commissary left the room, and then returned with an overcoat, hiding his tri-colored sash. He drew back to let Du Roy pass out first. But the journalist, who was preoccupied, declined to do so, and kept saying: "After you, sir, after you."

The commissary said: "Go first, sir, I am at home."

George bowed, and passed out. They went first to the police office to pick up three officers in plain clothes who were awaiting them, for George had given notice during the day that the surprise would take place that evening. One of the men got on the box beside the driver. The other two entered the cab, which reached the Rue des Martyrs. Du Roy said: "I have a plan of the rooms. They are on the second floor. We shall first find a little anteroom, then a dining-room, then the bedroom. The three rooms open into one another. There is no way out to facilitate flight. There is a locksmith a little further on. He is holding himself in readiness to be called upon by you."

When they arrived opposite the house it was only a quarter past eight, and they waited in silence for more than twenty minutes. But when he saw the three quarters about to strike, George said: "Let us start now."

They went up the stairs without troubling themselves about the doorkeeper, who, indeed, did not notice them. One of the officers remained in the street to keep watch on the front door. The four men stopped at the second floor, and George put his ear to the door and then looked through the keyhole. He neither heard nor saw anything. He rang the bell.

The commissary said to the officers: "You will remain in readiness till called on."

And they waited. At the end of two or three minutes George again pulled the bell several times in succession. They noted a noise from the further end of the rooms, and then a slight step approached. Someone was coming to spy who was there. The journalist then rapped smartly on the panel of the door. A voice, a woman's voice, that an attempt was evidently being made to disguise asked: "Who is there?"

The commissary replied: "Open, in the name of the law."

The voice repeated: "Who are you?"

"I am the commissary of police. Open the door, or I will have it broken in."

The voice went on: "What do you want?"

Du Roy said: "It is I. It is useless to seek to escape."

The light steps, the tread of bare feet, was heard to withdraw, and then in a few seconds to return.

George said: "If you won't open, we will break in the door."

He grasped the handle, and pushed slowly with his shoulder. As there was no longer any reply, he suddenly gave such a violent and vigorous shock that the old lock gave way. The screws were torn out of the wood, and he almost fell over Madeleine, who was standing in the ante-room, clad in a chemise and petticoat, her hair down, her legs bare, and a candle in her hand.

He exclaimed: "It is she, we have them," and darted forward into the rooms. The commissary, having taken off his hat, followed him, and the startled woman came after, lighting the way. They crossed a drawing-room, the uncleaned table of which displayed the remnants of a repast—empty champagne bottles, an open pot of fatted goose liver, the body of a fowl, and some half-eaten bits of bread. Two plates piled on the sideboard were piled with oyster shells.

The bedroom seemed disordered, as though by a struggle. A dress was thrown over a chair, a pair of trousers hung astride the arm of another. Four boots, two large and two small, lay on their sides at the foot of the bed. It was the room of a house let out in furnished lodgings, with commonplace furniture, filled with that hateful and sickening smell of all such places, the odor of all the people who had slept or lived there a day or six months. A plate of cakes, a bottle of chartreuse, and two liqueur glasses, still half full, encumbered the mantel-shelf. The upper part of the bronze clock was hidden by a man's hat.

The commissary turned round sharply, and looking Madeleine straight in the face, said: "You are Madame Claire Madeleine Du Roy, wife of Monsieur Prosper George Du Roy, journalist, here present?"

She uttered in a choking voice: "Yes, sir."

"What are you doing here?" She did not answer.

The commissary went on: "What are you doing here? I find you away from home, almost undressed, in furnished apartments. What did you come here for?" He waited for a few moments. Then, as she still remained silent, he continued: "Since you will not confess, madame, I shall be obliged to verify the state of things."

In the bed could be seen the outline of a form hidden beneath the clothes. The commissary approached and said: "Sir."

The man in bed did not stir. He seemed to have his back turned, and his head buried under a pillow. The commissary touched what seemed to be his shoulder, and said: "Sir, do not, I beg of you, force me to take action."

But the form still remained as motionless as a corpse. Du Roy, who had advanced quickly, seized the bed-clothes, pulled them down, and tearing away the pillow, revealed the pale face of Monsieur Laroche-Mathieu. He bent over him, and, quivering with the desire to seize him by the throat and strangle him, said, between his clenched teeth: "Have at least the courage of your infamy."

The commissary again asked: "Who are you?"

The bewildered lover not replying, he continued: "I am a commissary of police, and I summon you to tell me your name."

George, who was quivering with brutal wrath, shouted: "Answer, you coward, or I will tell your name myself."

Then the man in the bed stammered: "Mr. Commissary, you ought not to allow me to be insulted by this person. Is it with you or with him that I have to do? Is it to you or to him that I have to answer?"

His mouth seemed to be dried up as he spoke.

The commissary replied: "With me, sir; with me alone. I ask you who you are?"

The other was silent. He held the sheet close up to his neck, and rolled his startled eyes. His little, curled-up moustache showed up black upon his blanched face.

The commissary continued: "You will not answer, eh? Then I shall be forced to arrest you. In any case, get up. I will question you when you are dressed."

The body wriggled in the bed, and the head murmured: "But I cannot, before you."

The commissary asked: "Why not?"

The other stammered: "Because I am—I am—quite naked."

Du Roy began to chuckle sneeringly, and picking up a shirt that had fallen onto the floor, threw it onto the bed, exclaiming: "Come, get up. Since you have undressed in my wife's presence, you can very well dress in mine."

Then he turned his back, and returned towards the fireplace. Madeleine had recovered all her coolness, and seeing that all was lost, was ready to dare anything. Her eyes glittered with bravado, and twisting up a piece of paper she lit, as though for a reception, the ten candles in the ugly candelabra, placed at the corners of the mantel-shelf. Then, leaning against this, and holding out backwards to the dying fire one of her bare feet which she lifted up behind the petticoat, scarcely sticking to her hips, she took a cigarette from a pink paper case, lit it, and began to smoke. The commissary had returned towards her, pending that her accomplice got up.

She inquired insolently: "Do you often have such jobs as these, sir?"

He replied gravely: "As seldom as possible, madame."

She smiled in his face, saying: "I congratulate you; it is dirty work."

She affected not to look at or even to see her husband.

But the gentleman in the bed was dressing. He had put on his trousers, pulled on his boots, and now approached putting on his waistcoat. The commissary turned towards him, saying: "Now, sir, will you tell me who you are?"

He made no reply, and the official said: "I find myself obliged to arrest you."

Then the man exclaimed suddenly: "Do not lay hands on me. My person is inviolable."

Du Roy darted towards him as though to throw him down, and growled in his face: "Caught in the act, in the act. I can have you arrested if I choose; yes, I can." Then, in a ringing tone, he added: "This man is Laroche-Mathieu, Minister of Foreign Affairs."

The commissary drew back, stupefied, and stammered: "Really, sir, will you tell me who you are?"

The other had made up his mind, and said in forcible tones: "For once that scoundrel has not lied. I am, indeed, Laroche-Mathieu, the minister." Then, holding out his hand towards George's chest, in which a little bit of red ribbon showed itself, he added: "And that rascal wears on his coat the cross of honor which I gave him."

Du Roy had become livid. With a rapid movement he tore the bit of ribbon from his buttonhole, and, throwing it into the fireplace, exclaimed: "That is all that is fit for a decoration coming from a swine like you."

They were quite close, face to face, exasperated, their fists clenched, the one lean, with a flowing moustache, the other stout, with a twisted one. The commissary stepped rapidly between the pair, and pushing them apart with his hands, observed: "Gentlemen, you are forgetting yourselves; you are lacking in self-respect."

They became quiet and turned on their heels. Madeleine, motionless, was still smoking in silence.

The police official resumed: "Sir, I have found you alone with Madame Du Roy here, you in bed, she almost naked, with your clothes scattered about the room. This is legal evidence of adultery. You cannot deny this evidence. What have you to say for yourself?"

Laroche-Mathieu murmured: "I have nothing to say; do your duty."

The commissary addressed himself to Madeleine: "Do you admit, madame, that this gentleman is your lover?"

She said with a certain swagger: "I do not deny it; he is my lover."

"That is enough."

The commissary made some notes as to the condition and arrangement of the rooms. As he was finishing writing, the minister, who had finished dressing, and was waiting with his greatcoat over his arm and his hat in his hand, said: "Have you still need of me, sir? What am I to do? Can I withdraw?"

Du Roy turned towards him, and smiling insolently, said: "Why so? We have finished. You can go to bed again, sir; we will leave you alone." And placing a finger on the official's arm, he continued: "Let us retire, Mr. Commissary, we have nothing more to do in this place."

Somewhat surprised, the commissary followed, but on the threshold of the room George stopped to allow him to pass. The other declined, out of politeness. Du Roy persisted, saying: "Pass first, sir."

"After you, sir," replied the commissary.

The journalist bowed, and in a tone of ironical politeness, said: "It is your turn, sir; I am almost at home here."

Then he softly reclosed the door with an air of discretion.

An hour later George Du Roy entered the offices of the *Vie Francaise*. Monsieur Walter was already there, for he continued to manage and supervise with solicitude his paper, which had enormously increased in circulation, and greatly helped the schemes of his bank. The manager raised his head and said: "Ah! here you are. You look very strange. Why did you not come to dinner with us? What have you been up to?"

The young fellow, sure of his effect, said, emphasizing every word: "I have just upset the Minister of Foreign Affairs."

The other thought he was joking, and said: "Upset what?"

"I am going to turn out the Cabinet. That is all. It is quite time to get rid of that rubbish."

The old man thought that his leader-writer must be drunk. He murmured: "Come, you are talking nonsense."

"Not at all. I have just caught Monsieur Laroche-Mathieu committing adultery with my wife. The commissary of police has verified the fact. The minister is done for."

Walter, amazed, pushed his spectacles right back on his forehead, and said: "You are not joking?"

"Not at all. I am even going to write an article on it."

"But what do you want to do?"

"To upset that scoundrel, that wretch, that open evil-doer." George placed his hat on an armchair, and added: "Woe to those who cross my path. I never forgive."

The manager still hesitated at understanding matters. He murmured: "But—your wife?"

"My application for a divorce will be lodged to-morrow morning. I shall send her back to the departed Forestier."

"You mean to get a divorce?"

"Yes. I was ridiculous. But I had to play the idiot in order to catch them. That's done. I am master of the situation."

Monsieur Walter could not get over it, and watched Du Roy with startling eyes, thinking: "Hang it, here is a fellow to be looked after."

George went on: "I am now free. I have some money. I shall offer myself as a candidate at the October elections for my native place, where I am well known. I could not take a position or make myself respected with that woman, who was suspected by every one. She had caught me like a fool, humbugged and ensnared me. But since I became alive to her little game I kept watch on her, the slut." He began to laugh, and added: "It was poor Forestier who was cuckold, a cuckold without imagining it, confiding and tranquil. Now I am free from the leprosy he left me. My hands are free. Now I shall get on." He had seated himself astride a chair, and repeated, as though thinking aloud, "I shall get on."

And Daddy Walter, still looking at him with unveiled eyes, his spectacles remaining pushed up on his forehead, said to himself: "Yes, he will get on, the rascal."

George rose. "I am going to write the article. It must be done discreetly. But you know it will be terrible for the minister. He has gone to smash. He cannot be picked up again. The *Vie Francaise* has no longer any interest to spare him."

The old fellow hesitated for a few moments, and then made up his mind. "Do so," said he; "so much the worse for those who get into such messes."

XVII

Three months had elapsed. Du Roy's divorce had just been granted. His wife had resumed the name of Forestier, and, as the Walters were to leave on the 15th of July for Trouville, it was decided that he and they should spend a day in the country together before they started. A Thursday was selected, and they started at nine in the morning in a large traveling landau with six places, drawn by four horses with postilions. They were going to lunch at the Pavilion Henri-Quatre at Saint Germain. Pretty-boy had asked to be the only man of the party, for he could not endure the presence of the Marquis de Cazolles. But at the last moment it was decided that the Count de Latour-Yvelin should be called for on the way. He had been told the day before.

The carriage passed up the Avenue of the Champs Elyseés at a swinging trot, and then traversed the Bois de Boulogne. It was splendid summer weather, not too warm. The swallows traced long sweeping lines across the blue sky that one fancied one could still see after they had passed. The three ladies occupied the back seat, the mother between her daughters, and the men were with their backs to the horses, Walter between the two guests. They crossed the Seine, skirted Mount Valerien, and gained Bougival in order to follow the river as far as Le Pecq.

The Count de Latour-Yvelin, a man advancing towards middle-age, with long, light whiskers, gazed tenderly at Rose. They had been engaged for a month. George, who was very pale, often looked at Susan, who was pale too. Their eyes often met, and seemed to concert something, to understand one another, to secretly exchange a thought, and then to flee one another. Madame Walter was quiet and happy.

The lunch was a long one. Before starting back for Paris, George suggested a turn on the terrace. They stopped at first to admire the view. All ranged themselves in a line along the parapet, and went into ecstasies over the far-stretching horizon. The Seine at the foot of a long hill flowed towards Maisons-Lafitte like an immense serpent stretched in the herbage. To the right, on the summit of the slope, the aqueduct of Marly showed against the skyline its outline, resembling that of a gigantic, long-legged caterpillar, and Marly was lost beneath it in a thick cluster of trees. On the immense plain extending in front of them, villages could be seen dotted. The pieces of water at Le Vesinet showed like clear spots amidst the thin foliage of the little forest. To the left, away in the distance, the pointed steeple of Sastrouville could be seen.

Walter said: "Such a panorama is not to be found anywhere in the world. There is not one to match it in Switzerland."

Then they began to walk on gently, to have a stroll and enjoy the prospect. George and Susan remained behind. As soon as they were a few paces off, he said to her in a low and restrained voice: "Susan, I adore you. I love you to madness."

She murmured: "So do I you, Pretty-boy."

He went on: "If I do not have you for my wife, I shall leave Paris and this country."

She replied: "Ask Papa for my hand. Perhaps he will consent."

He made a gesture of impatience. "No, I tell you for the twentieth time that is useless. The door of your house would be closed to me. I should be dismissed from the paper, and we should not be able even to see one another. That is a pretty result, at which I am sure to arrive by a formal demand for you. They have promised you to the Marquis de Cazolles. They hope that you will end by saying 'yes,' and they are waiting for that."

She asked: "What is to be done?"

He hesitated, glancing at her, sidelong fashion. "Do you love me enough to run a risk?"

She answered resolutely: "Yes."

"A great risk?"

"Yes."

"The greatest of risks?"

"Yes."

"Have you the courage to set your father and mother at defiance?"

"Yes."

"Really now?"

"Yes."

"Very well, there is one way and only one. The thing must come from you and not from me. You are a spoilt child; they let you say whatever you like, and they will not be too much astonished at an act of daring the more on your part. Listen, then. This evening, on reaching home, you must go to your mamma first, your mamma alone, and tell her you want to marry me. She will be greatly moved and very angry—"

Susan interrupted him with: "Oh, mamma will agree."

He went on quickly: "No, you do not know her. She will be more vexed and angrier than your father. You will see how she will refuse. But you must be firm, you must not give way, you must repeat that you want to marry me, and no one else. Will you do this?"

"I will."

"On leaving your mother you must tell your father the same thing in a very serious and decided manner."

"Yes, yes; and then?"

"And then it is that matters become serious. If you are determined, very determined—very, very determined to be my wife, my dear, dear little Susan—I will—run away with you."

She experienced a joyful shock, and almost clapped her hands. "Oh! how delightful. You will run away with me. When will you run away with me?"

All the old poetry of nocturnal elopements, post-chaises, country inns; all the charming adventures told in books, flashed through her mind, like an enchanting dream about to be realized. She repeated: "When will you run away with me?"

He replied, in low tones: "This evening—to-night."

She asked, quivering: "And where shall we go to?"

"That is my secret. Reflect on what you are doing. Remember that after such a flight you can only be my wife. It is the only way, but is—it is very dangerous—for you."

She declared: "I have made up my mind; where shall I rejoin you?"

"Can you get out of the hotel alone?"

"Yes. I know how to undo the little door."

"Well, when the doorkeeper has gone to bed, towards midnight, come and meet me on the Place de la Concorde. You will find me in a cab drawn up in front of the Ministry of Marine."

"I will come."

"Really?"

"Really."

He took her hand and pressed it. "Oh! how I love you. How good and brave you are! So you don't want to marry Monsieur de Cazolles?"

"Oh! no."

"Your father was very angry when you said no?"

"I should think so. He wanted to send me back to the convent."

"You see that it is necessary to be energetic."

"I will be so."

She looked at the vast horizon, her head full of the idea of being ran off with. She would go further than that with him. She would be ran away with. She was proud of it. She scarcely thought of her reputation—of what shame might befall her. Was she aware of it? Did she even suspect it?

Madame Walter, turning round, exclaimed: "Come along, little one. What are you doing with Pretty-boy?"

They rejoined the others and spoke of the seaside, where they would soon be. Then they returned home by way of Chatou, in order not to go over the same road twice. George no longer spoke. He reflected. If the little girl had a little courage, he was going to succeed at last. For three months he had been enveloping her in the irresistible net of his love. He was seducing, captivating, conquering her. He had made himself loved by her, as he knew how to make himself loved. He had captured her childish soul without difficulty. He had at first obtained of her that she should refuse Monsieur de Cazolles. He had just obtained that she would fly with him. For there was no other way. Madame Walter, he well understood, would never agree to give him her daughter. She still loved him; she would always love him with unmanageable violence. He restrained her by his studied coldness; but he felt that she was eaten up by hungry and impotent passion. He could never bend her. She would never allow him to have Susan. But once he had the girl away he would deal on a level footing with her father. Thinking of all this, he replied by broken phrases to the remarks addressed to him, and which he did not hear. He only seemed to come to himself when they returned to Paris.

Susan, too, was thinking, and the bells of the four horses rang in her ears, making her see endless miles of highway under eternal moonlight, gloomy forests traversed, wayside inns, and the hurry of the hostlers to change horses, for every one guesses that they are pursued.

When the landau entered the court-yard of the mansion, they wanted to keep George to dinner. He refused, and went home. After having eaten a little, he went through his papers as if about to start on a long journey. He burnt some compromising letters, hid others, and wrote to some friends. From time to time he looked at the clock, thinking: "Things must be getting warm there." And a sense of uneasiness gnawed at his heart. Suppose he was going to fail? But what could he fear? He could always get out of it. Yet it was a big game he was playing that evening.

He went out towards eleven o'clock, wandered about some time, took a cab, and had it drawn up in the Place de la Concorde, by the Ministry of Marine. From time to time he struck a match to see the time by his watch. When he saw midnight approaching, his impatience became feverish. Every moment he thrust his head out of the window to look. A distant clock struck twelve, then another nearer, then two together, then a last one, very far away. When the latter had ceased to sound, he thought: "It is all over. It is a failure. She won't come." He had made up his mind, however, to wait till daylight. In these matters one must be patient.

He heard the quarter strike, then the half-hour, then the quarter to, and all the clocks repeated "one," as they had announced midnight. He no longer expected her; he was merely remaining, racking his brain to divine what could have happened. All at once a woman's head was passed through the window, and asked: "Are you there, Pretty-boy?"

He started, almost choked with emotion, "Is that you, Susan?"

"Yes, it is I."

He could not manage to turn the handle quickly enough, and repeated: "Ah! it is you, it is you; come inside."

She came in and fell against him. He said, "Go on," to the driver, and the cab started.

She gasped, without saying a word.

He asked: "Well, how did it go off?"

She murmured, almost fainting: "Oh! it was terrible, above all with mamma."

He was uneasy and quivering. "Your mamma. What did she say? Tell me."

"Oh! it was awful. I went into her room and told her my little story that I had carefully prepared. She grew pale, and then she cried: 'Never, never.' I cried, I grew angry. I vowed I would marry no one but you. I thought that she was going to strike me. She went on just as if she were mad; she declared that I should be sent back to the convent the next day. I had never seen her like that—never. Then papa came in, hearing her shouting all her nonsense. He was not so angry as she was, but he declared that you were not a good enough match. As they had put me in a rage, too, I shouted louder than they did. And papa told me to leave the room, with a melodramatic air that did not suit him at all. This is what decided me to run off with you. Here I am. Where are we going to?"

He had passed his arm gently round her and was listening with all his ears, his heart throbbing, and a ravenous hatred awakening within him against these people. But he had got their daughter. They should just see.

He answered: "It is too late to catch a train, so this cab will take us to Sevres, where we shall pass the night. To-morrow we shall start for La Roche-Guyon. It is a pretty village on the banks of the Seine, between Nantes and Bonnieres."

She murmured: "But I have no clothes. I have nothing."

He smiled carelessly: "Bah! we will arrange all that there."

The cab rolled along the street. George took one of the young girl's hands and began to kiss it slowly and with respect. He scarcely knew what to say to her, being scarcely accustomed to platonic love-making. But all at once he thought he noted that she was crying. He inquired, with alarm: "What is the matter with you, darling?"

She replied in tearful tones: "Poor mamma, she will not be able to sleep if she has found out my departure."

Her mother, indeed, was not asleep.

As soon as Susan had left the room, Madame Walter remained face to face with her husband. She asked, bewildered and cast down: "Good heavens! What is the meaning of this?"

Walter exclaimed furiously: "It means that that schemer has bewitched her. It is he who made her refuse Cazolles. He thinks her dowry worth trying for." He began to walk angrily up and down the room, and went on: "You were always luring him here, too, yourself; you flattered him, you cajoled him, you could not cosset him enough. It was Pretty-boy here, Pretty-boy there, from morning till night, and this is the return for it."

She murmured, livid: "I—I lured him?"

He shouted in her face: "Yes, you. You were all mad over him—Madame de Marelle, Susan, and the rest. Do you think I did not see that you could not pass a couple of days without having him here?"

She drew herself up tragically: "I will not allow you to speak to me like that. You forget that I was not brought up like you, behind a counter."

He stood for a moment stupefied, and then uttered a furious "Damn it all!" and rushed out, slamming the door after him. As soon as she was alone she went instinctively to the glass to see if anything was changed in her, so impossible and monstrous did what had happened appear. Susan in love with Pretty-boy, and Pretty-boy wanting to marry Susan! No, she was mistaken; it was not true. The girl had had a very natural fancy for this good-looking fellow; she had hoped that they would give him her for a husband, and had made her little scene because she wanted to have her own way. But he—he could not be an accomplice in that. She reflected, disturbed, as one in presence of great catastrophes. No, Pretty-boy could know nothing of Susan's prank.

She thought for a long time over the possible innocence or perfidy of this man. What a scoundrel, if he had prepared the blow! And what would happen! What dangers and tortures she foresaw. If he knew nothing, all could yet be arranged. They would travel about with Susan for six months, and it would be all over. But how could she meet him herself afterwards? For she still loved him. This passion had entered into her being like those arrowheads that cannot be withdrawn. To live without him was impossible. She might as well die.

Her thoughts wandered amidst these agonies and uncertainties. A pain began in her head; her ideas became painful and disturbed. She worried herself by trying to work things out; grew mad at not knowing. She looked at the clock; it was past one. She said to herself: "I cannot remain like this, I shall go mad. I must know. I will wake up Susan and question her."

She went barefooted, in order not to make a noise, and with a candle in her hand, towards her daughter's room. She opened the door softly, went in, and looked at the bed. She did not comprehend matters at first, and thought that the girl might still be arguing with her father. But all at once a horrible suspicion crossed her mind, and she rushed to her husband's room. She reached it in a bound, blanched and panting. He was in bed reading.

He asked, startled: "Well, what is it? What is the matter with you?"

She stammered: "Have you seen Susan?"

"I? No. Why?"

"She has—she has—gone! She is not in her room."

He sprang onto the carpet, thrust his feet into his slippers, and, with his shirt tails floating in the air, rushed in turn to his daughter's room. As soon as he saw it, he no longer retained any doubt. She had fled. He dropped into a chair and placed his lamp on the ground in front of him.

His wife had rejoined him, and stammered: "Well?"

He had no longer the strength to reply; he was no longer enraged, he only groaned: "It is done; he has got her. We are done for."

She did not understand, and said: "What do you mean? done for?"

"Yes, by Jove! He will certainly marry her now."

She gave a cry like that of a wild beast: "He, never! You must be mad!"

He replied, sadly: "It is no use howling. He has run away with her, he has dishonored her. The best thing is to give her to him. By setting to work in the right way no one will be aware of this escapade."

She repeated, shaken by terrible emotion: "Never, never; he shall never have Susan. I will never consent."

Walter murmured, dejectedly: "But he has got her. It is done. And he will keep her and hide her as long as we do not yield. So, to avoid scandal, we must give in at once."

His wife, torn by pangs she could not acknowledge, repeated: "No, no, I will never consent."

He said, growing impatient: "But there is no disputing about it. It must be done. Ah, the rascal, how he has done us! He is a sharp one. All the same, we might have made a far better choice as regards position, but not as regards intelligence and prospects. He will be a deputy and a minister."

Madame Walter declared, with savage energy: "I will never allow him to marry Susan. You understand—never."

He ended by getting angry and taking up, as a practical man, the cudgels on behalf of Pretty-boy. "Hold your tongue," said he. "I tell you again that it must be so; it absolutely must. And who knows? Perhaps we shall not regret it. With men of that stamp one never knows what may happen. You saw how he overthrew in three articles that fool of a Laroche-Mathieu, and how he did it with dignity, which was infernally difficult in his position as the husband. At all events, we shall see. It always comes to this, that we are nailed. We cannot get out of it."

She felt a longing to scream, to roll on the ground, to tear her hair out. She said at length, in exasperated tones: "He shall not have her. I won't have it."

Walter rose, picked up his lamp, and remarked: "There, you are stupid, just like all women. You never do anything except from passion. You do not know how to bend yourself to circumstances. You are stupid. I will tell you that he shall marry her. It must be."

He went out, shuffling along in his slippers. He traversed—a comical phantom in his nightshirt—the broad corridor of the huge slumbering house, and noiselessly re-entered his room.

Madame Walter remained standing, torn by intolerable grief. She did not yet quite understand it. She was only conscious of suffering. Then it seemed to her that she could not remain there motionless till daylight. She felt within her a violent necessity of fleeing, of running away, of seeking help, of being succored. She sought whom she could summon to her. What man? She could not find one. A priest; yes, a priest! She would throw herself at his feet, acknowledge everything, confess her fault and her despair. He would understand that this wretch must not marry Susan, and would prevent it. She must have a priest at once. But where could she find one? Whither could she go? Yet she could not remain like that.

Then there passed before her eyes, like a vision, the calm figure of Jesus walking on the waters. She saw it as she saw it in the picture. So he was calling her. He was saying: "Come to me; come and kneel at my feet. I will console you, and inspire you with what should be done."

She took her candle, left the room, and went downstairs to the conservatory. The picture of Jesus was right at the end of it in a small drawing-room, shut off by a glass door, in order that the dampness of the soil should not damage the canvas. It formed a kind of chapel in a forest of strange trees. When Madame Walter entered the winter garden, never having seen it before save full of light, she was struck by its obscure profundity. The dense plants of the tropics made the atmosphere thick with their heavy breath; and the doors no longer being open, the air of this strange wood, enclosed beneath a glass roof, entered the chest with difficulty; intoxicated, caused pleasure and pain, and imparted a confused sensation of enervation, pleasure, and death. The poor woman walked slowly, oppressed by the shadows, amidst which appeared, by the flickering light of her candle, extravagant plants, recalling monsters, living creatures, hideous deformities. All at once she caught sight of the picture of Christ. She opened the door separating her from it, and fell on her knees. She prayed to him, wildly, at first, stammering forth words of true, passionate, and despairing invocations. Then, the ardor of her appeal slackening, she raised her eyes towards him, and was struck with anguish. He resembled Pretty-boy so strongly, in the trembling light of this solitary candle, lighting the picture from below, that it was no longer Christ—it was her lover who was looking at her. They were his eyes, his forehead, the expression of his face, his cold and haughty air.

She stammered: "Jesus, Jesus, Jesus!" and the name "George" rose to her lips. All at once she thought that at that very moment, perhaps, George had her daughter. He was alone with her somewhere. He with Susan! She repeated: "Jesus, Jesus!" but she was thinking of them—her daughter and her lover. They were alone in a room, and at night. She saw them. She saw them so plainly that they rose up before her in place of the picture. They were smiling at one another. They were embracing. She rose to go towards them, to take her daughter by the hair and tear her from his clasp. She would seize her by the throat and strangle her, this daughter whom she hated—this daughter who was joining herself to this man. She touched her; her hands encountered the canvas; she was pressing the feet of Christ. She uttered a loud cry and fell on her back. Her candle, overturned, went out.

What took place then? She dreamed for a long time wild, frightful dreams. George and Susan continually passed before her eyes, with Christ blessing their horrible loves. She felt vaguely that she was not in her room. She wished to rise and flee; she could not. A torpor had seized upon her, which fettered her limbs, and only left her mind on the alert, tortured by frightful and fantastic visions, lost in an unhealthy dream—the strange and sometimes fatal dream engendered in human minds by the soporific plants of the tropics, with their strange and oppressive perfumes.

The next morning Madame Walter was found stretched out senseless, almost asphyxiated before "Jesus Walking on the Waters." She was so ill that her life was feared for. She only fully recovered the use of her senses the following day. Then she began to weep. The disappearance of Susan was explained to the servants as due to her being suddenly sent back to the convent. And Monsieur Walter replied to a long letter of Du Roy by granting him his daughter's hand.

Pretty-boy had posted this letter at the moment of leaving Paris, for he had prepared it in advance the evening of his departure. He said in it, in respectful terms, that he had long loved the young girl; that there had never been any agreement between them; but that finding her come freely to him to say, "I wish to be your wife," he considered himself authorized in keeping her, even in hiding her, until he had obtained an answer from her parents, whose legal power had for him less weight than the wish of his betrothed. He demanded that Monsieur Walter should reply, "post restante," a friend being charged to forward the letter to him.

When he had obtained what he wished he brought back Susan to Paris, and sent her on to her parents, abstaining himself from appearing for some little time.

They had spent six days on the banks of the Seine at La Roche-Guyon.

The young girl had never enjoyed herself so much. She had played at pastoral life. As he passed her off as his sister, they lived in a free and chaste intimacy—a kind of loving friendship. He thought it a clever stroke to respect her. On the day after their arrival she had purchased some linen and some country-girl's clothes, and set to work fishing, with a huge straw hat, ornamented with wild flowers, on her head. She thought the country there delightful. There was an old tower and an old chateau, in which beautiful tapestry was shown.

George, dressed in a boating jersey, bought ready-made from a local tradesman, escorted Susan, now on foot along the banks of the river, now in a boat. They kissed at every moment, she in all innocence, and he ready to succumb to temptation. But he was able to restrain himself; and when he said to her, "We will go back to Paris to-morrow; your father has granted me your hand," she murmured simply, "Already? It was so nice being your wife here."

XVIII

It was dark in the little suite of rooms in the Rue de Constantinople; for George Du Roy and Clotilde de Marelle, having met at the door, had gone in at once, and she had said to him, without giving him time to open the Venetian blinds: "So you are going to marry Susan Walter?"

He admitted it quietly, and added: "Did not you know it?"

She exclaimed, standing before him, furious and indignant:

"You are going to marry Susan Walter? That is too much of a good thing. For three months you have been humbugging in order to hide that from me. Everyone knew it but me. It was my husband who told me of it."

Du Roy began to laugh, though somewhat confused all the same; and having placed his hat on a corner of the mantel-shelf, sat down in an armchair. She looked at him straight in the face, and said, in a low and irritated tone: "Ever since you left your wife you have been preparing this move, and you only kept me on as a mistress to fill up the interim nicely. What a rascal you are!"

He asked: "Why so? I had a wife who deceived me. I caught her, I obtained a divorce, and I am going to marry another. What could be simpler?"

She murmured, quivering: "Oh! how cunning and dangerous you are."

He began to smile again. "By Jove! Simpletons and fools are always someone's dupes."

But she continued to follow out her idea: "I ought to have divined your nature from the beginning. But no, I could not believe that you could be such a blackguard as that."

He assumed an air of dignity, saying: "I beg of you to pay attention to the words you are making use of."

His indignation revolted her. "What? You want me to put on gloves to talk to you now. You have behaved towards me like a vagabond ever since I have known you, and you want to make out that I am not to tell you so. You deceive everyone; you take advantage of everyone; you filch money and enjoyment wherever you can, and you want me to treat you as an honest man!"

He rose, and with quivering lip, said: "Be quiet, or I will turn you out of here."

She stammered: "Turn me out of here; turn me out of here! You will turn me out of here—you—you?" She could not speak for a moment for choking with anger, and then suddenly, as though the door of her wrath had been burst open, she broke out with: "Turn me out of here? You forget, then, that it is I who have paid for these rooms from the beginning. Ah, yes, you have certainly taken them on from time to time. But who first took them? I did. Who kept them on? I did. And you want to turn me out of here. Hold your tongue, you good-for-nothing fellow. Do you think I don't know you robbed Madeleine of half Vaudrec's money? Do you think I don't know how you slept with Susan to oblige her to marry you?"

He seized her by the shoulders, and, shaking her with both hands, exclaimed: "Don't speak of her, at any rate. I won't have it."

She screamed out: "You slept with her; I know you did."

He would have accepted no matter what, but this falsehood exasperated him. The truths she had told him to his face had caused thrills of anger to run through him, but this lie respecting the young girl who was going to be his wife, awakened in the palm of his hand a furious longing to strike her.

He repeated: "Be quiet—have a care—be quiet," and shook her as we shake a branch to make the fruit fall.

She yelled, with her hair coming down, her mouth wide open, her eyes aglow: "You slept with her!"

He let her go, and gave her such a smack on the face that she fell down beside the wall. But she turned towards him, and raising herself on her hands, once more shouted: "You slept with her!"

He rushed at her, and, holding her down, struck her as though striking a man. She left off shouting, and began to moan beneath his blows. She no longer stirred, but hid her face against the bottom of the wall and uttered plaintive cries. He left off beating her and rose up. Then he walked about the room a little to recover his coolness, and, an idea occurring to him, went into the bedroom, filled the basin with cold water, and dipped his head into it. Then he washed his hands and came back to see what she was doing, carefully wiping his fingers. She had not budged. She was still lying on the ground quietly weeping.

"Shall you have done grizzling soon?"

She did not answer. He stood in the middle of the room, feeling somewhat awkward and ashamed in the presence of the form stretched out before him. All at once he formed a resolution, and took his hat from the mantel-shelf, saying: "Good-night. Give the key to the doorkeeper when you leave. I shan't wait for your convenience."

He went out, closed the door, went to the doorkeeper's, and said: "Madame is still there. She will be leaving in a few minutes. Tell the landlord that I give notice to leave at the end of September. It is the 15th of August, so I am within the limits."

And he walked hastily away, for he had some pressing calls to make touching the purchase of the last wedding gifts.

The wedding was fixed for the 20th of October after the meeting of the Chambers. It was to take place at the Church of the Madeleine. There had been a great deal of gossip about it without anyone knowing the exact truth. Different tales were in circulation. It was whispered that an elopement had taken place, but no one was certain about anything. According to the servants, Madame Walter, who would no longer speak to her future son-in-law, had poisoned herself out of rage the very evening the match was decided on, after having taken her daughter off to a convent at midnight. She had been brought back almost dead. Certainly, she would never get over it. She had now the appearance of an old woman; her hair had become quite gray, and she had gone in for religion, taking the Sacrament every Sunday.

At the beginning of September the *Vie Francaise* announced that the Baron Du Roy de Cantel had become chief editor, Monsieur Walter retaining the title of manager. A battalion of well-known writers, reporters, political editors, art and theatrical critics, detached from old important papers by dint of monetary influence, were taken on. The old journalists, the serious and respectable ones, no longer shrugged their shoulders when speaking of the *Vie Francaise*. Rapid and complete success had wiped out the contempt of serious writers for the beginnings of this paper.

The marriage of its chief editor was what is styled a Parisian event, George Du Roy and the Walters having excited a great deal of curiosity for some time past. All the people who are written about in the papers promised themselves to be there.

The event took place on a bright autumn day.

At eight in the morning the sight of the staff of the Madeleine stretching a broad red carpet down the lofty flight of steps overlooking the Rue Royale caused passers-by to pause, and announced to the people of Paris that an important ceremony was about to take place. The clerks on the way to their offices, the work-girls, the shopmen, paused, looked, and vaguely speculated about the rich folk who spent so much money over getting spliced. Towards ten o'clock idlers began to halt. They would remain for a few minutes, hoping that perhaps it would begin at once, and then moved away. At eleven squads of police arrived and set to work almost at once to make the crowd move on, groups forming every moment. The first guests soon made their appearance—those who wanted to be well placed for seeing everything. They took the chairs bordering the main aisles. By degrees came others, ladies in rustling silks, and serious-looking gentlemen, almost all bald, walking with well-bred air, and graver than usual in this locality.

The church slowly filled. A flood of sunlight entered by the huge doorway lit up the front row of guests. In the choir, which looked somewhat gloomy, the altar, laden with tapers, shed a yellow light, pale and humble in face of that of the main entrance. People recognized one another, beckoned to one another, and gathered in groups. The men of letters, less respectful than the men in society, chatted in low tones and looked at the ladies.

Norbert de Varenne, who was looking out for an acquaintance, perceived Jacques Rival near the center of the rows of chair, and joined him. "Well," said he, "the race is for the cunning."

The other, who was not envious, replied: "So much the better for him. His career is safe." And they began to point out the people they recognized.

"Do you know what became of his wife?" asked Rival.

The poet smiled. "Yes, and no. She is living in a very retired style, I am told, in the Montmartre district. But—there is a but—I have noticed for some time past in the *Plume* some political articles terribly like those of Forestier and Du Roy. They are by Jean Le Dal, a handsome, intelligent young fellow, of the same breed as our friend George, and who has made the acquaintance of his late wife. From whence I conclude that she had, and always will have, a fancy for beginners. She is, besides, rich. Vaudrec and Laroche-Mathieu were not assiduous visitors at the house for nothing."

Rival observed: "She is not bad looking, Madeleine. Very clever and very sharp. She must be charming on terms of intimacy. But, tell me, how is it that Du Roy comes to be married in church after a divorce?"

Norbert replied: "He is married in church because, in the eyes of the Church, he was not married before."

"How so?"

"Our friend, Pretty-boy, from indifference or economy, thought the registrar sufficient when marrying Madeleine Forestier. He therefore dispensed with the ecclesiastical benediction, which constituted in the eyes of Holy Mother Church a simple state of concubinage. Consequently he comes before her to-day as a bachelor, and she lends him all her pomp and ceremony, which will cost Daddy Walter a pretty penny."

The murmur of the augmented throng swelled beneath the vaulted room. Voices could be heard speaking almost out loud. People pointed out to one another celebrities who attitudinized, pleased to be seen, and carefully maintained the bearing adopted by them towards the public accustomed to exhibit themselves thus at all such gatherings, of which they were, it seemed to them, the indispensable ornaments.

Rival resumed: "Tell me, my dear fellow, you who go so often to the governor's, is it true that Du Roy and Madame Walter no longer speak to one another?"

"Never. She did not want to give him the girl. But he had a hold, it seems, on the father through skeletons in the house—skeletons connected with the Morocco business. He threatened the old man with frightful revelations. Walter recollected the example he made of Laroche-Mathieu, and gave in at once. But the mother, obstinate like all women, swore that she would never again speak a word to her son-in-law. She looks like a statue, a statue of Vengeance, and he is very uneasy at it, although he puts a good face on the matter, for he knows how to control himself, that fellow does."

Fellow-journalists came up and shook hands with them. Bits of political conversation could be caught. Vague as the sound of a distant sea, the noise of the crowd massed in front of the church entered the doorway with the sunlight, and rose up beneath the roof, above the more discreet murmur of the choicer public gathered within it.

All at once the beadle struck the pavement thrice with the butt of his halberd. Every one turned round with a prolonged rustling of skirts and a moving of chairs. The bride appeared on her father's arm in the bright light of the doorway.

She had still the air of a doll, a charming white doll crowned with orange flowers. She stood for a few moments on the threshold, then, when she made her first step up the aisle, the organ gave forth a powerful note, announcing the entrance of the bride in loud metallic tones. She advanced with bent head, but not timidly; vaguely moved, pretty, charming, a miniature bride. The women smiled and murmured as they watched her pass. The men muttered: "Exquisite! Adorable!" Monsieur Walter walked with exaggerated dignity, somewhat pale, and with his spectacles straight on his nose. Behind them four bridesmaids, all four dressed in pink, and all four pretty, formed the court of this gem of a queen. The groomsmen, carefully chosen to match, stepped as though trained by a ballet master. Madame Walter followed them, giving her arm to the father of her other son-in-law, the Marquis de Latour-Yvelin, aged seventy-two. She did not walk, she dragged herself along, ready to faint at each forward movement.

It could be felt that her feet stuck to the flagstones, that her legs refused to advance, and that her heart was beating within her breast like an animal bounding to escape. She had grown thin. Her white hair made her face appear still more blanched and her cheeks hollower. She looked straight before her in order not to see any one—in order not to recall, perhaps, that which was torturing her.

Then George Du Roy appeared with an old lady unknown. He, too, kept his head up without turning aside his eyes, fixed and stern under his slightly bent brows. His moustache seemed to bristle on his lip. He was set down as a very good-looking fellow. He had a proud bearing, a good figure, and a straight leg. He wore his clothes well, the little red ribbon of the Legion of Honor showing like a drop of blood on his dress coat.

Then came the relations, Rose with the Senator Rissolin. She had been married six weeks. The Count de Latour-Yvelin accompanied by the Viscountess de Percemur. Finally, there was a strange procession of the friends and allies of Du Roy, whom he introduced to his new family; people known in the Parisian world, who became at once the intimates, and, if need be, the distant cousins of rich parvenus; gentlemen ruined, blemished; married, in some cases, which is worse. There were Monsieur de Belvigne, the Marquis de Banjolin, the Count and Countess de Ravenel, Prince Kravalow, the Chevalier, Valréali; then some guests of Walter's, the Prince de Guerche, the Duke and the Duchess de Ferraciné, the beautiful Marchioness des Dunes. Some of Madame Walter's relatives preserved a well-to-do, countrified appearance amidst the throng.

The organ was still playing, pouring forth through the immense building the sonorous and rhythmic accents of its glittering throats, which cry aloud unto heaven the joy or grief of mankind. The great doors were closed, and all at once it became as gloomy as if the sun had just been turned out.

Now, George was kneeling beside his wife in the choir, before the lit-up altar. The new Bishop of Tangiers, crozier in hand and miter on head, made his appearance from the vestry to join them together in the Eternal name. He put the customary questions, exchanged the rings, uttered the words that bind like chains, and addressed the newly-wedded couple a Christian allocution. He was a tall, stout man, one of those handsome prelates to whom a rounded belly lends dignity.

The sound of sobs caused several people to look round. Madame Walter was weeping, with her face buried in her hands. She had to give way. What could she have done else? But since the day when she had driven from her room her daughter on her return home, refusing to embrace her; since the day when she had said, in a low voice, to Du Roy, who had greeted her ceremoniously on again making his appearance: "You are the vilest creature

I know of; never speak to me again, for I shall not answer you," she had been suffering intolerable and unappeasable tortures. She hated Susan with a keen hatred, made up of exasperated passion and heartrending jealousy, the strange jealousy of a mother and mistress—unacknowledgable, ferocious, burning like a new wound. And now a bishop was marrying them—her lover and her daughter—in a church, in presence of two thousand people, and before her. And she could say nothing. She could not hinder it. She could not cry out: "But that man belongs to me; he is my lover. This union you are blessing is infamous!"

Some ladies, touched at the sight, murmured: "How deeply the poor mother feels it!"

The bishop was declaiming: "You are among the fortunate ones of this world, among the wealthiest and most respected. You, sir, whom your talent raises above others; you who write, who teach, who advise, who guide the people, you who have a noble mission to fulfill, a noble example to set."

Du Roy listened, intoxicated with pride. A prelate of the Roman Catholic Church was speaking thus to him. And he felt behind him a crowd, an illustrious crowd, gathered on his account. It seemed to him that some power impelled and lifted him up. He was becoming one of the masters of the world—he, the son of two poor peasants at Canteleu. He saw them all at once in their humble wayside inn, at the summit of the slope overlooking the broad valley of Rouen, his father and mother, serving the country-folk of the district with drink, He had sent them five thousand francs on inheriting from the Count de Vaudrec. He would now send them fifty thousand, and they would buy a little estate. They would be satisfied and happy.

The bishop had finished his harangue. A priest, clad in a golden stole, ascended the steps of the altar, and the organ began anew to celebrate the glory of the newly-wedded couple. Now it gave forth long, loud notes, swelling like waves, so sonorous and powerful that it seemed as though they must lift and break through the roof to spend abroad into the sky. Their vibrating sound filled the church, causing body and spirit to thrill. Then all at once they grew calmer, and delicate notes floated through the air, little graceful, twittering notes, fluttering like birds; and suddenly again this coquettish music waxed once more, in turn becoming terrible in its strength and fullness, as if a grain of sand had transformed itself into a world. Then human voices rose, and were wafted over the bowed heads— Vauri and Landeck, of the Opera, were singing. The incense shed abroad a delicate odor, and the Divine Sacrifice was accomplished on the altar, to consecrate the triumph of the Baron George Du Roy!

Pretty-boy, on his knees beside Susan, had bowed his head. He felt at that moment almost a believer, almost religious; full of gratitude towards the divinity who had thus favored him, who treated him with such consideration. And without exactly knowing to whom he was addressing himself, he thanked him for his success.

When the ceremony was concluded he rose up, and giving his wife his arm, he passed into the vestry. Then began the interminable defiling past of the visitors. George, with wild joy, believed himself a king whom a nation had come to acclaim. He shook hands, stammered unmeaning remarks, bowed, and replied: "You are very good to say so."

All at once he caught sight of Madame de Marelle, and the recollection of all the kisses that he had given her, and that she had returned; the recollection of all their caresses, of her pretty ways, of the sound of her voice, of the taste of her lips, caused the desire to have her once more for his own to shoot through his veins. She was so pretty and elegant, with her boyish air and bright eyes. George thought to himself: "What a charming mistress, all the same."

She drew near, somewhat timid, somewhat uneasy, and held out her hand. He took it in his, and retained it. Then he felt the discreet appeal of a woman's fingers, the soft pressure that forgives and takes possession again. And for his own part, he squeezed it, that little hand, as though to say: "I still love you; I am yours."

Their eyes met, smiling, bright, full of love. She murmured in her pleasant voice: "I hope to have the pleasure of seeing you again soon, sir."

He replied, gayly: "Soon, madame."

She passed on. Other people were pushing forward. The crowd flowed by like a stream. At length it grew thinner. The last guests took leave.

George took Susan's arm in his to pass through the church again. It was full of people, for everyone had regained their seats in order to see them pass together. They went by slowly, with calm steps and uplifted heads, their eyes fixed on the wide sunlit space of the open door. He felt little quiverings run all over his skin those cold shivers caused by over-powering happiness. He saw no one. His thoughts were solely for himself. When he gained the threshold he saw the crowd collected—a dense, agitated crowd, gathered there on his account—on account of George Du Roy. The people of Paris were gazing at and envying him. Then, raising his eyes, he could see afar off, beyond the Palace de la Concorde, the Chamber of Deputies, and it seemed to him that he was going to make but one jump from the portico of the Madeleine to that of the Palais Bourbon.

He slowly descended the long flight of steps between two ranks of spectators. But he did not see them; his thoughts had now flown backwards, and before his eyes, dazzled by the brilliant sun, now floated the image of Madame de Marelle, re-adjusting before the glass the little curls on her temples, always disarranged when she rose.